M000314232

EARLY GREEK PHILOSOPHY

IX

LCL 532

EARLY GREEK PHILOSOPHY

VOLUME IX

SOPHISTS

PART 2

EDITED AND TRANSLATED BY

ANDRÉ LAKS AND GLENN W. MOST

IN COLLABORATION WITH
GÉRARD JOURNÉE

AND ASSISTED BY
DAVID LÉVYSTONE

HARVARD UNIVERSITY PRESS
CAMBRIDGE, MASSACHUSETTS
LONDON, ENGLAND
2016

Library of Congress Control Number 2015957358
CIP data available from the Library of Congress

ISBN 978-0-674-99710-3

*Composed in ZephGreek and ZephText by
Technologies 'N Typography, Merrimac, Massachusetts.
Printed on acid-free paper and bound by
The Maple-Vail Book Manufacturing Group*

CONTENTS

THE 'SOPHISTS'
PART 2

37. ANTIPHON [ANTIPH.]

Already the ancients disagreed on the question of how many Antiphons were active in Athens in the second half of the fifth century BC, and even today the problem remains unresolved. An Antiphon from the Athenian deme of Rhamnous who lived from ca. 480 until 411 BC is well known from various historical sources that mention his activities as an orator and politician, and a collection of three of his political speeches as well as three judiciary tetralogies survives. Is this Antiphon the same person as the Antiphon who is called a 'sophist' and to whom writings are attributed on epistemology, natural phenomena, mathematics, moral theory, and political life (*On Truth, On Concord*), to say nothing of a variety of other activities such as soothsaying and dream interpretation (which some people have assigned to yet another Antiphon)? Modern scholars (following ancient ones) have cited numerous arguments both for the identification of these two men and for their separation. None of the arguments in support of their separation seems decisive, and the improbability of two men of the same name operating in Athens at the same time in such closely related fields as rhetoric and politics suggests instead that it is one and the same man at issue. We have therefore, like a number of recent scholars, assigned to a single Antiphon reports that other scholars distribute among different persons. However, for the sake

2

of prudence, we have placed in the section **R** a number of reports, notably on Antiphon's place in the history of rhetoric, which could in principle also have been located in **D**, in order to collect in **D** what are for the most part only original texts. For reasons of space, we do not include the preserved and fragmentary political and judicial speeches transmitted under Antiphon's name, as the hypothesis of a single author would suggest doing; these are easily available in volume 1 of the Loeb Classical Library *Minor Attic Orators* (LCL 308) and elsewhere. Instead, we limit ourselves to the fragments surviving from both of Antiphon's major treatises and from his other works; indeed, we are rather well informed about *On Truth* because an Oxyrhynchus papyrus transmits a continuous portion of its text and, more marginally, because later lexicographers were interested in the idiosyncratic use Antiphon made of numerous terms. Xenophon reports a discussion between Socrates and Antiphon; given the difficulty of assessing how reliable this report is, we include it not in the main section on Antiphon's doctrines, but in an appendix to it.

BIBLIOGRAPHY

Edition with Commentary

G. J. Pendrick. *Antiphon the Sophist. The Fragments* (Cambridge, 2002).

The Papyrus

G. Bastianini and F. Decleva Caizzi. "Antipho," in *Corpus dei Papiri Filosofici Greci e Latini* (*CPF*), part I, vol. 1* (Florence, 1989), pp. 176–222.

Speeches

F. Decleva Caizzi. *Antiphontis Tetralogiae* (Milan, 1969).
L. Gernet. Antiphon, *Discours. Suivis des Fragments d'Antiphon le sophiste* (Paris, 1923).

See also the titles listed in the General Introduction to Chapters 31–42.

OUTLINE OF THE CHAPTER

P

D

ANTIPHON [87 DK]

P

How Many Antiphons? (P1–P2)

P1 *Suda*

a (< A1) A.2744

Ἀντιφῶν Ἀθηναῖος τερατοσκόπος καὶ ἐποποιὸς καὶ σοφιστής· ἐκαλεῖτο δὲ Λογομάγειρος.

b (T3 Pendrick) A.2745

Ἀντιφῶν, Σοφίλου, Ἀθηναῖος, τῶν δήμων Ῥαμνούσιος· διδάσκαλος δὲ αὐτοῦ οὐδεὶς προγινώσκεται· ἀλλ᾽ ὅμως ἦρξε τοῦ δικανικοῦ χαρακτῆρος μετὰ Γοργίαν. λέγεται δὲ καὶ Θουκυδίδου γενέσθαι διδάσκαλος. ἐκαλεῖτο δὲ Νέστωρ.

c (< A1) A.2746

Ἀντιφῶν Ἀθηναῖος ὀνειροκρίτης· Περὶ κρίσεως ὀνείρων ἔγραψεν.

ANTIPHON

P

How Many Antiphons? (P1–P2)

P1 *Suda*

a (< A1)

Antiphon, Athenian, soothsayer, poet, and sophist. He was called 'Speech Chef.'

b (≠ DK)

Antiphon, son of Sophilus, Athenian, from the deme Rhamnous. No earlier teacher of his is known; nonetheless, he began the judicial genre after Gorgias. He is also said to have been Thucydides' teacher. He was called 'Nestor.'

c (< A1)

Antiphon, Athenian, interpreter of dreams. He wrote *On the Interpretation of Dreams.*

P2 (< A2) Hermog. *Ideis* 2.11 (399.18–400.21 Rabe)

περὶ δὲ Ἀντιφῶντος λέγοντας ἀνάγκη προειπεῖν, ὅτι
καθάπερ ἄλλοι τέ φασιν οὐκ ὀλίγοι καὶ Δίδυμος ὁ
γραμματικός, πρὸς δὲ καὶ ἀπὸ ἱστορίας φαίνεται,
πλείους μὲν γεγόνασιν Ἀντιφῶντες, δύο δὲ οἱ σοφι-
στεύσαντες, ὧν καὶ λόγον ἀνάγκη ποιήσασθαι. ὧν εἷς
μέν ἐστιν ὁ ῥήτωρ, οὗπερ οἱ φονικοὶ φέρονται λόγοι
καὶ ‹οἱ›[1] δημηγορικοὶ[2] καὶ ὅσοι τούτοις ὅμοιοι, ἕτερος
δὲ ὁ καὶ τερατοσκόπος καὶ ὀνειροκρίτης λεγόμενος
γενέσθαι, οὗπερ οἵ τε Περὶ τῆς ἀληθείας εἶναι λέγονται λόγοι καὶ ὁ Περὶ ὁμονοίας[3] καὶ ὁ Πολιτικός.[4] ἐγὼ
δὲ ἕνεκα μὲν τοῦ διαφόρου τῶν ἐν τοῖς λόγοις τούτοις
ἰδεῶν πείθομαι δύο τοὺς Ἀντιφῶντας γενέσθαι (πολὺ
γὰρ ὡς ὄντως τὸ παραλλάττον τῶν ἐπιγραφομένων
τῆς Ἀληθείας λόγων πρὸς τοὺς λοιπούς), ἕνεκα δὲ τοῦ
καὶ παρὰ Πλάτωνι καὶ παρ' ἄλλοις ἱστορουμένου πάλιν οὐ πείθομαι. Θουκυδίδην γὰρ Ἀντιφῶντος εἶναι
τοῦ Ῥαμνουσίου μαθητὴν ἀκούω πολλῶν λεγόντων,
καὶ τὸν μὲν Ῥαμνούσιον εἰδὼς ἐκεῖνον, οὗπερ εἰσὶν οἱ
φονικοί, τὸν Θουκυδίδην δὲ πολλῷ κεχωρισμένον[5] καὶ
κεκοινωνηκότα τῷ εἴδει τῶν τῆς Ἀληθείας λόγων, πάλιν οὐ πείθομαι. οὐ μὴν ἀλλ' εἴτε εἷς ὁ Ἀντιφῶν ἐγέ-

---

[1] ‹οἱ› Waltz et Spengel   [2] καὶ ὁ πολιτικὸς post δημηγορικοὶ add. Waltz et Spengel   [3] καὶ οἱ δημηγορικοὶ post
ὁμονοίας hab. mss. plerique, del. Sauppe, post λέγονται λόγοι
transp. Lb   [4] καὶ οἱ πολιτικοί Md   [5] ‹τούτου› κεχωρισμένον Blass

P2 (< A2) Hermogenes, *On Types of Style*

When one speaks about Antiphon, it is necessary to state beforehand that, as Didymus the grammarian and many other authors say, and as is apparent from historical research as well, there were several Antiphons, of whom two were sophists, who must be taken account of. One of these is the orator, whose homicide speeches, public speeches, and all the other speeches of the same kind are extant; while the other is the one who is also said to have been a soothsayer and interpreter of dreams, and to whom the discourses *On Truth,* and *On Concord* and *Politicus,* are attributed. As for me, when I consider the difference in style among these discourses, I am persuaded that there were two Antiphons; for the disparity between the discourses entitled *On Truth* and the other ones is really very large. But then again, because of what Plato[1] and other authors report, once again I am persuaded of the opposite view [i.e. I am persuaded that there was only one Antiphon]. For I have read in many authors that Thucydides was a student of Antiphon of Rhamnous, and I am aware that it is the one from Rhamnous to whom the homicide speeches belong but that Thucydides is very remote from these and shares the style of writing of the discourses *On Truth;* so that once again I am persuaded of the opposite view. But whether there was one Antiphon who used two

---

[1] Plato, *Menexenus* 236a: "the man who learned music from Lamprus and rhetoric from Antiphon of Rhamnous."

νετο, δύο λόγων εἴδεσι τοσοῦτον ἀλλήλων διεστη-
κόσι[6] χρησάμενος, εἴτε καὶ δύο, χωρὶς ἑκάτερος ὁ μὲν
τοῦτο, ὁ δὲ ἐκεῖνο μετελθών, ἀνάγκη χωρὶς περὶ ἑκατέρου διελθεῖν· πλεῖστον γὰρ ὡς ἔφαμεν τὸ μεταξύ.

[6] διεστηκότων mss., corr. Blass

Origin and Chronology of the Orator (P3–P5)

P3 (≠ DK) Clem. Alex. *Strom.* 1.79.3

[. . . = **R5**] Ἀντιφῶντα ⟨Σω⟩φίλου[1] Ῥαμνούσιον, ὥς
φησι Διόδωρος[2] [. . .].

[1] φίλου ms., corr. Potter   [2] Ἀπολλόδωρος Wilamowitz

P4 (≠ DK) Hermog. *Ideis* 2.11, p. 401.5–6

[. . . = **R3**] καὶ γάρ ἐστι τοῖς χρόνοις τῶν δέκα ῥητόρων τούτων πρεσβύτατος ἁπάντων [. . . = **R8**].

P5 (> 82 A6) Ps.-Plut. *Vit. X Orat.* 832F

γέγονε δὲ κατὰ τὰ Περσικὰ καὶ Γοργίαν τὸν σοφι-
στήν, ὀλίγῳ[1] νεώτερος αὐτοῦ, καὶ παρατέτακεν ἕως
καταλύσεως τῆς δημοκρατίας ὑπὸ τῶν τετρακοσίων
γενομένης [. . .].

[1] ὀλίγῳ ⟨ὢν⟩ Herwerden

kinds of discourses so different from each other, or two, of whom separately the one adopted this kind of style and the other that one, each of them must be discussed separately, for the distance between them is, as we said, very large.

Origin and Chronology of the Orator (P3–P5)

P3 (≠ DK) Clement of Alexandria, *Stromata*

[. . .] Antiphon of Rhamnous, the son of Sophilus, as Diodorus[1] says [. . .].

See also **R4**

[1] Not identified. Wilamowitz proposed correcting to Apollodorus.

P4 (≠ DK) Hermogenes, *On Types of Style*

[. . .] in terms of chronology he is the oldest of all of these ten [scil. Attic] orators [. . .].

P5 (> 82 A6) Ps.-Plutarch, *Lives of the Ten Orators*

He was born at the time of the Persian Wars [i.e. 480 BC] and of Gorgias the sophist, being a little younger than the latter; and he lived until the Four Hundred overthrew the democracy [i.e. 411] [. . .].

The Soothsayer and Interpreter
of Dreams (P6–P7)

P6 (T5 Pendrick) Arist. Frag. 75 Rose in Diog. Laert. 2.46

τούτῳ τις, καθά φησιν Ἀριστοτέλης ἐν τρίτῳ Περὶ ποιητικῆς, ἐφιλονείκει Ἀντίλοχος Λήμνιος καὶ Ἀντιφῶν ὁ τερατοσκόπος [. . .].

P7 (A8) Clem. Alex. *Strom.* 7.24.4

χαρίεν τὸ τοῦ Ἀντιφῶντος· οἰωνισαμένου τινός, ὅτι κατέφαγεν ὗς τὰ δελφάκια, θεασάμενος αὐτὴν ὑπὸ λιμοῦ διὰ μικροψυχίαν τοῦ τρέφοντος κατισχναμένην· "χαῖρε," εἶπεν, "ἐπὶ τῷ σημείῳ, ὅτι οὕτω πεινῶσα τὰ σὰ οὐκ ἔφαγεν τέκνα."

The Poet? (P8)

P8 (< A6) Ps.-Plut. *Vit. X Orat.* 833C

λέγεται δὲ τραγῳδίας συνθεῖναι καὶ ἰδίᾳ καὶ σὺν Διονυσίῳ τῷ τυράννῳ· [. . . = **P10**].

ANTIPHON

The Soothsayer and Interpreter of Dreams (P6–P7)

P6 (≠ DK) Aristotle, Fragment of *On Poetry* in Diogenes Laertius

As Aristotle says in Book 3 of his *On Poetry,* a certain Antilochus of Lemnos and Antiphon the soothsayer engaged in rivalry with him [i.e. Socrates] [. . .].

P7 (A8) Clement of Alexandria, *Stromata*

Antiphon's remark is pleasant: when someone took as an omen the fact that a sow had eaten its piglets, he observed that it was emaciated from starvation because of its keeper's stinginess and said, "Rejoice at this omen: hungry as it was, it was not your own children that it ate."

See also **P1a, P1c, P2**

The Poet? (P8)

P8 (< A6) Ps.-Plutarch, *Lives of the Ten Orators*

He is said to have composed tragedies, both on his own and in collaboration with Dionysius the tyrant [. . .].

The Psychotherapist (P9–P11)

P9 (A6) Philostr. *Vit. soph.* 1.15, pp. 15.32–16.3 Kayser

πιθανώτατος δὲ ὁ Ἀντιφῶν γενόμενος καὶ προσρηθεὶς
Νέστωρ ἐπὶ τῷ περὶ παντὸς εἰπὼν ἂν πεῖσαι νηπεν-
θεῖς ἀκροάσεις ἐπήγγειλεν, ὡς οὐδὲν οὕτω δεινὸν
ἐρούντων ἄχος, ὃ μὴ ἐξελεῖν τῆς γνώμης.

P10 (< A6) Ps.-Plut. *Vit. X Orat.* 833C–D

[. . . = **P8**] ἔτι δ' ὢν πρὸς τῇ ποιήσει τέχνην ἀλυπίας
συνεστήσατο, ὥσπερ τοῖς νοσοῦσιν ἡ παρὰ τῶν ἰα-
τρῶν θεραπεία ὑπάρχει· ἐν Κορίνθῳ τε κατεσκευα-
σμένος οἴκημά τι παρὰ τὴν ἀγορὰν προέγραψεν, ὅτι
δύναται τοὺς λυπουμένους διὰ λόγων θεραπεύειν, καὶ
πυνθανόμενος τὰς αἰτίας παρεμυθεῖτο τοὺς κάμνον-
τας. νομίζων δὲ τὴν τέχνην ἐλάττω ἢ καθ' αὑτὸν εἶναι
ἐπὶ ῥητορικὴν ἀπετράπη [. . .].

P11 (< B93) Philod. *Poem.* (P. Herc. 994), xxxviii.14–23
(p. 113 Sbordone)

εὔδη|λος ἡ τῶν ἄλλων φλη|ναφ[ία φ]αίνεται τῶν ἢ |
ταὐτὰ τέρπειν καὶ ὀχλεῖν | ἢ διάφορα κατηξιωκό|των,
ὡς καί τινος τῶν | ἀρχαίων Ἀντιφῶντος, | εἴτ' οὖν ῥη-
τορικὸς εἴτε | καὶ φιλόσοφος ἠβούλε|τ' εἶναι.

ANTIPHON

The Psychotherapist (P9–P11)

P9 (A6) Philostratus, *Lives of the Sophists*

When Antiphon had attained a great degree of persuasive power and was nicknamed 'Nestor' because he could succeed in persuading people when he spoke about anything, he announced that he would give lectures capable of eliminating pain, as he supposed that no one could name to him a grief so terrible that he could not banish it from that man's thought.

P10 (< A6) Ps.-Plutarch, *Lives of the Ten Orators*

[. . .] While he was still engaged in poetry he invented an art of eliminating pain, just as there is a kind of treatment provided by doctors for people who are sick. In Corinth he established an office next to the marketplace and advertised that he was able to treat grief-stricken people by means of his speeches. And he inquired into the causes and thereby consoled those people who were suffering. But then, considering that this art was beneath him, he turned to rhetoric [. . .].

P11 (< B93) Philodemus, *On Poems*

It is easy to see the nonsense those other people utter who have claimed that either the same ones [i.e. sounds] or different ones cause pleasure and pain, like for example one of the ancients, Antiphon, whether he wanted to be thought of as a rhetorician or as a philosopher.

The Politician (P12–P14)

P12 (≠ DK) Thuc. 8.68.1

ἦν δὲ ὁ μὲν τὴν γνώμην ταύτην εἰπὼν Πείσανδρος,
καὶ τἆλλα ἐκ τοῦ προφανοῦς προθυμότατα ξυγκατα-
λύσας τὸν δῆμον· ὁ μέντοι ἅπαν τὸ πρᾶγμα ξυνθεὶς
ὅτῳ τρόπῳ κατέστη ἐς τοῦτο καὶ ἐκ πλείστου ἐπιμε-
ληθεὶς Ἀντιφῶν ἦν ἀνὴρ Ἀθηναίων τῶν καθ᾽ ἑαυτὸν
ἀρετῇ τε οὐδενὸς ὕστερος καὶ κράτιστος ἐνθυμηθῆναι
γενόμενος καὶ ἃ γνοίη εἰπεῖν, καὶ ἐς μὲν δῆμον οὐ
παριὼν οὐδ᾽ ἐς ἄλλον ἀγῶνα ἑκούσιος οὐδένα, ἀλλ᾽
ὑπόπτως τῷ πλήθει διὰ δόξαν δεινότητος διακείμενος,
τοὺς μέντοι ἀγωνιζομένους καὶ ἐν δικαστηρίῳ καὶ ἐν
δήμῳ πλεῖστα εἷς ἀνήρ, ὅστις ξυμβουλεύσαιτό τι,
δυνάμενος ὠφελεῖν [. . . = **P15**].

P13 (≠ DK) Arist. *Ath. Pol.* 32.2

ἡ μὲν οὖν ὀλιγαρχία τοῦτον κατέστη τὸν τρόπον, ἐπὶ
Καλλίου μὲν ἄρχοντος, ἔτεσι δ᾽ ὕστερον τῆς τῶν
τυράννων ἐκβολῆς μάλιστα ἑκατόν, αἰτίων μάλιστα
γενομένων Πεισάνδρου καὶ Ἀντιφῶντος καὶ Θηραμέ-
νους, ἀνδρῶν καὶ γεγενημένων εὖ καὶ συνέσει καὶ
γνώμῃ δοκούντων διαφέρειν.

P14 (≠ DK) Philostr. *Vit. soph.* 1.15, p. 15.16–26 Kayser

Ἀντιφῶντα δὲ τὸν Ῥαμνούσιον οὐκ οἶδ᾽, εἴτε χρηστὸν
δεῖ προσειπεῖν, εἴτε φαῦλον. χρηστὸς μὲν γὰρ προσ-

ANTIPHON

The Politician (P12–P14)

P12 (≠ DK) Thucydides, *The Peloponnesian War*

The man who proposed this resolution [scil. to establish the regime of the Four Hundred] was Peisander, who on other occasions too had publicly demonstrated great eagerness to overthrow the democracy. But the man who contrived the whole plan to bring matters to this point and who had devoted his attention to it for the longest time was Antiphon, a man second to none of the Athenians of his time in excellence and one who was extremely forceful in thinking and in saying what he thought; and though he did not willingly appear before the assembly or take part in any other debate, and was suspect in the eyes of the populace because of his reputation for great cleverness, he was nonetheless the one man who was most able to help whoever asked his advice when they were involved in contests, both in the law court and in the assembly [. . .].

P13 (≠ DK) Aristotle, *The Constitution of the Athenians*

So this is how the oligarchy was established, under the archonship of Callias, about one hundred years after the expulsion of the tyrants; the principal men responsible were Peisander, Antiphon, and Theramenes, men who were well born and were thought to possess superior intelligence and judgment.

P14 (≠ DK) Philostratus, *Lives of the Sophists*

As for Antiphon of Rhamnous, I do not know whether he should be called a good man or a wicked one. For on the

19

εἰρήσθω διὰ τάδε· ἐστρατήγησε πλεῖστα, ἐνίκησε
πλεῖστα, ἑξήκοντα τριήρεσι πεπληρωμέναις ηὔξησεν
Ἀθηναίοις τὸ ναυτικόν, ἱκανώτατος ἀνθρώπων ἔδοξεν
εἰπεῖν τε καὶ γνῶναι· διὰ μὲν δὴ ταῦτα ἐμοί τε ἐπαι-
νετέος καὶ ἑτέρῳ. κακὸς δ' ἂν εἰκότως διὰ τάδε φαί-
νοιτο· κατέλυσε τὴν δημοκρατίαν, ἐδούλωσε τὸν Ἀθηναίων δῆμον, ἐλακώνισε κατ' ἀρχὰς μὲν ἀφανῶς,
ὕστερον δ' ἐπιδήλως, τυράννων τετρακοσίων δῆμον
ἐπαφῆκε τοῖς Ἀθηναίων πράγμασιν.

Trial and Death (P15–P18)

P15 (≠ DK) Thuc. 8.68.2

[. . . = **P12**] καὶ αὐτός τε, ἐπειδὴ τὰ τῶν τετρακοσίων
ἐν ὑστέρῳ μεταπεσόντα ὑπὸ τοῦ δήμου ἐκακοῦτο, ἄριστα φαίνεται τῶν μέχρι ἐμοῦ ὑπὲρ αὐτῶν τούτων
αἰτιαθείς, ὡς ξυγκατέστησε, θανάτου δίκην ἀπολογη-
σάμενος.

P16 (≠ DK) Ps.-Plut. Vit. X Orat. 833D–F, 834A–B

ψήφισμα ἐπὶ Θεοπόμπου ἄρχοντος, ἐφ' οὗ οἱ τετρα-
κόσιοι κατελύθησαν, καθ' ὃ[1] ἔδοξεν[2] Ἀντιφῶντα κρι-
θῆναι, ὃ Καικίλιος παρατέθειται. "ἔδοξε τῇ βουλῇ μιᾷ
καὶ εἰκοστῇ τῆς πρυτανείας· Δημόνικος Ἀλωπεκῆθεν

[1] ψήφισμα ante καθ' ὃ hab. mss.: secl. Duebner
[2] ἔδοξαν mss., corr. Reiske

one hand he is to be called a good man for the following reasons: he often held the office of general, he often gained victories, he increased the Athenian fleet by sixty fully equipped triremes, he was considered to be, of all men, the one most capable of speaking and understanding. For these reasons he deserves to be praised by me and by anyone else. But on the other hand he showed himself to be a wicked man in the following ways: he overthrew the democracy, he enslaved the Athenian populace, he supported the Spartan cause, at first in secret, but later in public, and he set loose the mob of the Four Hundred against the Athenian state.

Trial and Death (P15–P18)

P15 (≠ DK) Thucydides, *The Peloponnesian War*

[. . .] And later, when the actions of the Four Hundred had been reversed and were being assailed by the assembly and he was accused because he had helped to establish that regime, he was clearly the man who delivered the best speech of those who lived before me, when he defended himself on a capital charge regarding these same matters.

P16 (≠ DK) Ps.-Plutarch, *Lives of the Ten Orators*

Caecilius has preserved the decree dating from the archonship of Theopompus [= 411 BC], when the regime of the Four Hundred was overthrown, which resolved that Antiphon should be tried: "Resolved by the Council on the twenty-first day of the prytany, Demonicus of Alo-

ἐγραμμάτευε, Φιλόστρατος Παλληνεὺς³ ἐπεστάτει·
Ἄνδρων εἶπε περὶ τῶν ἀνδρῶν, οὓς ἀποφαίνουσιν
οἱ στρατηγοὶ πρεσβευομένους εἰς Λακεδαίμονα ἐπὶ
κακῷ τῆς πόλεως τῆς Ἀθηναίων, καὶ ἐκ⁴ τοῦ στρατο-
πέδου πλεῖν ἐπὶ πολεμίας νεὼς καὶ πεζεῦσαι διὰ Δε-
κελείας, Ἀρχεπτόλεμον καὶ Ὀνομακλέα καὶ Ἀντιφῶ-
ντα⁵ συλλαβεῖν καὶ ἀποδοῦναι εἰς τὸ δικαστήριον,
ὅπως δῶσι δίκην [. . .]." τούτῳ ὑπογέγραπται τῷ δόγ-
ματι ἡ καταδίκη. "προδοσίας ὦφλον Ἀρχεπτόλεμος
Ἱπποδάμου Ἀγρύληθεν παρών, Ἀντιφῶν Σωφίλου
Ῥαμνούσιος παρών· τούτοιν ἐτιμήθη τοῖς ἕνδεκα πα-
ραδοθῆναι καὶ τὰ χρήματα δημόσια εἶναι καὶ τῆς
θεοῦ τὸ ἐπιδέκατον, καὶ τὼ οἰκία κατασκάψαι αὐτῶν
καὶ ὅρους θεῖναι τοῖν οἰκοπέδοιν, ἐπιγράψαντας ΑΡ-
ΧΕΠΤΟΛΕΜΟΥ ΚΑΙ ΑΝΤΙΦΩΝΤΟΣ ΤΟΙΝ ΠΡΟ-
ΔΟΝΤΟΙΝ. [. . .] μὴ ἐξεῖναι θάψαι Ἀρχεπτόλεμον καὶ
Ἀντιφῶντα Ἀθήνησι, μηδ᾽ ὅσης Ἀθηναῖοι κρατοῦσι·
καὶ ἄτιμον εἶναι Ἀρχεπτόλεμον καὶ Ἀντιφῶντα καὶ
γένος τὸ ἐκ τούτοιν, καὶ νόθους καὶ γνησίους· καὶ ἐάν
τις ποιήσηταί τινα τῶν ἐξ Ἀρχεπτολέμου καὶ Ἀντιφῶντος, ἄτιμος ἔστω ὁ ποιησάμενος. ταῦτα δὲ γράψαι
ἐν στήλῃ χαλκῇ· καὶ ᾗπερ ἀνάκειται τὰ ψηφίσματα
τὰ περὶ Φρυνίχου, καὶ τοῦτο θέσθαι."

3 Πελληνεὺς mss., corr. Taylor
4 ἐκ secl. Reiske
5 Ὀνομαλέα et Ἀρχιφῶντα mss., corr. edd.

pece being secretary and Philostratus of Pallene chairman. Andron moved concerning those men—Archeptolemus, Onomacles, and Antiphon—who the generals declare went as ambassadors to Lacedaemon to the detriment of the city of Athens, sailed from the camp on an enemy ship, and traveled by land through Decelia: that they be arrested and confined in prison in order to be punished. [. . .]" After this decree there follows the sentence: "Archeptolemus of Agryle, son of Hippodamus, present, and Antiphon of Rhamnous, son of Sophilus, present, were condemned for treason. They were sentenced to be delivered to the Eleven [i.e. the executioners], their property to be confiscated after one tenth had been dedicated to the goddess [i.e. Athena], their houses to be demolished, and boundary stones to be placed on their estates, bearing the inscription, '[scil. the property] of Archeptolemus and Antiphon, the traitors.' [. . .] it is forbidden to bury Archeptolemus and Antiphon in Athens or in any other land ruled by the Athenians. Archeptolemus and Antiphon are to be deprived of their civic rights and so too their descendants, both illegitimate and legitimate ones; and anyone who adopts any of the descendants of Archeptolemus and Antiphon shall himself be deprived of his civic rights. This is to be inscribed on a bronze column; and this as well is to be erected in the place where the decrees regarding Phrynichus[1] are set up."

[1] One of the principal instigators of the oligarchic coup of June 411.

P17 (≠ DK) Arist. *EE* 3.5 1232b6–9

[. . .] καὶ μᾶλλον ἂν φροντίσειεν ἀνὴρ μεγαλόψυχος,
τί δοκεῖ ἑνὶ σπουδαίῳ ἢ πολλοῖς τοῖς τυγχάνουσιν,
ὥσπερ Ἀντιφῶν ἔφη πρὸς Ἀγάθωνα κατεψηφισμένος
τὴν ἀπολογίαν ἐπαινέσαντα.

P18 (≠ DK) Ps.-Plut. *Vit. X Orat.* 833A–C

οἱ δ᾽ ὑπὸ τῶν τριάκοντα ἀνῃρῆσθαι αὐτὸν ἱστοροῦ-
σιν, ὥσπερ Λυσίας ἐν τῷ ὑπὲρ τῆς Ἀντιφῶντος θυγα-
τρὸς λόγῳ [Frag. 25a Carey]· ἐγένετο γὰρ αὐτῷ θυγά-
τριον, οὗ Κάλλαισχρος ἐπεδικάσατο. ὅτι δ᾽ ὑπὸ τῶν
τριάκοντα ἀπέθανεν, ἱστορεῖ καὶ Θεόπομπος ἐν τῇ
πεντεκαιδεκάτῃ τῶν Φιλιππικῶν [FGrHist 115 F120]·
ἀλλ᾽ οὗτός γ᾽ ἂν εἴη ἕτερος, Λυσιδωνίδου πατρός
[. . .]. ἔστι δὲ καὶ ἄλλος λόγος περὶ τῆς τελευτῆς
αὐτοῦ. πρεσβευτὴν γὰρ ὄντα αὐτὸν εἰς Συρακούσας
πλεῦσαι, ἡνίκα ἤκμαζεν ἡ τοῦ προτέρου Διονυσίου
τυραννίς· γενομένης δὲ παρὰ πότον ζητήσεως, τίς
ἄριστός ἐστι χαλκός, καὶ τῶν πολλῶν διαφερομένων,
αὐτὸν εἰπεῖν ἄριστον εἶναι ἐξ οὗ Ἁρμόδιος καὶ Ἀρι-
στογείτων πεποίηνται· τοῦτο δ᾽ ἀκούσαντα τὸν Διονύ-
σιον καὶ ὑπονοήσαντα προτροπὴν εἰς ἐπίθεσιν εἶναι
τὸ ῥηθὲν προστάξαι ἀναιρεθῆναι αὐτόν· οἱ δέ, ὅτι τὰς
τραγῳδίας αὐτοῦ διέσυρε, χαλεπήναντα.

ANTIPHON

P17 (≠ DK) Aristotle, *Eudemian Ethics*

[. . .] a great-souled man would be much more concerned about the opinion of a single serious man than about that of a multitude of ordinary ones, as Antiphon said, when he had been condemned, to Agathon, who was praising his defense speech.

P18 (≠ DK) Ps.-Plutarch, *Lives of the Ten Orators*

Others report that he was killed by the Thirty, for example Lysias in his speech on Antiphon's daughter;[1] for he left behind a young daughter, whom Callaeschrus sought to marry. Theopompus too, in Book 15 of his *Philippics,* reports that he was put to death by the Thirty; but this must be a different one [i.e. a different Antiphon], the son of Lysidonides [. . .]. There is also another story about his death: viz. that he sailed as ambassador to Syracuse, when the tyranny of the earlier Dionysius was at its height. During drinks the question arose, what was the best bronze, and many people proposed different answers; but he said that the best kind was that from which [scil. the statues of] Harmodius and Aristogeiton were made. When Dionysius heard this, he suspected that these words were an instigation to assassinate him and he ordered that he be killed. Others say that he was angry with him because he was disparaging his tragedies.

[1] This speech is lost.

ANTIPHON [87 DK]

D

Fragments Attested for or Attributable to
On Truth *(D1–D40)*
Fragments Attested for or Attributable to
Book 1 *(D1–D16)*
Thought *(D1)*

D1 Gal. *In Hipp. Med. off.* (XVIII.2, p. 656 Kühn)

a (> B1)

καὶ πολλάκις [. . .] ἀντιδιαιρῶν ταῖς αἰσθήσεσι τὴν
γνώμην, πολλάκις εἴρηκεν, ὥσπερ καὶ ὁ Ἀντιφῶν ἐν
τῷ προτέρῳ τῆς Ἀληθείας οὕτω λέγων· "ταῦτα δὲ
γνοὺς εἴσ‹η›ἔν τι οὐδὲν αὐτῶν, οὔτε ὧν ὄψει ὁρᾷ ‹ὁ
ὁρῶν› μακρότατα οὔτε ὧν γνώμῃ γιγνώσκει ὁ μακρότατα γιγνώσκων"[1] [. . . = **D1b**].

[1] οὕτω λέγων. . . γιγνώσκων] locum variis corruptelis
adfectum ita restituit Pendrick post Diels

---

[1] The text of this sentence is very corrupt in the manuscripts
and is very uncertain.

ANTIPHON

D

Fragments Attested for or Attributable to
On Truth *(D1–D40)*[1]

[1] Most of these texts are explicitly attributed by their sources.
For the others, especially for the papyri fragments, the attribution
is based on inference.

Fragments Attested for or Attributable to
Book 1 (D1–D16)
Thought (D1)

D1 Galen, *Commentary on Hippocrates'* On the Office
of the Doctor

a (> B1)

[. . .] often distinguishing 'thought' (*gnômê*) from the sen-
sations, he [scil. Critias, 88 B40] has often used the term,
just like Antiphon, who says in the first book of *Truth:*
**"even if you perceive these things, you will not know
at all any one of them, neither those which ⟨he who
sees⟩ farthest sees by sight nor those which he who
perceives farthest perceives by thought** (*gnômê*)"[1]
[. . .].

b (B2)

[. . . = **D1a**] καὶ "πᾶσι γὰρ ἀνθρώποις ἡ γνώμη τοῦ σώματος ἡγεῖται[1] καὶ εἰς ὑγίειαν καὶ νόσον καὶ εἰς τὰ ἄλλα πάντα."

[1] ἡρεῖται M: αιειται P, corr. edd.

Some Epistemological Terms (D2–D6)

D2 (B4) Harpocr. A.167

ἄοπτα· ἀντὶ τοῦ ἀόρατα καὶ οὐκ ὀφθέντα, ἀλλὰ δόξαντα ὁρᾶσθαι. Ἀντιφῶν Ἀληθείας α΄.

D3 (B5) Harpocr. A.170

ἀπαθῆ· ἀντὶ τοῦ τὰ μὴ ὡς ἀληθῶς γεγονότα πάθη. Ἀντιφῶν Ἀληθείας α΄.

D4 (B6) Pollux *Onom.* 2.58–59

[. . .] καὶ **διοπτεύειν** Κριτίας καὶ Ἀντιφῶν, Ἀντιφῶν δὲ καὶ **εἴσοπτοι.**

D5 (B7) Pollux *Onom.* 2.57

Ἀντιφῶν δὲ καὶ τὸ **ὀψόμενον** εἶπε καὶ τῇ **ὄψει** οἷον τοῖς ὀφθαλμοῖς καὶ **ὀπτὴρ** καὶ **ἄοπτα.**

b (B2)

[. . .] and **"for thought leads the body, for all humans, toward health and disease and toward everything else."**

Some Epistemological Terms (D2–D6)

D2 (B4) Harpocration, *Lexicon of the Ten Orators*

'unseen things': instead of 'invisible ones' and 'ones that are not seen, but are thought to be seen.' Antiphon, Book 1 of *Truth*.

D3 (B5) Harpocration, *Lexicon of the Ten Orators*

'things not experienced': instead of 'experiences which did not truly happen.' Antiphon, Book 1 of *Truth*.

D4 (B6) Pollux, *Onomasticon*

[. . .] and **'to inspect,'** Critias and Antiphon; and Antiphon also **'visible.'**

D5 (B7) Pollux, *Onomasticon*

Antiphon also said **"what will see,"** and **"by sight"** to mean 'by the eyes,' and **"eyewitness,"**[1] and **"unseen things"** [cf. **D2**].

[1] The term is used by Antiphon the orator (5.27).

D6 (< B8) Pollux *Onom.* 2.76

παρὰ μόνῳ δ᾽ Ἀντιφῶντι ὀδμὰς καὶ εὐοδμίαν εὕροι τις
ἄν.

Nature and Matter (D7–D8)

D7 (B15) Harpocr. E.42

ἔμβιος· Ἀντιφῶν Ἀληθείας α΄· "καὶ ἡ[1] σηπεδὼν τοῦ
ξύλου ἔμβιος γένοιτο" ἀντὶ τοῦ ἐν τῷ ζῆν, τούτεστι
ζήσειε καὶ μὴ ξηρανθείη μηδ᾽ ἀποθάνοι.

[1] γῆ post ἡ hab. A, del. Dindorf post Bekker: ἐν γῇ prop.
Sedley

D8 (< B15) Arist. *Phys.* 2.1 193a9–14

δοκεῖ δ᾽ ἡ φύσις καὶ ἡ οὐσία τῶν φύσει ὄντων ἐνίοις
εἶναι τὸ πρῶτον ἐνυπάρχον ἑκάστῳ ἀρρύθμιστον
⟨ὂν⟩[1] καθ᾽ ἑαυτό, οἷον κλίνης φύσις τὸ ξύλον, ἀνδρι-
άντος δ᾽ ὁ χαλκός. σημεῖον δέ φησιν Ἀντιφῶν ὅτι, εἴ
τις κατορύξειε κλίνην καὶ λάβοι δύναμιν ἡ σηπεδὼν
ὥστε ἀνεῖναι βλαστόν, οὐκ ἂν γενέσθαι κλίνην ἀλλὰ
ξύλον [. . .].

[1] ⟨ὂν⟩ Ross

D6 (< B8) Pollux, *Onomasticon*

Antiphon is the only one [scil. among the Attic prose authors] in whom one would find **'smells'** and **'fragrance.'**[1]

1 Poetic terms found also in non-Attic prose.

Nature and Matter (D7–D8)

D7 (B15) Harpocration, *Lexicon of the Ten Orators*

'alive': Antiphon, Book 1 of *Truth:* **"and the rotting of the wood would be alive"** instead of 'in the condition of life,' that is, 'would live and not dry out or die.'

D8 (< B15) Aristotle, *Physics*

Some people think that the nature and the substance of the things that are by nature is what is present first of all in each thing, without possessing configuration (*arrhuthmistos*) in itself, as the nature of a bed is the wood, and that of a statue the bronze. Antiphon says that evidence of this is the fact that if one were to bury a bed and the rotting could acquire the power of sending up a shoot, it would not become a bed, but wood [. . .].

Other Isolated Words Attested
for Book 1 (D9–D16)

D9 (B10)

a *Suda* A.435

ἀδέητος· ὁ μηδενὸς δεόμενος καὶ πάντα ἔχων. Ἀντιφῶν ἐν α΄ Ἀληθείας· "διὰ τοῦτο οὐδενὸς δεῖται, οὐδὲ[1]
προσδέχεται οὐδενός τι, ἀλλ' ἄπειρος καὶ ἀδέητος."

[1] οὔτε mss., corr. Bernhardy

b Harpocr. A.26

ἀδέητος· ἀντὶ τοῦ ἀνενδεής, παρ' Ἀντιφῶντι Ἀληθείας
α΄.

D10 (B11) Harpocr. Δ.8

δεήσεις· ἀντὶ τοῦ ἐνδείας. Ἀντιφῶν Ἀληθείας α΄.

D11 (B17) Anecd. Gr. 1.173.5 Bachmann

Ἀφροδίτης· ἀντὶ τοῦ ἀφροδισίων. οὕτως Ἀντιφῶν ἐν
Ἀληθείας πρώτῳ[1].

[1] πρῶτα ms., corr. Bachmann

*Other Isolated Words Attested
for Book 1 (D9–D16)*

D9 (B10)

a *Suda*

'unlacking': he who lacks nothing and possesses every-thing. Antiphon in Book 1 of *Truth:* **"that is why he** [i.e. perhaps: god] **lacks nothing and receives nothing from anyone, but is unlimited and unlacking."**

b Harpocration, *Lexicon of the Ten Orators*

'unlacking': instead of 'lacking nothing,' in Antiphon, Book 1 of *Truth*.

D10 (B11) Harpocration, *Lexicon of the Ten Orators*

'lackings': instead of 'needs.' Antiphon, Book 1 of *Truth*.

D11 (B17) *Anecdota Graeca*

'of Aphrodite': instead of 'of sexual acts.' So Antiphon in the first book of *Truth*.

D12 (B18)

a Harpocr. A.121

ἀναποδιζόμενα· ἀντὶ τοῦ[1] ἐξεταζόμενα, ἢ ἀντὶ τοῦ
ἄνωθεν τὰ αὐτὰ πολλάκις λεγόμενα ἢ πραττόμενα.
Ἀντιφῶν Ἀληθείας α΄.

[1] τοῦ ‹πάλιν› Diels (cf. D12b)

b Pollux *Onom.* 2.196

ἀναποδιζόμενα Ἀντιφῶν τὰ πάλιν ἐξεταζόμενα.

D13 (B19)

a Harpocr. A.140

ἀνήκει· παρ᾽ Ἀντιφῶντι Ἀληθείας α΄ ἀντὶ ἁπλοῦ τοῦ
ἥκει, ἢ οἷον ἀνεβιβάσθη καὶ προελήλυθεν.

b Anecd. Gr. 1.96.25 Bachmann

ἀνήκει· Ἀντιφῶν μὲν ἀντὶ τοῦ καθήκει [. . .].

D14 (B14) Harpocr. Δ.42

διάθεσις· [. . . = **R1**] καὶ γὰρ τὸ ῥῆμα διαθέσθαι
λέγουσιν ἐπὶ τοῦ διοικῆσαι. Ἀντιφῶν Ἀληθείας α΄·
"γυμνωθεῖσα δὲ ἀφορμῆς πολλὰ ἂν καὶ καλὰ κακῶς
διαθεῖτο."

D12 (B18)

a Harpocration, *Lexicon of the Ten Orators*

[scil. things] **'reexamined':** instead of 'closely examined' or instead of 'the same things being said or done many times from the beginning.' Antiphon, Book 1 of *Truth.*

b Pollux, *Onomasticon*

[scil. things] **'reexamined':** Antiphon, "closely examined again."

D13 (B19)

a Harpocration, *Lexicon of the Ten Orators*

'comes up': in Antiphon, Book 1 of *Truth,* instead of the simple form 'comes,' or like 'has stepped up' and 'has gone forward.'

b *Anecdota Graeca*

'comes up': Antiphon instead of 'arrives' [. . .].

D14 (B14) Harpocration, *Lexicon of the Ten Orators*

'organization': [. . .] For they use the verb **'to organize'** for 'to arrange.' Antiphon, Book 1 of *Truth:* **"stripped of resources** (*aphormê*) **it** [i.e. thought?] **would organize badly many fine things."**

35

D15 (B20) Harpocr. E.77

ἐπαλλάξεις· ἀντὶ τοῦ συναλλαγὰς ἢ μίξεις. Ἀντιφῶν
Ἀληθείας αʹ.

D16 (B21) Harpocr. O.31

ὀριγνηθῆναι· ἀντὶ τοῦ ἐπιθυμῆσαι. Ἀντιφῶν Ἀληθείας αʹ.

Fragments Attested for or Attributable
to Book 2 (D17–D35)
Time and Eternity (D17–D18)

D17 (< B9) Aët. 1.22.6 (Stob.) [περὶ οὐσίας χρόνου]

Ἀντιφῶν [. . .] νόημα ἢ μέτρον τὸν χρόνον [. . .].

D18 (cf. B22) Phot. *Lex.* A.422 (cf. Harpocr. A.38)

ἀειεστώ· Ἀντιφῶν τὴν ἀϊδιότητα ἐν Ἀληθείας βʹ καὶ
τὸ ἐπὶ τῶν αὐτῶν ἀεὶ ἑστάναι [. . .].

The World Order (D19–D20)

D19 Harpocr.

a (B23) Δ.40

διάστασις· Ἀντιφῶν Ἀληθείας βʹ· "περὶ τῆς νῦν κρα-
τούσης διαστάσεως" ἀντὶ τοῦ διακοσμήσεως τῶν
ὅλων.

D15 (B20) Harpocration, *Lexicon of the Ten Orators*

'interchanges': instead of 'exchanges' or 'mixtures.' Antiphon, Book 1 of *Truth*.

D16 (B21) Harpocration, *Lexicon of the Ten Orators*

'to stretch toward': instead of 'to desire.' Antiphon, Book 1 of *Truth*.

*Fragments Attested for or Attributable
to Book 2 (D17–D35)
Time and Eternity (D17–D18)*

D17 (< B9) Aëtius

Antiphon [. . .]: time is a thought or a measure [. . .].

D18 (cf. B22) Harpocration, *Lexicon of the Ten Orators*

'eternal being': Antiphon in the second book of *Truth*, eternity and always being in the same condition [. . .].

The World Order (D19–D20)

D19 Harpocration, *Lexicon of the Ten Orators*

a (B23)

'separation': Antiphon, Book 2 of *Truth:* **"about the separation prevailing now"** instead of 'the ordering of the world.'

b (B24) A.30

ἀδιάστατον· τὸ μήπω διεστηκὸς μηδὲ διακεκριμένον Ἀντιφῶν εἶπεν.

D20 (B24a) *Suda* Δ.557

διάθεσις καὶ διατίθεσθαι· [. . . = **D41b**] ἐν τῷ β΄ τῆς Ἀληθείας ὁ αὐτὸς κέχρηται αὐτῷ καὶ ἐπὶ τῆς διακοσμήσεως.

The Vortex (D21)

D21 (B25) Harpocr. Δ.12

δίνῳ· ἀντὶ τοῦ δινήσει. Ἀντιφῶν Ἀληθείας β΄.

The Heavenly Bodies (D22–D24)
The Sun (D22)

D22 (B26) Aët. 2.20.15 (Stob.) [περὶ οὐσίας ἡλίου]

Ἀντιφῶν πῦρ ἐπινεμόμενον μὲν τὸν περὶ τὴν γῆν ὑγρὸν ἀέρα, ἀνατολὰς δὲ καὶ δύσεις ποιούμενον τῷ τὸν μὲν ἐπικαιόμενον ἀεὶ προλείπειν, τοῦ δ᾽ ὑπονοτιζομένου πάλιν ἀντέχεσθαι.

b (B24)

'unseparated': Antiphon called by this term what has not yet been separated nor differentiated.

D20 (B24a) *Suda*

'organization' and **'to be organized':** [. . .] In Book 2 of *Truth* the same man [i.e. Antiphon] has also applied the term to the world ordering.

The Vortex (D21)

D21 (B25) Harpocration, *Lexicon of the Ten Orators*

'by the vortex': instead of 'by the whirling motion.' Antiphon, Book 2 of *Truth*.

The Heavenly Bodies (D22–D24)
The Sun (D22)

D22 (B26) Aëtius

Antiphon: [scil. the sun consists of] fire that is nourished by the moist air surrounding the earth, and that rises and sets because each time it leaves behind the air that has been burned and in turn adheres to the air that possesses some moisture.

The Moon (D23–D24)

D23 (B27) Aët. 2.28.4 (Stob.; cf. Plut.) [περὶ φωτισμῶν σελήνης]

Ἀντιφῶν ἰδιοφεγγῆ μὲν τὴν σελήνην, τὸ δὲ ἀποκρυπτόμενον περὶ αὐτὴν ὑπὸ τῆς προσβολῆς τοῦ ἡλίου ἀμαυροῦσθαι, πεφυκότος τοῦ ἰσχυροτέρου πυρὸς[1] τὸ ἀσθενέστερον ἀμαυροῦν· ὃ δὴ συμβαίνειν καὶ περὶ τὰ ἄλλα ἄστρα.

[1] πυρὸς om. Stob.

D24 (B28) Aët. 2.29.3 (Stob.) [περὶ ἐκλείψεως σελήνης]

[. . .] Ἀντιφῶν κατὰ τὴν τοῦ σκαφοειδοῦς στροφὴν καὶ τὰς περικλίσεις.

Meteorology (D25)

D25 (< B29) Gal. In Hipp. Epid. 3.33, p. 129.1–6

οὕτω [scil. εἰλλόμενον] δὲ καὶ παρ' Ἀντιφῶντι κατὰ τὸ δεύτερον τῆς Ἀληθείας ἔστιν εὑρεῖν γεγραμμένην τὴν προσηγορίαν ἐν τῇδε τῇ ῥήσει· "ὅταν οὖν γένωνται ἐν τῷ ἀέρι ὄμβροι τε καὶ πνεύματα ὑπεναντία ἀλλήλοις, τότε συστρέφεται τὸ ὕδωρ καὶ πυκνοῦται κατὰ πολλά· ὅ τι δ' ἂν τῶν ξυμπιπτόντων κρατηθῇ,[1] τοῦτ' ἐπυκνώθη καὶ συνεστράφη ὑπό τε τοῦ πνεύματος εἰλλόμενον[2] καὶ ὑπὸ τῆς βίας."

The Moon (D23–D24)

D23 (B27) Aëtius

Antiphon: the moon possesses its own light, but the ob-
scured area around it is made dim by the impact of the
sun, since what is stronger by nature makes dim what is
weaker. This is what happens in the case of the other celestial bodies as well.

D24 (B28) Aëtius

[. . .] Antiphon: [scil. the lunar eclipse occurs] because of
the rotation of the bowl-shaped body and its inclinations.

Meteorology (D25)

D25 (< B29) Galen, *Commentary on Hippocrates'* Epi-
demics

In Antiphon too [scil. as in Plato], in the second book of
Truth, one can find the term [i.e. 'compressed'] written in
this way [scil. *eillomenon*] in the following passage: **"so
whenever rains and winds that oppose one another
form in the air, the water comes together and con-
denses in many places; and, among the aggregates,
whatever is dominated, undergoes condensation
and aggregation, being compressed by both the air
and its violence."**[1]

[1] This probably describes the formation of hail.

---

[1] κρατήσῃ mss., corr. Sauppe, ut corruptum not. Pendrick
[2] verbum leviter corruptum in mss. rest. Wenkebach

The Earth (D26)

D26

a (B30) Harpocr. Γ.18

γρυπάνιον· Ἀντιφῶν Ἀληθείας β´· "καῖον γὰρ τὴν γῆν καὶ συντῆκον γρυπάνιον ποιεῖ."

b (cf. B31) Phot. *Lex.* Γ.220 (et al.)

γρυπανίζειν· σείεσθαι τὴν γῆν παλλομένην[1] καὶ ὥσπερ ῥυσοῦσθαι[2] ἀπὸ σεισμοῦ· οὕτως ἐχρήσατο Ἀντιφῶν.

[1] παλλομένην Anecd. Gr. 1.228 Bekker et *Etym. Mag.* s.v. γυπάνειν: βαλλομένην ms.   [2] ῥυσοῦσθαι *Etym. Gen.* et *Etym. Mag.*: ῥυποῦσθαι ms.: γρυποῦσθαι Theodoridis

The Sea (D27)

D27 (B32) Aët. 3.16.4 (Plut.) [περὶ θαλάσσης πῶς συνέστη καὶ πῶς ἐστι πικρά]

Ἀντιφῶν ἱδρῶτα τοῦ θερμοῦ, ἐξ οὗ τὸ περιληφθὲν ὑγρὸν ἀπεκρίθη, τῷ καθεψηθῆναι παραλυκίσαντα,[1] ὅπερ ἐπὶ παντὸς ἱδρῶτος συμβαίνει.

[1] παραλυκίσασα Mm: παρακυλίσασα Π: corr. Xylander

The Earth (D26)

D26

a (B30) Harpocration, *Lexicon of the Ten Orators*

'wrinkled': Antiphon, Book 2 of *Truth:* **"for burning the earth and making it melt, it makes it wrinkled."**

b (cf. B31) Photius, *Lexicon*

'to become wrinkled': for the earth, to quake when it is shaken and as it were to shrivel because of an earthquake. This is how Antiphon used it.

The Sea (D27)

D27 (B32) Aëtius

Antiphon: [scil. the sea is] the sweat that comes from heat from which the enclosed moisture has separated out, and that has turned salty from having been boiled, which is what happens to every kind of sweat.

Human Anatomy and Medicine (D28–D35)

D28 (B29a, Nachtrag, vol. II, p. 426.17–35) Gal. *Nom. med.*, p. 34.9–38 Meyerhof-Schacht

وإن احتجت مني إلى شهادة استدل بها من كلام أصحاب الريطوريقي لتعلم أن أولئك أيضا كانوا يريدون بقولهم حمى الحرارة النارية الخارجةَ عن الطبع فاسمع قول أنطيفون حيث يقول فهذه أشياء قد أخبرتك أن المرة كانت تفعلها لأنها كانت في اليدين والرجلين وأما التي كانت تتأدى إلى اللحم فإنما كانت إذا كان مقدارها كثيرا أحدثت حميات دائمة لأن اللحم إذا صارت إليه حدث به منها فساد في نفس جوهره وتورم فالحرارة الخارجة عن الطبع تكون من هذا الموضع فأما دوامها وأطباقها فيكون من قبل المرة إذا كانت كثيرة في اللحم لم تنصب وتخف سريعا بل كانت تبقى بأن تصبر عند الحرارة الخارجة عن الطبع . فأنت تجد أنطيفون في كلامه هذا لم يقتصر على أن يسمي الحرارة الخارجة عن الطبع بالاسم الذي يسميها به جميع اليونانيين من أهل اللغة المعروفة بأطيقي وهو بُريتي فقال إن في جميع المحمومين حرارة تسمى بهذا الاسم دون أن أخبرك كيف تكون هذه الحرارة فنسب السبب في كونها إلى المرار . وكذلك قال أيضا في هذه المقالة

Human Anatomy and Medicine (D28–D35)

D28 (B29a, Nachtrag, vol. II, p. 426.17–35) Galen, *On Medical Names*

If you require me to provide you with a quotation from the rhetoricians that illustrates that when they say 'fever' they mean 'an unnatural fiery heat' (so that you can know this), then listen to what Antiphon said: "I have informed you that these are things that bile produces, because it is present in the hands and feet. If the quantity of bile which reaches the flesh is great, it brings about constant fevers. For if it arrives at the flesh, this produces putrefaction in its very essence, so that it [i.e. the flesh] swells. Unnatural heat is generated from this location [i.e. where the flesh putrefies and produces a swelling]. Their [scil. the fevers'] length and extent is determined by the bile: if it is plentiful in the flesh, they do not dissipate and diminish quickly, but rather remain, because the unnatural heat endures." You can see that Antiphon does not limit himself to calling 'unnatural heat' by the word used by all Greeks speaking the dialect known as Attic, namely *puretoi*.[1] For he said that in all patients suffering from fever, there is a heat called by this word, before informing you how this heat is generated: he attributes the cause for its generation to bile. In the same second book of his treatises *On Truth,* he has a passage attributing the cause for the generation of fever to bile, saying: "Whatever [scil. bile] reaches the flesh, generates severe and long-lasting fevers." After-

---

[1] The Arabic text only offers traces of letters (the so-called *rasm*), and can be read in a variety of ways; the previous editors restored '$\theta\acute{\epsilon}\rho\mu\eta$,' but they recognized that this makes little sense in this context.

الثانية بعينها من مقالاته في الحق قول لا نسب فيه السبب في كون الحمى إلى المرار
فقال وأما كل شيء منها يتأدى إلى اللحم فإنه يولد حميات شديدة طويلة المدة. ثم
إنه من بعد هذا إذا أمعن في القول قليلا يلقب الحرارة التي تكون على غير المجرى
الطبيعي في النقرس بغير اللقب الذي يلقب به جميع أصحابه فيسميها فلغموني
وحمى وهذان اسمان يدلان في هذا الموضع على اللهيب. [. . .] وأما أنهم كانوا
يسمون ذلك أيضا حمى فأنت تستدل على ذلك من هذا القول الذي أنسخه لك من
قول أنطيفون فالعروق إذا وردها أكثر مما تحتمل انفتحت وبسبب هذا يحدث بها
فلغموني فإذا حدث بها فلغموني وصارت توجع صاحبها وإذا استحكم ذلك سميت
هذه العلة نقرسا.

D29 (B33) Harpocr. Π.65; cf. Φ.25 (F33b Pendrick)

[. . .] ὅτι γὰρ καὶ ἐπ' ἀνθρώπων τάσσουσι τὴν φορίνην
δῆλον ποιεῖ Ἀντιφῶν ἐν β΄ Ἀληθείας.

D30 (B38) Pollux *Onom.* 2.7

[. . .] καὶ ἄμβλωμα ὡς Ἀντιφῶν.

D31 (B34) Pollux Onom. 2.41

[. . .] καὶ καρηβαρικὸν ποτὸν ἢ βρῶμα· τὸ δὲ τοῦτο
ποιεῖν καροῦν Ἀντιφῶν φησίν.

ward, he continues his discussion for quite a while, employing a term for the unnatural heat during gout which is different from that used by all the patients having it [i.e. the unnatural heat]: he calls it *'phlegmonê'* and 'fever.' At this place, these two words refer to 'burning [*lahīb*].' [. . .] They [scil. the ancients] used to call this [scil. *phlegmonê*] also fever. You can deduce this from the quotation from Antiphon which I have copied for you [scil. here]: "If more than they can tolerate comes to the blood vessels, they burst. For this reason, *phlegmonê* occurs in them. When *phlegmonê* occurs and they [i.e. the blood vessels] cause the patient pain, and if it [i.e. the *phlegmonê*] becomes inveterate, then this disease is called gout."[2]

2 Translated by Peter E. Pormann.

D29 (B33) Harpocration, *Lexicon of the Ten Orators*

[. . .] For Antiphon makes it clear in Book 2 of *Truth* that they also apply the term **'hide'**[1] to human beings.

1 Usually used for the thick skin of certain animals, like the tortoise or elephant.

D30 (B38) Pollux, *Onomasticon*

[. . .] and **'abortion,'** like Antiphon.

D31 (B34) Pollux, *Onomasticon*

[. . .] and a drink or food that causes headache: this effect Antiphon calls **'stupefying.'**

D32 (B39) Pollux *Onom.* 2.61

Ἀντιφῶν δ' ἐν τοῖς Περὶ ἀληθείας καὶ ἀνάπηρα εἴρηκεν.

D33 (B35) Pollux *Onom.* 2.215

[. . .] καὶ ἐναιμῶδες παρὰ Ἀντιφῶντι.

D34 (B36) Pollux *Onom.* 2.223

καὶ Ἀντιφῶν δ' εἴρηκεν "ἐν ᾧ τὸ ἔμβρυον αὐξάνεταί
τε καὶ τρέφεται, καλεῖται 'χόριον.'"

D35 (B37) Pollux *Onom.* 2.224

[. . .] ἐπίπλους [. . .] Ἀντιφῶν δ' αὐτὸν καὶ ἀρρενικῶς
καὶ οὐδετέρως καλεῖ.

*Fragments Not Assigned to a Specific
Book of* On Truth *(D36–D40)
Geometry (D36)*

D36 (< B13)

a Arist. *Phys.* 1.2 185a16–17

[. . . = **R16a**] τὸν τετραγωνισμὸν τὸν μὲν διὰ τῶν τμημάτων γεωμετρικοῦ διαλῦσαι, τὸν δὲ Ἀντιφῶντος οὐ
γεωμετρικοῦ.

D32 (B39) Pollux, *Onomasticon*

Antiphon in his books *On Truth* has also said **'mutilated.'**

D33 (B35) Pollux, *Onomasticon*

[. . .] and **'blood-like'** in Antiphon.

D34 (B36) Pollux, *Onomasticon*

And Antiphon has said, **"that in which the fetus grows and is nourished is called the 'chorium'** ('afterbirth')."

D35 (B37) Pollux, *Onomasticon*

[. . .] **epiplous**[1] [. . .] Antiphon uses the word both as masculine and as neuter.

[1] The omentum, a fold of peritoneum that connects the stomach with other organs of the abdomen.

*Fragments Not Assigned to a Specific
Book of* On Truth *(D36–D40)
Geometry (D36)*

D36 (< B13)

a Aristotle, *Physics*

[. . .] it is up to the geometer to refute the squaring [scil. of the circle] by means of segments, but it is not up to the geometer [scil. to refute] that of Antiphon.[1]

[1] Aristotle also mentions Antiphon's procedure, without giving further details, at *Sophistic Refutations* 172a7.

b Simpl. *In Phys.*, p. 54.12, 20–22

τὸν γὰρ τετραγωνισμὸν τοῦ κύκλου πολλῶν ζητού-
ντων [. . . cf. **R16b**], ὁ δὲ Ἀντιφῶν γράψας κύκλον
ἐνέγραψέ τι χωρίον εἰς αὐτὸν πολύγωνον τῶν ἐγγράφεσθαι δυναμένων [. . . = **R15**].

Rejection of Divine Providence (D37)

D37 (< B12) Orig. *Cels.* 4.25

[. . .] Ἀντιφῶν ἄλλος ῥήτωρ νομιζόμενος εἶναι καὶ τὴν
πρόνοιαν ἀναιρῶν ἐν τοῖς ἐπιγεγραμμένοις Περὶ ἀληθείας [. . . = **R17**].

Justice and Nature (D38)

D38 (B44) P.Oxy. 1364 + 3647 + 1797 (*CPF* Antipho 1–2)

a (B44A) P.Oxy. 1364, Frag. 1

[Col. 1] μι [. . .]¹ δικα[ιοσ]ύνη | [δ' οὖ]ν τὰ² τῆς πόλ[λε-
ω]ς νόμιμα, | [ἐν ᾗ] ἂν πολι[τεύ]ηταί τις, μὴ | [παρ]-
αβαίνειν. | χρῷτ' ἂν οὖν | ἄνθρωπος μάλιστα ἑαυτῷ

ordo fragmentorum **D38a, b, c** incertus; frustula cum paucis
litteris omittimus; supplementa variorum virorum doctorum non
indicamus nominatim   Col. 1 ¹]νόμι[μον·] *CPF*
    ² δ' οὖ]ν τὰ *CPF*: πάν]τα ‹τὰ› Grenfell et Hunt (= GrH)

b Simplicius, *Commentary on Aristotle's* Physics

Many people were looking for how to square the circle [. . .]. Antiphon drew a circle and then inscribed within it one of the polygons that can be inscribed in it [. . .] [cf. **R14–R16**].

Rejection of Divine Providence (D37)

D37 (< B12) Origen, *Against Celsus*

[. . .] Antiphon, who is thought to be another orator [scil. besides Demosthenes], and who abolishes providence in his books entitled *On Truth* [. . .].

Justice and Nature (D38)

D38 (B44) Oxyrhynchus papyri[1]

[1] The original sequence of the fragments printed here as **D38a** and **b** is uncertain: we adopt the order proposed by the first editors, Grenfell and Hunt, followed by DK, but Funghi has argued that the sequence of the fragments should be inverted (cf. *CPF* Antipho 1–2, vol. 1*, p. 183).

a (B44A)

[Col. 1] . . . ⟨therefore⟩ **justice is not to ⟨trans⟩gress against the legal institutions** (*nomima*) **⟨of whatever⟩ city one happens to be a citizen of. So a man would make use of justice in the way that would be most advantageous for himself if, in the presence of witnesses, he considered that it is the laws that are great, but, alone and without witnesses, that it is what belongs to nature. For what belongs to the laws**

| ξυμφ[ε]ρόντως | δικαιο[σ]ύνη, εἰ | μετὰ μὲν μαρ|τύ-
ρων τ[ο]ὺς νό|μους μεγά[λο]υς | ἄγοι,³ μονούμε|νος
δὲ μαρτύ|ρων τὰ τῆς φύ|σεως· τὰ μὲν γὰρ | τῶν
νόμων | [ἐπίθ]ετα, τὰ δὲ | [τῆς] φύσεως ἀ|[ναγ]καῖα·
καὶ τὰ | [μὲν] τῶν νό|[μω]ν ὁμολογη|[θέντ]α ̣ οὐ φύν|[τα
ἐστί]ν, τὰ δὲ | [τῆς φύσ]εως φύν|[τα οὐχ] ὁμολο-
γη|[Col. 2]θ[έ]ντα. τὰ οὖν νόμι|μα παραβαίνων | εἰ ἂν¹
λάθη τοὺς | ὁμολογήσαντας | καὶ αἰσχύνης | καὶ
ζημίας ἀ|πήλλακται, μὴ | λαθὼν δ' οὔ· τῶν | δὲ τῇ
φύσει ξυμ|φύτων ἐάν τι² | παρὰ τὸ δυνατὸν | βιάζε-
ται, ἐάν | τε πάντας ἀν|θρώπους λάθη, | οὐδὲν ἔλατ-
τον | τὸ κακόν, ἐάν τε | πάντες ἴδωσιν, | οὐδὲν μεῖζον·
| οὐ γὰρ διὰ δόξαν | βλάπτεται, ἀλλὰ | δι' ἀλήθειαν.
ἔστι | δὲ τῶνδε πάντων³ ἕνε|κα τούτων ἡ σκέψις, ὅτι
τὰ πολλὰ | τῶν κατὰ νό|μον δικαίων | πολεμίως τῇ |
φύσ[ει] κεῖται· νε|νο[μο]θ[έ]τηται | γὰρ [ἐ]πί τε τοῖς |
ὀ|φ[θ]αλμοῖς, ἃ δεῖ | [Col. 3] αὐτο[ὺ]ς ὁρᾶν καὶ | ἃ οὐ
[δε]ῖ· καὶ ἐπὶ | τοῖς ὠσίν, ἃ δεῖ αὐ|τὰ ἀκούειν καὶ |
ἃ οὐ δεῖ· καὶ ἐπὶ τῇ | γλώττῃ, ἅ τ[ε] | δεῖ αὐτὴν λέγειν
| καὶ ἃ οὐ δεῖ· καὶ ἐ|πὶ ταῖς χερσίν, | ἅ τε δεῖ αὐτὰς
δρᾶν | καὶ ἃ οὐ δεῖ· καὶ | ἐπὶ τοῖς ποσίν, ἐφ' ἅ τε
δεῖ αὐτοὺς | ἰέναι καὶ ἐφ' ἃ οὐ | δεῖ· καὶ ἐπὶ τῷ νῷ,
| ὧν τε δεῖ αὐτὸν | ἐπιθυμεῖν καὶ | ὧν μή. [ἧττο]ν¹ οὖν
| οὐδὲν τ[ῇ] φύσει | φιλιώτ[ερ]α οὐδ' οἰ|κειότε[ρα] ἀφ'

³ cf. Harpocration A.7 (Anecd. Gr. 13 Bachmann): Ἀντιφῶν
ἐν τῷ Περὶ Ἀληθείας φησὶ τοὺς νόμους μεγάλους ἄγοι, ἀντὶ
τοῦ ἡγοῖτο.

is ‹adventi›tious, but what belongs to nature is necessary. And what belongs to the laws is the product of
an agreement, not of nature, but what ‹belongs to
nature› is the product of nature, not of an agreement. [Col. 2] So if someone transgresses against legal institutions without being noticed by those who
agreed upon them, he escapes shame and punishment; but if they notice, he does not. But if, contra-
vening what is possible, he does violence to anything
produced by nature, the harm is not less if no man
notices him, and it is not greater if all men see him.
For it is not because of opinion that he is harmed,
but because of the truth. Our examination of all
these points is for the sake of the following thesis:
that most of the things that are just according to the
law are established in a way that is hostile to nature.
For laws have been established regarding the eyes,
[Col. 3] saying what they must see and what they
‹must› not; and regarding the ears, what they must
hear and what they must not; and regarding the
tongue, what it must say and what it must not; and
regarding the hands, what they must do and what
they must not; and regarding the feet, where they
must go and where they must not; and regarding
thought, what it must desire and what it must not.
But what the laws deter people from is not ‹less›

Col. 2 ¹ εἰ ἂν *CPF*: ἢ ante: ἢι post corr.: ἐὰν Pendrick: εἰὰν
Wilamowitz   ² ἐάν τι GrH: εαντε pap.

³ τωνδε a.c.: παντων p.c. (παν suprascr.): πάν‹τως› τῶνδε
Diels   Col. 3 ¹[ἤττο]ν *CPF*: [ἔστι]ν GrH, Pendrick: [οὐ μὲ]ν
Diels: [οὐ]κ Wilamowitz

53

ὧν | οἱ νόμο[ι ἀ]ποτρέ|πουσι τ[οὺς] ἀν[θ]ρώπ[ους] | ἢ
ἐφ᾽ ἃ [ἐπιτρέ]²|πουσ[ιν]· τ[ὸ γὰρ³] | ζῆν [ἔ]στὶ τῆς
φύ|σεως κ[αὶ τ]ὸ ἀπο|θαν[εῖ]ν· καὶ τὸ | μὲν [ζ]ῆν
αὐτ[οῖς⁴] | ἐστι[ν ἀ]πὸ τῶν | ξυμ[φερό]ντῳ[ν,] | τὸ δὲ
ἀ[ποθανεῖν] | ἀπὸ τ[ῶν μὴ ξυμ-]||[Col. 4]φερόντῳ[ν. τὰ
| δὲ ξυμφέρ[οντα] | τὰ μὲν ὑπ[ὸ τῶν] | νόμων | κε[ί]|-
μενα¹ δεσμ[οὶ]² | τῆς φύσεώς ἐ[στι,] | τὰ δ᾽ ὑπὸ τῆς
φύ|σεως ἐλεύθερα. [οὔ]|κουν τὰ ἀλγύ|νοντα ὀρθῷ γε
λ[ό]|γῳ ὀνίνησιν τὴ[ν] | φύσιν μᾶλλον | ἢ τὰ εὐφραί-
νον|τα· οὔκουν [ἀ]ν οὐ|δὲ ξυμφέρον|τ᾽ εἴη τὰ λυποῦ[-
ντα] | μᾶλλον ἢ τ[ὰ ἥ]|δοντ[α]· τὰ γὰρ τῷ | ἀλη[θε]ῖ
ξυμφέ|ρ[οντ]α οὐ βλά|π[τει]ν δεῖ ἀλ[λ᾽ ὠ]|φ[ε]λεῖν.
τὰ τοίνυ[ν] | τῇ φύσει ξυμ|φέροντα τ[α]υτ[. . . [25–31a
illegible] [. . . . . .]ηται· κα[ὶ] | [οἵτινε]ς ἂν | πα|[Col. 5]
[θόν]τες ἀμύνων|[ται κ]αὶ μὴ αὐτοὶ | [ἄρχ]ωσι τοῦ
δρᾶν· | [καὶ ο]ἵτινε[ς] ἂν | [τοὺς] γεινᾶμέ|[νου]ς καὶ
κακοὺς | ὄντας εἰς αὐτοὺς | εὖ ποιῶσιν· καὶ οἱ | κα-
τόμνυσθαι | διδόντες ἑτέ|ροις, αὐτοὶ δὲ μὴ | κατομνύ-
με|[νοι.] καὶ τούτων | τῶν εἰρημένων | πόλλ᾽ ἄν τις
εὔ|ροι πολέμια τῇ | φύσει· ἔνι τ᾽ ἐν αὐ|τοῖς ἀλγύνε-
σθαί | τε μᾶλλον ἐξὸν | ἥττω, καὶ ἐλάτ|τω ἥδεσθαι
ἐξὸν | πλείω, καὶ κακῶς | πάσχειν ἐξὸν | μὴ πάσχειν.
| εἰ μὲν οὖν τις | [τ]οῖς τοιαῦτα προ<σ>|[ι]εμένοις¹
ἐπικού|[ρ]ησις ἐγίγνε|[το] παρὰ τῶν νό|[μ]ων, τοῖς δὲ
μὴ | [π]ρο<σ>ιεμένοις,² ἀλ|[λ᾽ ἐ]ναντιουμέ|[ν]οις ἐλάτ-

---

² [ἐπιτρέ]- Schöne, *CPF*: [προτρέ]- GrH

ANTIPHON

agreeable or akin to nature than what they ⟨indu⟩ce
them toward. ⟨For⟩ to live and to die belong to nature; and to live comes ⟨for them⟩ from what is
be⟨ne⟩ficial, ⟨to die⟩ from ⟨what is not [Col. 4]
bene⟩ficial. As for what is beneficial, what is established ⟨by the⟩ laws are fetters upon nature, while
what is established by nature is free. If one reasons
correctly, what causes pain does ⟨not⟩ help nature
more than what causes pleasure; and so what causes
pain would not be more beneficial either than what
pleases. For what is truly beneficial must be not
harmful but helpful. So what is beneficial to nature
. . . and ⟨those who⟩ [Col. 5] defend themselves after
they have suffered some harm, and do not themselves ⟨seize the init⟩iative in acting; ⟨and those⟩ who
treat ⟨their⟩ parents well, even if these have been
bad to them; and those who allow other people to
swear an oath, but do not themselves swear an oath.
And many of the things mentioned will be found to
be hostile to nature: for they entail that people suffer more pain, when less would be possible, and that
they have less pleasure, when more would be possible, and that they undergo suffering, when it would
be possible not to do so. Well then, if the laws provided some help for those who submit to such situations, and loss for those who do not submit to them

---

³ τ[ὸ γὰρ] GrH, *CPF*: τ[ὸ δὲ] Pendrick: τ[ὸ δ’ αὖ] Diels:
π[άλιν τὸ] Wilamowitz   ⁴ αὐτ[οῖς] GrH, *CPF*: αὐτ[ῇ] Pendrick

Col. 4 ¹κε[ί]μενα GrH: κεκ[ρι]μένα von Arnim: κεκ[ελευσ]-
μένα Diels   ² δεσμ[οὶ] *CPF*: δεσμ[ὰ] GrH

Col. 5 ¹,² προ⟨σ⟩[ι]εμένοις GrH

τωσις, | [Col. 6] οὐκ ἀν[ωφελὲς ἂν][1] | ἦν τ[ὸ ἐν τοῖς
νό]|μοις πεῖ[σμα· νῦν][2] | δὲ φαίνε[ται τοῖς] | προσι-
εμ[ένοις] | τὰ τοιαῦτα τὸ ἐ[κ] | νόμου δίκαι[ον] | οὐχ
ἱκανὸν ἐπι|κουρεῖν· ὅ γε πρῶ|τον μὲν ἐπιτρέ|πει τῷ
πάσχον|τι παθεῖν καὶ τῷ | δρῶντι δρᾶσαι· | καὶ οὔτε
ἐνταῦ|θα διεκώλυε τὸν | πάσχοντα μὴ | παθεῖν οὔτε
τὸν | δρῶντα δρᾶσαι· | εἴς τε τὴν τιμω|ρίαν ἀναφερό|-
μενον οὐδὲν | ἰδιώτερον ἐπὶ | [τ]ῷ πεπονθότι | ἢ[3]
τῷ δεδρακό|[τι·] πεῖ[σ]αι γὰρ δ[εῖ] | α̣[ὐ̣]τ̣ὸ̣ν̣[4] [το]ὺς
τ[ιμω]ρ[ήσοντ]ας[5] ὡς ἔ|παθεν, [ἢ][6] δύνα|σθαι ἀπ[άτ]
ῃ δί|κην [ἔχει]ν. ταῦ|τὰ[7] δὲ κ̣[α]ταλεί|πεται[ι] καὶ
τῷ δρά|σαντ[ι ἀ]ρνεῖσθαι | [Col. 7] [1–4 illegible]
[. . . . . τῷ | [ἀπο]λ̣ο̣γ̣[οῦντί ἐ]|σ̣τ̣ι̣ν̣ ἡ ἀπ̣[ολο-
γία] | ὅσηπερ τ[ῷ κα]|τηγοροῦν[τι ἡ] | κατηγορ[ία, ἡ
δὲ] | πειθὼ ἀν̣[τίπαλος] | τῷ γε πε̣[πονθό]|τι καὶ τῷ
[δεδρα]|κότι· ἐγίγ[νετο][1] | γὰρ ν[

Col. 6 [1] ἀν[ωφελὲς ἂν] GrH: ἀν[όνητον ἂν] Diels   [2] τ[ὸ
ἐν τοῖς νό]μοις πεῖ[σμα· νῦν] CPF: τ[ὸ τοῖς νό]μοις πεῖ[σμα·
νῦν] Diels: τ[ὸ τοῖς νό]μοις πεί[θεσθαι· νῦν] GrH   [3] Δ (i.e.
l. 400) ante ἢ hab. in marg. pap.   [4] πεῖ[σ]αι γὰρ δ[εῖ] α[ὐ]τὸν
CPF: πεῖ[σ]αι γὰρ ἁ[ν ἔ]λ[οι]το Diels   [5] [το]ὺς τ[ιμω]-
ρ[ήσοντ]ας CPF post Diels: [το]ὺς τ[ιμω]ρ[οῦντ]ας GrH
        [6] [ἢ] CPF: [καὶ] Diels   [7] ταῦτὰ CPF: ταῦτα Janko,
Pendrick   Col. 7 [1] ἐγίγ[νετο CPF: γίγ[νεται GrH

b (B44 Fragment B) P.Oxy. 1364, Frag. 2 + P.Oxy. 3647

[Col. 1] [Illegible]
[Col. 2] . . . ρων[1] ἐπ[ιστάμε]|θά τε κ[αὶ σέβομεν·] | τοὺς

but who oppose them, [Col. 6] it would not ⟨be use⟩less ⟨to obey the laws. But as it is,⟩ it is evident that, for those who submit to such situations, a just outcome deriving from a law is not enough to provide them help. First, it permits the sufferer to suffer and the doer to do. And just as, at that time [i.e. before the crime], it did not prevent either the sufferer from suffering or the doer from doing, so too when reference is made to it for the purpose of punishment, it is not more on the side of the one who has suffered than on that of the one who has done. For it is necessary that he persuade ⟨those people who will exact punishment⟩ that he has suffered, ⟨or⟩ that he be capable of ⟨obtaining⟩ justice by deceit. But the doer too is permitted to deny the same things. [Col. 7] . . . exactly as much of a ⟨defense⟩ is available to the ⟨defendant⟩ as the accusation that is available to the accuser, and persuasiveness is ⟨balanced⟩ for the one ⟨who has suffered⟩ and for the one ⟨who has done⟩. For it happened . . .

b (B44B)

[Col. 1] [Illegible]
[Col. 2] . . . ⟨we know them and we respect them⟩; but

Col. 2 ¹ [τῶν μὲν ἐγγυτέ]ρρων vel [οἰκειοτέ]ρων Funghi: [τῶν πατέ]ρων CPF: [τῶν ἐγχώ]ρων Pendrick, alii alia

δὲ [τῶν τη]|λοῦ οἰκ[ούν]των | οὔτε ἐπι[στ]άμε|θα οὔτε
σέβομεν. | ἐν τ[ο]ύτῳ οὖν | πρὸς ἀλλήλους | βεβαρ-
βαρώμε|θα· ἐπεὶ φύσει γε | πάντα πάντες | ὁμοίως
πεφύκ[α]|μεν καὶ βάρβα|ροι καὶ Ἕλλην[ες] | εἶναι.
σκοπεῖν | δ[ὲ] παρέχει τὰ | τῶν φύσει [ὄντων]² | ἀναγ-
καῖ[α ἐν]³ | πᾶσιν ἀν[θρώ]|ποις π[οριζόμενά] | τε κατὰ
τ[ὰς αὐτὰς] | δυνά[μεις ἅπασι,] | καὶ ἐν [αὐτοῖς
τού]|τοις οὔτε β[άρβα]|ρος ἀφώρι[σται] | ἡμῶν ο[ὐ-
δεὶς] | οὔτε Ἕλλην· ἀ|ναπνέομέν | τε γὰρ εἰς τὸν
ἀ|έρ[α] ἅπαντες | κατὰ τὸ στόμ[α] | [κ]αὶ κατ[ὰ] τὰς
ῥῖ|νας· κ[αὶ γελῶ]|[με]ν⁴ χ[αίροντες τῷ]⁵ | [νῷ ἢ] δα-
κρύ|[Col. 3]ομε[ν] λυπού|μενοι· καὶ τῇ ἀ|κοῇ τοὺς
φθόγ|γους εἰσδεχόμε|θα· καὶ τῇ αὐγῇ | μετὰ τῆς
ὄψε|ως ὁρῶμεν· καὶ | ταῖς χερσὶν ἐρ|γαζόμεθα· καὶ |
τοῖς ποσὶν βαδ[ίζο]|μεν. υβ[

² [ὄντων] GrH: [ὁμοίως] Fränkel   ³ ἀναγκαῖα[α ἐν] CPF:
ἀναγκαί[ων] GrH: ἀναγκαῖ[α] Funghi   ⁴ κ[αὶ γελῶμε]ν
Funghi   ⁵ χ[αίροντες τῷ] Funghi: χ[αίρον- Luppe

c (B44) P.Oxy. 1797

[Col. 1]. . . . . .] τοῦ δικαίου | [. . . . . .]. ον δοκουν| [. . .
τὸ] μαρτυρεῖν | [ἀ]λλήλοις¹ τἀληθῆ | [δίκαιο]ν νομίζε-
ται | [εἶναι] καὶ χρήσιμον | [οὐδὲν] ἧττον εἰς | [τὰ τῶν]
ἀνθρώπων | [ἐπιτ]ηδεύματα. | [τοῦτο] τοίνυν οὐ
δί|[καιος] ἔσται ὁ ποιῶν, | [εἴπε]ρ² τὸ μὴ ἀδικεῖν |
[μηδ]ένα μὴ ἀδι|[κού]μενον αὐτὸν | [δίκ]αιόν ἐστιν·
ἀνάγ|[κη] γὰρ τὸν μαρτυ|[ροῦ]ντα, κἂν ἀλη|[θῆ] μαρ-

those [scil. probably laws] **of those people who live far
away we neither know nor do we respect them. Thus
in this regard we have become barbarians toward
each other, since, in nature at least, we are all fitted
similarly by nature in all regards to be both barbarians and Greeks. But it is possible to examine what
is necessary** ⟨in what exists⟩ **by nature for all humans
and** ⟨what is provided to them⟩ **in conformity with** ⟨the
same⟩ **properties, and in** ⟨these things none⟩ **of us has
been defined as either b**⟨arbaria⟩**n or Greek. For we
all breathe into the air through our mouth and nose;**
⟨we laugh when we are happy in our mind⟩ [Col. 3] **or we
weep when we are grieved; we take in sounds by our
hearing, and we see by means of light with our vi-
sion; we do work with our hands and we walk with
our feet** . . .

c (B44)

[Col. 1] . . . **of what is just . . . to provide true testimony
to one another is considered** ⟨to be just⟩ **and to be**
⟨not at all⟩ **less useful for people's** ⟨act⟩**ivities. But a
man who does** ⟨this⟩ **will not be** ⟨just, if it is true that⟩
**not to commit injustice against anyone, if one has
not suffered injustice oneself, is just. For necessarily a man who provides testimony, even if he provides true testimony, all the same commits injustice**

τυρῇ, ὅμως | [ἄλλον π]ως ἀδικεῖν | [. . . . . . a]ὐτὸν[3]
ἀ|[δι]κεῖσθαι [ ] | [. .] νενε[. . . . . . .][4] | [ἐ]ν ᾧ διὰ τ[ὰ
ὑπ' ἐκεί]|[ν]ου μαρτ[υρηθέν]|τα ἁλίσκ[ε]ται ὁ κα|τα-
μαρτυρούμενος | καὶ ἀπόλλυσιν ἢ | χρήματα ἢ αὐτὸν
| [δ]ιὰ τοῦτον ὃν οὐδὲν | [ἀ]δικεῖ· ἐν μὲν οὖν | τούτῳ
τὸν κατα|[μ]αρτυρούμενον | [ἀ]δικεῖ, ὅτι οὐκ ἀδι|[κο]-
ῦντα ἑαυτὸν ἀ|[δι]κεῖ· αὐτὸς δ' ἀδικεῖ|[ται ὑ]πὸ τοῦ
καταμαρ|[τυρηθ]έντος, ὅτι μι|[σεῖται] ὑπ' αὐτοῦ
τἀ|[Col. 2]ληθῆ μαρτυ[ρή]|σας· καὶ οὐ μόν[ον] | τῷ
μίσει, ἀλλὰ [καὶ] | ὅτι δεῖ αὐτὸν τ[ὸν] | αἰῶνα πάντα
φυ|λάττεσθαι τοῦτο[ν] | οὗ κατεμαρτύρ[η]|σεν· ὡς
ὑπάρχε[ι] | γ' αὐτῷ ἐχθρὸς τοιο[ῦ]|τος, οἷος καὶ λέ-
γειν | καὶ δρᾶν εἴ τι δύν[αι]|το κακὸν αὐτόν. κα[ί]|τοι
ταῦτα φαίνεται | οὐ σμικρὰ ὄντα τἀ|δικήματα, οὔτε
| ἃ αὐτὸς ἀδικεῖται | οὔτε ἃ ἀδικεῖ· οὐ γὰρ | οἷόν τε
ταῦτά τε δί|καια εἶναι καὶ τὸ μη|[δ]ὲν ἀδικεῖν μη|[δὲ]
αὐτὸν ἀδικεῖσθαι, |[ἀλ]λ' ἀνάγκη ἐστὶν |[ἢ] τὰ ἕτερα
αὐτῶν | [δ]ίκαια εἶναι ἢ ἀμ|φότερα ἄδικα. φαίνεται
δὲ καὶ τὸ δικά|ζειν καὶ τὸ κρίνειν | καὶ τὸ διαιτᾶν,
ὅπως | ἂν περαίνηται, οὐ | δίκαια ὄντα· τὸ γὰρ | [ἄ]-
λλους ὠφελοῦν ἄλ|[λο]υς βλάπτει· ἐν δὲ | [τού]τῳ οἱ
μὲν ὠφελού|[μενο]ι οὐκ ἀδικοῦ[ν]|[ται, οἱ] δὲ βλαπτό-
με[νοι] | [ἀδικο]ῦνται[ι. . . . . .

---

[3] [εἶτα δὲ a]ὐτὸν CPF
[4] [ἐν μίσει οὖ]ν ἐνε[χόμενος CPF

against ⟨another person⟩ **in some way**. . . . **to suffer injustice himself** . . . **in which,** ⟨because of the testimony that man provides,⟩ **the one against whom he testifies is convicted and loses either his money or his life because of this man against whom he commits no injustice. Thus in this case he commits injustice against the one against whom he provides testimony, because he commits injustice against someone who is not committing injustice against himself; and he himself suffers injustice from the one against whom he provides testimony, because he** ⟨is hated⟩ **by him for having** [Col. 2] **provided true testimony— and not only because of the hatred, but** ⟨also⟩ **because for the rest of his whole life he must be on his guard against this man against whom he has provided testimony, for he has the sort of enemy who would do him any harm he could, in word and in deed. And yet it is evident that these are not petty injustices, neither the ones that he himself suffers nor the ones he commits. For it is not possible both that these things be just, and at the same time that one not commit injustice nor suffer injustice oneself;** ⟨but⟩ **it is necessary** ⟨either⟩ **that** [scil. only] **one of them be just or that both of them be unjust. It is also evident that judging, deciding, and adjudicating, in whatever way these are performed, are not just. For what benefits some harms others; and in this case, the ones who are benefited do not suffer injustice, while those who are harm**⟨ed do suffer injust⟩**ice** . . .

Wealth (D39)

D39

a (< B43) Harpocr. A.2

ἄβιος· τὸν ἄβιον Ἀντιφῶν ἐπὶ[1] τοῦ πολὺν τὸν[2] βίον κεκτημένου ἔταξεν [. . .].

[1] ἐπὶ Epitome Harp.: ἀντὶ mss.   [2] τὸν Epitome Harp.: om. mss.

b (B43) Hesych. A.127

ἄβιος· πλούσιος ὡς Ἀντιφῶν ἐν Ἀληθείᾳ.

Precautions (D40)

D40 (B3) Pollux *Onom.* 6.143

[. . .] ἀπαρασκεύῳ γνώμῃ ἐν τοῖς Περὶ ἀληθείας Ἀντιφῶν εἶπεν, ἀπαρασκεύαστον δ᾽ ἐν ταῖς ῥητορικαῖς τέχναις—δοκοῦσι δ᾽ οὐ γνήσιαι [. . .].

Fragments Attested for On Concord *(D41–D49)*
Organization of the Discourse (D41)

D41

a (B63) Harpocr. Δ.42

διάθεσις· [. . .] ἀντὶ τοῦ διοίκησις ὁ αὐτὸς ἐν τῷ Περὶ ὁμονοίας· "ἀλλὰ εἰδότες τὴν διάθεσιν ἀκούουσιν."

Wealth (D39)

D39

a (< B43) Harpocration, *Lexicon of the Ten Orators*

'opulent' (*abios*): Antiphon applied 'opulent' to the man who possesses a large livelihood (*bios*) [. . .].

b (B43) Hesychius, *Lexicon*

'opulent': 'wealthy,' as Antiphon in *Truth*.

Precautions (D40)

D40 (B3) Pollux, *Onomasticon*

[. . .] 'with unprepared thought,' says Antiphon in his writings *On Truth*, but 'unreadied' in his technical handbooks of rhetoric (but these are considered to be inauthentic) [. . .].

Fragments Attested for On Concord *(D41–D49)*
Organization of the Discourse (D41)

D41

a (B63) Harpocration, *Lexicon of the Ten Orators*

'organization': [. . .] instead of 'arrangement,' the same man [i.e. Antiphon] in his *On Concord:* **"but, knowing the organization, they listen."**

b (B24a) *Suda* Δ.557

διάθεσις καὶ διατίθεσθαι· [. . .] Ἀντιφῶν δὲ τῇ διαθέσει ἐχρήσατο ἐπὶ γνώμης ἢ διανοίας· ὁ αὐτὸς καὶ ἐπὶ
τοῦ διαθεῖναι λόγον, τουτέστιν ἐπὶ τοῦ ἐξαγγεῖλαί τι.
[. . . = **D20**]

Human Pretentions (D42)

D42 (B48) Phot. *Lex.* Θ.48

θεειδέστατον· θεοῦ ἰδέαν ἔχον. εἶπε δὲ Ἀντιφῶν ἐν τῷ
Περὶ ὁμονοίας οὕτως· ἄνθρωπος, ὅς φησι μὲν πάντων
θηρίων θεειδέστατον γενέσθαι.

*Human Realities: Names of
Barbarian Peoples (D43–D45)*

D43 (B45) Harpocr. Σ.28

Σκιάποδες· Ἀντιφῶν ἐν τῷ Περὶ ὁμονοίας. ἔθνος ἐστὶ
Λιβυκόν.

D44 (B46) Harpocr. M.2

Μακροκέφαλοι· Ἀντιφῶν ἐν τῷ Περὶ ὁμονοίας. ἔθνος
ἐστὶν οὕτω καλούμενον [. . .].

b (B24a) *Suda*

'organization' and **'to be organized'**: [. . .] Antiphon applied **'organization'** to an intention or thought. The same man also applied it to organizing a discourse, that is, to proclaiming something. [. . .]

Human Pretentions (D42)

D42 (B48) Photius, *Lexicon*

'most godlike': possessing the outward appearance of a god. Antiphon spoke as follows in his *On Concord:* **"a human being, who on the one hand claims to be the most godlike of all the beasts."**

Human Realities: Names of Barbarian Peoples (D43–D45)

D43 (B45) Harpocration, *Lexicon of the Ten Orators*

'Shadowfeet': Antiphon in his *On Concord;* it is a people of Libya.

D44 (B46) Harpocration, *Lexicon of the Ten Orators*

'Longheads': Antiphon in his *On Concord.* There exists a people called by this name [. . .].

D45 (< B47) Harpocr. Υ.8

ὑπὸ γῆν οἰκοῦντες· λέγοι ἂν τοὺς [. . .] λεγομένους
Τρωγοδύτας[1] [. . .]. Ἀντιφῶν ἐν τῷ Περὶ ὁμονοίας.

[1] Τρωγλοδύτας mss., corr. Untersteiner

*Good and Bad Characteristics
and Sentiments (D46–D49)
Moderation (D46)*

D46 (B70) Harpocr. E.156

εὐηνιώτατα· Ἀντιφῶν ἐν τῷ Περὶ ὁμονοίας. εὐήνιος ὁ[1]
πρᾶος καὶ μέτριος καὶ μὴ ταραχώδης. ἡ μεταφορὰ
ἀπὸ τῶν ἵππων.

[1] ὁ Epit. Harp: ἐστι mss.

Hesitation (D47)

D47

a (B55) Phot. *Lex.* I.133

ἵνα· ὅπου. Ἀντιφῶν ἐν τῷ Περὶ τῆς ὁμονοίας· "ὀκνεῖν[1]
ἵνα οὐδὲν ἔργον ὀκνεῖν."

[1] ὀκνεῖν Suda I.360: om. Phot.

D45 (B47) Harpocration, *Lexicon of the Ten Orators*

'Those who dwell under the earth' (perhaps he is speaking of the ones [. . .] called 'Trogodytes' [. . .]. Antiphon in his *On Concord.*

Good and Bad Characteristics
and Sentiments (D46–D49)
Moderation (D46)

D46 (B70) Harpocration, *Lexicon of the Ten Orators*

'most obedient to the reins': Antiphon in his *On Concord.* Obedient to the reins is someone who is tame, moderate, and not disordered. The metaphor comes from horses.

Hesitation (D47)

D47

a (B55) Photius, *Lexicon*

'where': in the place in which. Antiphon in his *On Concord:* **"to hesitate where it does no good to hesitate."**

b (B56) *Suda* O.116

ὀκνῶ· φοβοῦμαι. [. . .] καὶ οἱ ῥήτορες οὐκ ἐπὶ δειλίας καὶ ῥᾳθυμίας ἐχρήσαντο τῷ ὀνόματι, ἀλλ' ἐπὶ τοῦ φόβου καὶ τοῦ φοβεῖσθαι. Ἀντιφῶν· "κακὸς δ' ἄν, εἰ[1] ἀποῦσι μὲν καὶ μέλλουσι τοῖς κινδύνοις τῇ γλώττῃ θρασύνεται καὶ τῷ θέλειν ἐπείγει, τὸ δ' ἔργον ἂν παρῇ, ὀκνεῖ."

[1] ἄν, εἰ] ἀεὶ Gaisford: ἂν <εἴη> εἰ Diels: ἂν εἰ <ἐπ'> Sauppe

Regret (D48)

D48 (B52) Harpocr. A.111

ἀναθέσθαι· Ἀντιφῶν Περὶ ὁμονοίας· "ἀναθέσθαι δὲ ὥσπερ πεττὸν τὸν βίον οὐκ ἔστιν" ἀντὶ τοῦ ἄνωθεν βιῶναι μετανοήσαντας ἐπὶ τῷ προτέρῳ βίῳ. εἴρηται δὲ ἐκ μεταφορᾶς τῶν πεττευομένων.

False Friends (D49)

D49 (B65) *Suda* Θ.434

θωπεία· κολακεία [. . .] Ἀντιφῶν ἐν τῷ Περὶ ὁμονοίας· "πολλοὶ δ' ἔχοντες φίλους οὐ γινώσκουσιν, ἀλλ' ἑταίρους ποιοῦνται θῶπας πλούτου καὶ τύχης κόλακας."

b (B56) *Suda*

'I hesitate': I am afraid. [. . .] and the orators did not use the word for cowardice and laziness, but for fear and being afraid. Antiphon: **"he would be worthless, if about absent and future dangers he is bold with his tongue and presses on with desire, but hesitates when the task is at hand."**

Regret (D48)

D48 (B52) Harpocration, *Lexicon of the Ten Orators*

'to retract': Antiphon, *On Concord:* **"it is not possible to retract one's life like a move in checkers,"** instead of 'to live one's life again as one regrets one's earlier life.' The expression comes from the metaphor of checkers.

False Friends (D49)

D49 (B65) *Suda*

'flattery': adulation. [. . .] Antiphon in his *On Concord:* **"many men who have friends do not know them, but they take as their companions people who flatter their wealth and adulate their good fortune."**

Fragments Attributable to
On Concord (*D50–D63*)
The Unsuccessful Life (D50–D59)
The Defects of Human Life (D50–D51)

D50 (B51) Stob. 4.34.56

Ἀντιφῶντος.[1] εὐκατηγόρητος πᾶς ὁ βίος θαυμαστῶς,
ὦ μακάριε, καὶ οὐδὲν ἔχων περιττὸν οὐδὲ μέγα καὶ
σεμνόν, ἀλλὰ πάντα σμικρὰ καὶ ἀσθενῆ καὶ ὀλιγο-
χρόνια καὶ ἀναμεμειγμένα λύπαις μεγάλαις.

[1] Ἀντιφῶντος ed. Trincav.: ἀντιφάνους mss.

D51 (B50) Stob. 4.34.63

Ἀντιφῶντος. τὸ ζῆν ἔοικε φρουρᾷ ἐφημέρῳ τό τε μῆκος τοῦ βίου ἡμέρᾳ μιᾷ, ὡς ἔπος εἰπεῖν, ᾗ ἀναβλέψαν-
τες πρὸς τὸ φῶς παρεγγυῶμεν τοῖς ἐπιγιγνομένοις
ἑτέροις.

Anxieties (D52–D53)

D52 (B53) Stob. 3.10.39

Ἀντιφῶντος. οἱ δὲ ἐργαζόμενοι μὲν καὶ φειδόμενοι καὶ

ANTIPHON

Fragments Attributable to
On Concord *(D50–D63)*
The Unsuccessful Life (D50–D59)
The Defects of Human Life (D50–D51)

D50 (B51) Stobaeus, *Anthology*[1]

Of Antiphon: It is astonishingly easy to find fault with all of life, my friend, since it possesses nothing exceptional nor great and imposing, but everything in it is little, weak, ephemeral, and mixed with great pains.

[1] There is some doubt in the case of this and the following quotations from Stobaeus regarding which Antiphon is involved, which work, and whether they are genuine: cf. Pendrick 2002, pp. 39–40. But the grounds for suspicion about their authenticity seem less weighty than in the case of e.g. Pythagoras (cf. **PYTHS. R36**) or Democritus (cf. **ATOM. D227** and the following), and we have therefore not printed these fragments in italics (but we have not set them in boldface either).

D51 (B50) Stobaeus, *Anthology*

Of Antiphon: Living is like a day-long sentry duty,[1] and the whole length of life is like a single day, as it were, during which no sooner have we raised our eyes toward the light than we pass on the baton to other people who come after us.

[1] Cf. Plato, *Phaedo* 62b.

Anxieties (D52–D53)

D52 (B53) Stobaeus, *Anthology*

Of Antiphon: People who work and economize, and toil

71

ταλαιπωροῦντες καὶ προστιθέντες ἥδονται οἷα δή τις
ἂν εἰκάσειεν ἥδεσθαι· ἀφαιροῦντες δὲ καὶ χρώμενοι
ἀλγοῦσιν, ὥσπερ ἀπὸ τῶν σαρκῶν ἀφαιρούμενοι.

D53 (B53a) Stob. 3.16.20

Ἀντιφῶντος. εἰσί τινες οἳ τὸν παρόντα μὲν βίον οὐ
ζῶσιν, ἀλλὰ παρασκευάζονται πολλῇ σπουδῇ ὡς ἕτε-
ρόν τινα βίον βιωσόμενοι, οὐ τὸν παρόντα· καὶ ἐν
τούτῳ παραλειπόμενος ὁ χρόνος οἴχεται.

Cowardice (D54)

D54 (B57) Stob. 3.8.18

Ἀντιφῶντος. νόσος δειλοῖσιν ἑορτή· οὐ γὰρ ἐκπορεύ-
ονται ἐπὶ πρᾶξιν.

False and True Temperance (D55–D56)

D55 (B58) Stob. 3.20.66

Ἀντιφῶντος. ὅστις δὲ ἰὼν ἐπὶ τὸν πλησίον κακῶς ποιήσων δειμαίνει μὴ ἃ θέλει ποιῆσαι ἁμαρτὼν τούτων
ἃ μὴ θέλει ἀπενέγκηται, σωφρονέστερος. ἐν ᾧ γὰρ
δειμαίνει, μέλλει· ἐν ᾧ δὲ μέλλει, πολλάκις ὁ διὰ μέ-
σου χρόνος ἀπέστρεψε τὸν νοῦν τῶν θελημάτων· καὶ
ἐν μὲν τῷ γεγενῆσθαι οὐκ ἔνεστιν, ἐν δὲ τῷ μέλλειν

and accumulate, feel a pleasure of the sort that one might guess them to feel. But when they take some of it [scil. what they have acquired] away and make use of it, they feel a pain as though it were some of their own flesh they were taking away.

D53 (B53a) Stobaeus, *Anthology*

Of Antiphon: There are some people who do not live the present life but make preparations with great effort as though they were going to live some different life, and not the present one. And while they are doing this, the time that they are neglecting is gone.

Cowardice (D54)

D54 (B57) Stobaeus, *Anthology*

Of Antiphon: For cowards, illness is a holiday; for then they do not have to set out for action.

False and True Temperance (D55–D56)

D55 (B58) Stobaeus, *Anthology*

Of Antiphon: Someone who sets out against another man intending to do him harm, and fears that he will fail in his purpose and will obtain what he does not want, demonstrates a certain temperance. For as long as he fears, he hesitates; and while he hesitates, it often happens that the lapse of time deters his mind from its intentions. And this is not possible for what is past, but it is possible for this to

ἐνδέχεται[1] γενέσθαι. ὅστις δὲ δράσειν μὲν οἴεται τοὺς
πέλας κακῶς, πείσεσθαι δ' οὔ, οὐ[2] σωφρονεῖ. ἐλπίδες
δ' οὐ πανταχοῦ ἀγαθόν· πολλοὺς γὰρ τοιαῦται ἐλπίδες κατέβαλον εἰς ἀνηκέστους συμφοράς, ἃ δ' ἐδό-
κουν τοὺς[3] πέλας ποιήσειν, παθόντες ταῦτα ἀνεφάνη-
σαν αὐτοί. σωφροσύνην δὲ ἀνδρὸς οὐκ ἂν ἄλλου[4]
ὀρθότερόν τις κρίνειεν, ἢ ὅστις τοῦ θυμοῦ ταῖς παραχρῆμα ἡδοναῖς ἐμφράσσει αὐτὸς ἑαυτὸν κρατεῖν τε
καὶ νικᾶν ἠδυνήθη αὐτὸς ἑαυτόν. ὃς δὲ θέλει χαρίσα-
σθαι τῷ θυμῷ παραχρῆμα θέλει τὰ κακίω ἀντὶ τῶν
ἀμεινόνων.

[1] ἐνδέχεται ‹μὴ› Bücheler   [2] οὐ om. MA   [3] τοὺς
Meineke: τοῖς S   [4] ἄλλου Jacoby: ἄλλος S

D56 (B59) Stob. 3.5.57

Ἀντιφῶντος. ὅστις δὲ τῶν αἰσχρῶν ἢ τῶν κακῶν μήτε
ἐπεθύμησε μήτε ἥψατο, οὐκ ἔστι σώφρων· οὐ γὰρ
ἔσθ' ὅτου κρατήσας αὐτὸς ἑαυτὸν κόσμιον παρέχεται.

Marriage and Family (D57–D58)

D57 (B49) Stob. 4.22.66

Ἀντιφῶντος. φέρε δὴ προελθέτω ὁ βίος εἰς τὸ πρόσθεν καὶ γάμων καὶ γυναικὸς ἐπιθυμησάτω. αὕτη ἡ
ἡμέρα, αὕτη ἡ νὺξ καινοῦ δαίμονος ἄρχει, καινοῦ
πότμου. μέγας γὰρ ἀγὼν γάμος ἀνθρώπῳ. εἰ γὰρ τύχοι μὴ ἐπιτηδεία γενομένη, τί χρὴ τῇ συμφορᾷ χρῆ-

happen for something in the future. But someone who supposes that he can do harm to other men, without himself suffering, does ‹not› show temperance. Hopes are not always a good thing: for hopes of this sort have cast many men into incurable misfortunes, and the evil they expected to inflict on others they turned out to suffer themselves. One would attribute temperance most correctly only to that man who blocks himself from the immediate pleasures of his desire and is himself capable of dominating and defeating himself. But someone who wants to satisfy his desire immediately wants what is worse instead of what is better.

D56 (B59) Stobaeus, *Anthology*

Of Antiphon: Someone who has not desired nor touched what is shameful or evil is not temperate: for there is nothing in which he shows himself to be well-ordered by dominating it.

Marriage and Family (D57–D58)

D57 (B49) Stobaeus, *Anthology*

Of Antiphon: Come then, let us suppose that someone's life has moved forward and that he feels a desire for marriage and a wife. This very day, this very night is the beginning of a new personal fortune, of a new destiny. For marriage is a great trial for a man. For if the woman turns out to be unsuitable, what is he to do about this misfor-

σθαι; χαλεπαὶ μὲν ἐκπομπαί, τοὺς φίλους ἐχθροὺς
ποιῆσαι, ἴσα φρονοῦντας ἴσα πνέοντας, ἀξιώσαντα
καὶ ἀξιωθέντα· χαλεπὸν δὲ καὶ ἐκτῆσθαι[1] κτῆμα τοιοῦτον, δοκοῦντα ἡδονὰς κτᾶσθαι λύπας ἄγεσθαι.

φέρε δή, μὴ τὰ παλίγκοτα λέγωμεν, λεγέσθω τὰ
πάντων ἐπιτηδειότατα. τί γὰρ ἥδιον ἀνθρώπῳ γυναικὸς καταθυμίας; τί δὲ γλυκύτερον ἄλλως τε καὶ νέῳ;
ἐν τῷ αὐτῷ δέ γε τούτῳ, ἔνθα τὸ ἡδύ, ἔνεστι πλησίον
που καὶ τὸ λυπηρόν· αἱ γὰρ ἡδοναὶ οὐκ ἐπὶ σφῶν
αὐτῶν ἐμπορεύονται, ἀλλ' ἀκολουθοῦσιν αὐταῖς λῦπαι
καὶ πόνοι. ἐπεὶ καὶ ὀλυμπιονῖκαι καὶ πυθιονῖκαι καὶ
οἱ τοιοῦτοι ἀγῶνες καὶ σοφίαι καὶ πᾶσαι ἡδοναὶ ἐκ
μεγάλων λυπημάτων ἐθέλουσι παραγίνεσθαι· τιμαὶ
γάρ, ἆθλα—δελέατα, ἃ ὁ θεὸς ἔδωκεν ἀνθρώποις—
μεγάλων πόνων καὶ ἱδρώτων εἰς ἀνάγκας καθιστᾶ-
σιν.[2] ἐγὼ γάρ, εἴ μοι γένοιτο σῶμα ἕτερον τοιοῦτον[3]
οἷον ἐγὼ ἐμαυτῷ, οὐκ ἂν δυναίμην ζῆν, οὕτως ἐμαυτῷ
πολλὰ πράγματα παρέχων ὑπέρ τε τῆς ὑγιείας τοῦ
σώματος ὑπέρ τε τοῦ καθ' ἡμέραν βίου ἐς τὴν ξυλλο-
γὴν ὑπέρ τε δόξης καὶ σωφροσύνης καὶ εὐκλείας καὶ
τοῦ εὖ ἀκούειν· τί οὖν, εἴ μοι γένοιτο σῶμα ἕτερον
τοιοῦτον, ὅ γέ μοι οὕτως ἐπιμελὲς εἴη; οὐκ οὖν δῆλον,
ὅτι γυνὴ ἀνδρί, ἐὰν ᾖ καταθυμία, οὐδὲν ἐλάττους τὰς
φιλότητας παρέχεται καὶ τὰς ὀδύνας ἢ αὐτὸς αὑτῷ
ὑπέρ τε τῆς ὑγιείας δισσῶν σωμάτων ὑπέρ τε τοῦ
βίου τῆς συλλογῆς[4] ὑπέρ τε τῆς σωφροσύνης καὶ τῆς
εὐκλείας;

tune? Divorce is difficult: to make enemies out of his
friends, people who think the same as he does and who
breathe the same, after he has given them his esteem and
received theirs. But it is also difficult to hold onto a pos-
session of this sort, when, imagining that he was acquiring
pleasures, he brings home pains.

Come then, let us not speak of disagreeable matters,
let it be the most suitable things of all that we speak of.
For what is more pleasant for a man than a woman that is
in accord with his own heart? And what is sweeter, especially for a young man? And yet precisely where there is
pleasure, pain too is somewhere near at hand. For pleasures do not travel on their own, but are accompanied
by pains and toils. Olympian and Pythian victories, other
contests of this sort, the forms of wisdom (*sophiai*), and
all pleasures tend to be attained at the cost of great sufferings. For honors, prizes—these lures that god has set
out for humans—impose on them the constraint of great
toil and sweat. As for me, if I had a second body like the
one I have for myself, I could not live, so many are the
troubles I give myself for my body's health, for earning a
living every day, and for a reputation, for temperance, for
renown, and for a good name. What then if I had a second
body like this to which I had to devote such care? Is it not
evident that a wife causes her husband, when she is in
accord with his spirit, just as many pleasures and pains as
he causes himself for the sake of the health of two bodies
and for earning a living, for temperance, and renown?

---

1 καὶ ἐκτῆσθαι Diels: κεκτῆσθαι mss.   2 καθιστῶσιν
mss., corr. Sauppe   3 τοιοῦτον ‹ἐπιμελὲς ὂν› Diels, alii alia
4 καὶ post συλλογῆς hab. mss., secl. Sauppe

φέρε δὴ καὶ παῖδες γενέσθωσαν· φροντίδων ἤδη
πάντα πλέα καὶ ἐξοίχεται τὸ νεοτήσιον σκίρτημα ἐκ
τῆς γνώμης καὶ ⟨τὸ⟩[5] πρόσωπον οὐκέτι τὸ αὐτό.

[5] ⟨τὸ⟩ Sauppe

D58 (B66) Clem. Alex. *Strom.* 6.19.7

Ἀντιφῶν ὁ ῥήτωρ λέγει· **"γηροτροφία γὰρ προσέοι-
κεν παιδοτροφίᾳ."**

Wealth and Foolishness (D59)

D59 (B54) Stob. 3.16.30

Ἀντιφῶντος. ἔστι δέ τις λόγος, ὡς ἄρα ἰδὼν ἀνὴρ
ἄνδρα ἕτερον ἀργύριον ἀναιρούμενον πολὺ ἐδεῖτό οἱ
δανεῖσαι ἐπὶ τόκῳ· ὁ δ᾽ οὐκ ἠθέλησεν, ἀλλ᾽ ἦν οἷος
ἀπιστεῖν τε καὶ μὴ ὠφελεῖν μηδένα· φέρων δ᾽ ἀπέθετο
ὅποι[1] δή· καί τις καταμαθὼν τοῦτο ποιοῦντα ὑφείλετο·
ὑστέρῳ δὲ χρόνῳ ἐλθὼν οὐχ εὕρισκε τὰ χρήματα ὁ
καταθέμενος. περιαλγῶν οὖν τῇ συμφορᾷ τά τε ἄλλα
καὶ ὅτι οὐκ ἔχρησε τῷ δεομένῳ, ὃ ἂν αὐτῷ καὶ σῷον
ἦν καὶ ἕτερον προσέφερεν, ἀπαντήσας δὲ τῷ ἀνδρὶ τῷ
τότε δανειζομένῳ ἀπωλοφύρετο τὴν συμφοράν, ὅτι
ἐξήμαρτε καὶ ὅτι οἱ μεταμέλει οὐ χαρισαμένῳ, ἀλλ᾽
ἀχαριστήσαντι, ὡς[2] πάντως οἱ ἀπολόμενον[3] τὸ ἀργύ-

[1] ποῖ mss., corr. Blass   [2] ὡς Blass: καὶ mss.
[3] οἱ ἀπολόμενον: verba leviter corrupta in mss. corr. Gesner

Come then, and let us suppose that children are born too: now everything is full of worries, youthful frolicking is gone from the mind, and one's face is no longer the same.

D58 (B66) Clement of Alexandria, *Stromata*

Antiphon the orator says, **"Taking care of the elderly is like taking care of children."**

Wealth and Foolishness (D59)

D59 (B54) Stobaeus, *Anthology*

Of Antiphon: There is a story that when one man saw another man taking out some money, he implored him to lend it to him at interest. But the other man refused—he was a distrustful kind of man, disinclined to help anyone. He carried the money away and hid it somewhere; but someone noticed him doing this and stole it. When the man who had hidden the money came back later he could not find it. In great distress at his misfortune—especially because he had not lent his money to the man who needed it, for it would not only have been safe for him, it would also have brought in more—he ran into the man who had wanted to borrow money at that time and he lamented his misfortune, saying that he had made a mistake and that he regretted that he had refused to do this favor instead of granting it, since in any case he had lost the money. The

ριον. ὁ δ' αὐτὸν ἐκέλευε μὴ φροντίζειν, ἀλλὰ νομίζειν
αὐτῷ εἶναι καὶ μὴ ἀπολωλέναι καταθέμενον λίθον εἰς
τὸ αὐτὸ χωρίον· "πάντως γὰρ οὐδ' ὅτε ἦν σοι, ἐχρῶ
αὐτῷ, ὅθεν μηδὲ νῦν νόμιζε στέρεσθαι μηδενός." ὅτῳ
γάρ τις μὴ ἐχρήσατο μηδὲ χρήσεται, ὄντος ἢ μὴ
ὄντος αὐτῷ οὐδὲν οὔτε πλέον οὔτε ἔλασσον βλάπτε-
ται. ὅταν γὰρ ὁ θεὸς μὴ παντελῶς βούληται ἀγαθὰ
διδόναι ἀνδρί, χρημάτων πλοῦτον παρασχών, τοῦ
φρονεῖν ⟨δὲ⟩[4] καλῶς πένητα ποιήσας, τὸ ἕτερον ἀφε-
λόμενος ἑκατέρων ἀπεστέρησεν.

[4] ⟨δὲ⟩ Sauppe

Aspects of Life in Society (D60–D63)
Friendship (D60–D61)

D60 (B62) Stob. 2.31.41

ὅτῳ[1] τις ἂν τὸ πλεῖστον τῆς ἡμέρας συνῇ, τοιοῦτον
ἀνάγκη γενέσθαι καὶ αὐτὸν τοὺς τρόπους.

haec sententia caret lemmate in Stob., sed sequitur duas
sententias Antiphonti attributas; eam refinxit Spengel ut duos
versus Menandri   [1] (ὅ)τω ms., corr. Pendrick

D61 (B64) Φιλοσόφων λόγοι 62 (11 Schenkl) = Ex-
cerpta Vind. 44 (4.293 Meineke)

Ἀντιφῶν· αἱ νέαι φιλίαι ἀναγκαῖαι μέν, αἱ δὲ παλαιαὶ
ἀναγκαιότεραι.

other man told him not to worry but to imagine that he still possessed his money and had not lost it, and to set down a stone in the same place: "In any case, when you had it, you did not use it; so don't think that you have been deprived of anything now either." For someone who has not used something and will not use it is not harmed either more or less, whether he possesses it or not. For when a god does not wish to give entirely good things to a man, he gives him wealth of money but makes him poor in good sense, thereby depriving him of both things by taking away one of them.

Aspects of Life in Society (D60–D63)
Friendship (D60–D61)

D60 (B62) Stobaeus, *Anthology*

One necessarily oneself becomes similar in character to whomever one spends most of the day with.

D61 (B64) *Words of Philosophers*

Antiphon: New friendships constrain, but old ones constrain even more.

Education (D62–D63)

D62 (B60) Stob. 2.31.39

Ἀντιφῶντος. πρῶτον, οἶμαι, τῶν ἐν ἀνθρώποις¹ ἐστὶ
παίδευσις· ὅταν γάρ τις πράγματος κἂν ὁτουοῦν τὴν
ἀρχὴν ὀρθῶς ποιήσηται, εἰκὸς καὶ τὴν τελευτὴν ὀρθῶς γίγνεσθαι· καὶ γὰρ τῇ γῇ οἷον ἄν τις τὸ σπέρμα
ἐναρόσῃ, τοιαῦτα καὶ τὰ ἔκφορα δεῖ προσδοκᾶν· καὶ
ἐν νέῳ σώματι ὅταν τις τὴν παίδευσιν γενναίαν ἐναρόσῃ, ζῇ τοῦτο καὶ θάλλει διὰ παντὸς τοῦ βίου, καὶ
αὐτὸ οὔτε ὄμβρος οὔτε ἀνομβρία ἀφαιρεῖται.

¹ ἀνθρώποις Pflugk: οὐρανοῖς ms.

D63 (B61) Stob. 2.31.40

τοῦ αὐτοῦ. ἀναρχίας δ᾽ οὐδὲν κάκιον ἀνθρώποις·
ταῦτα γινώσκοντες οἱ πρόσθεν ἄνθρωποι ἀπὸ τῆς ἀρχῆς εἴθιζον τοὺς παῖδας ἄρχεσθαι καὶ τὸ κελευόμενον
ποιεῖν, ἵνα μὴ ἐξανδρούμενοι εἰς μεγάλην μεταβολὴν
ἰόντες ἐκπλήσσοιντο.

Other Isolated Words Attested for
On Concord (D64–D68)

D64 (B67) Harpocr. A.43

ἀθεώρητος· ἀντὶ τοῦ ἀθέατος παρ᾽ Ἀντιφῶντι ἐν τῷ
Περὶ ὁμονοίας.

Education (D62–D63)

D62 (B60) Stobaeus, *Anthology*

Of Antiphon: The foremost thing in human affairs, I think, is education. For in any action whatsoever, if one begins in the right way, then it is likely that the end will turn out right too. For so too whatever kind of seed one sows in the earth, one should expect the same kind of produce. And if someone sows a noble education in a young body, it lives and flourishes for his whole life, and neither rain nor drought destroys it.

D63 (B61) Stobaeus, *Anthology*

Of the same man [i.e. Antiphon]: Nothing is worse for human beings than the lack of rules. The men of earlier times, recognizing this, accustomed their children from the beginning to obey and to do what they were told, so that when they became adults they would not be thrown into turmoil if they encountered some great change.

Other Isolated Words Attested for
On Concord *(D64–D68)*

D64 (B67) Harpocration, *Lexicon of the Ten Orators*

'unobserved': instead of 'unseen' in Antiphon in his *On Concord*.

D65 (B67a) Harpocr. A.131 (et Epit.)

ἀνδρεία· ἡ τῶν ἀνδρῶν ἡλικία. Ἀντιφῶν ἐν τῷ Περὶ ὁμονοίας.

D66 (B68) Harpocr. A.265

αὐλιζόμενοι· ἀντὶ τοῦ κοιμώμενοι. Ἀντιφῶν Περὶ ὁμονοίας.

D67 (B69) Harpocr. B.1 (et Epit.)

βαλβῖσιν· Ἀντιφῶν Περὶ ὁμονοίας ἀντὶ τοῦ ταῖς ἀρχαῖς.

D68 (B71) Harpocr. Φ.12

φηλώματα· Ἀντιφῶν ἐν τῷ Περὶ ὁμονοίας ἐξαπάτας· φηλοῦν γὰρ τὸ ἐξαπατᾶν.

Fragments Attested for or Attributable
to Politicus *(D69–D74)*
Computation (D69–D70)

D69 (B74) Harpocr. E.168

εὐσύμβολος· ἀντὶ τοῦ ῥᾳδίως καὶ εὖ συμβάλλων, τουτέστιν ἀγαθὸς συμβάλλειν. Ἀντιφῶν Πολιτικῷ.

D65 (B67a) Harpocration, *Lexicon of the Ten Orators*
'manhood': the age of men. Antiphon in his *On Concord*.

D66 (B68) Harpocration, *Lexicon of the Ten Orators*
'spending the night': instead of 'sleeping.' Antiphon *On Concord*.

D67 (B69) Harpocration, *Lexicon of the Ten Orators*
'starting lines' [scil. of a race]: Antiphon *On Concord* instead of 'beginnings.'

D68 (B71) Harpocration, *Lexicon of the Ten Orators*
'cheatings': Antiphon in his *On Concord,* deceits. For to cheat is to deceive.

*Fragments Attested for or Attributable
to* Politicus *(D69–D74)*
Computation *(D69–D70)*

D69 (B74) Harpocration, *Lexicon of the Ten Orators*
'good at computing': instead of 'computing easily and well,' that is, good at performing computation. Antiphon *Politicus.*

D70 (B75) Harpocr. H.12 (et Epit.)

ἡμιολιασμός· Ἀντιφῶν Πολιτικῷ· 'διπλασιασμοῦ' καὶ
'ἡμιολιασμοῦ'[1] ἀντὶ τοῦ 'τὸ ἡμιόλιον δοῦναι' ἐν τοῖς
λογισμοῖς.

[1] ἡμιόλιστον mss., corr. Schneider

Disorderliness (D71)

D71 (B72) Anecd. Gr. 1.78.20 Bekker

ἀπειθαρχία· Ἀντιφῶν Πολιτικῷ.

Intemperance and Wastefulness (D72–D74)

D72 (< B76) Prisc. *Inst.* 18.230

Ἀντιφῶν ἐν τῷ Πολιτικῷ· μήτε φιλοπότην κληθῆναι
καὶ δοκεῖν τὰ πράγματα καταμελεῖν ὑπὸ οἴνου ἡσ-
σώμενον.

D73 (B73) Athen. *Deipn.* 10 423A

καταριστᾶν δὲ εἴρηκεν ἐν τῷ Πολιτικῷ Ἀντιφῶν οὕ-
τως· "ὅτε δή[1] τις πράγματα τὰ ἑαυτοῦ ἢ τὰ τῶν
φίλων κατηρίστηκεν."

[1] ὅτ' ἄν ms., corr. Kaibel

D70 (B75) Harpocration, *Lexicon of the Ten Orators*

'multiplying by one and a half': Antiphon *Politicus*. 'multiplying by two' and 'multiplying by one and a half' instead of 'making one a half times as much,' in calculations.

Disorderliness (D71)

D71 (B72) *Anecdota Graeca*

'disobedience to authority': Antiphon *Politicus*.

Intemperance and Wastefulness (D72–D74)

D72 (< B76) Priscian, *The Institutions*

Antiphon in his *Politicus:* "and not to be called bibulous either, and to have the reputation of neglecting one's affairs because one is overcome by wine."

D73 (B73) Athenaeus, *Deipnosophists*

Antiphon said, "to consume in breakfasts" in his *Politicus* as follows: "when someone has consumed in breakfasts his own property or his friends'."

D74 (B77) Plut. *Ant.* 28

ἀναλίσκειν καὶ καθηδυπαθεῖν τὸ πολυτελέστατον, ὡς
Ἀντιφῶν εἶπεν, ἀνάλωμα, τὸν χρόνον.

Fragments Attributable to Interpretation
of Dreams *(D75–D77)*
Theory of the Interpretation of Dreams (D75)

D75

a (< B79) Cic. *Div.* 1.51.116

hic magna quaedam exoritur neque ea naturalis sed arti-
ficiosa somniorum Antiphontis[1] interpretatio eodemque
modo et oraculorum et vaticinationum.

[1] Antiphontis *secl. edd.*

b (< A9) *Gnomol. Vind.* 50 (14 Wachsmuth) = *Gnomol.*
Vat. 71, p. 1 Sternbach

Ἀντιφῶν ἐρωτηθείς, τί ἐστι μαντική, εἶπεν· "ἀνθρώ-
που φρονίμου εἰκασμός."

Reported Interpretations of Dreams (D76–D77)

D76 (B78) Artem. *Oneiro.* 1.14

σηπία· αὕτη δὲ μόνη καὶ τοὺς ἀποδρᾶναι πειρωμένους
ὠφελεῖ διὰ τὸν θολόν, ᾧ χρωμένη πολλάκις φεύγει.
μέμνηται δὲ τούτου τοῦ ὀνείρου καὶ Ἀντιφῶν ὁ Ἀθηναῖος.

D74 (B77) Plutarch, *Antony*

To use up and squander what, as Antiphon said, is **the expense that costs the most—time.**

Fragments Attributable to Interpretation
of Dreams *(D75–D77)*
Theory of the Interpretation of Dreams (D75)

D75

a (< B79) Cicero, *On Divination*

At this point one should mention Antiphon's celebrated interpretation of dreams, which is based not on a natural capacity but on a technical skill, just like that of oracles and prophecies.

b (< A9) Vienna and Vatican Gnomologies

When Antiphon was asked what divination is, he said, "It is the conjecture of an intelligent human being."

Reported Interpretations of Dreams (D76–D77)

D76 (B78) Artemidorus, *Interpretation of Dreams*

Cuttlefish: Only this one also helps those who are trying to run away, because of its ink by making use of which it often escapes. Antiphon of Athens too mentions this dream.

D77

a (< B80) Cic. *Div.* 2.70.144

cursor ad Olympia proficisci cogitans visus est in somnis
curru quadrigarum vehi. mane ad coniectorem. at ille
"vinces," inquit; "id enim celeritas significat et vis equo-
rum." post idem ad Antiphontem. is autem "vincare,"
inquit, "necesse est; an non intellegis quattuor ante te
cucurrisse?" ecce alius cursor [. . .]: ad interpretem detulit
aquilam se in somnis visum esse factum. at ille: "vicisti; ista
enim avis volat nulla vehementius." huic eidem[1] Antipho
"baro," inquit, "victum te esse non vides? ista enim avis
insectans alias avis et agitans semper ipsa postrema est."

[1] huic equidem *vel* est quidem *mss.*: *corr. Lambinus*

b (F80b Pendrick) Diog. Oen. 24.II–III Smith

. . . | [Col. II] δη μέλλοντος ['Ο]λυμ|πίασιν ἀγωνιεῖσθαι
| ὅτι λελείψεται. ὁ μὲν | γάρ, φησίν, ἀετὸν ἔφη | [5]
δόξαι διώκειν ἐν τοῖς | ὀνείροις, ἐπερωτῶν | τὸν Ἀντι-
φῶντα· ὁ δ᾽ αὐ|[τ]όθεν κε̣λ̣ . . . [ἐπε]|[Col. III]ρω[τη-
θέντα οὐκ] ἄν|τικρυς εἰπεῖν τῷ | δρομεῖ τὸν θεὸν | ὅτι
λελείψῃ, καὶ | [5] τὸν ἀετὸν μηδὲν | ὀχλεῖν. εἰ μή τι δι᾽
| Ἀντιφῶντα παρέ|[δ]ε̣ι̣ξεν αὐτόν, ἵν᾽ ε . . .

Col. II et III suppl. dub. Smith   II.8 κε̣λ̣[εύσας] vel
κε̣λ̣[εύει] Smith

D77

a (< B80) Cicero, *On Divination*

[Cicero reporting examples found in the Stoics:] A runner who was thinking of setting out for the Olympian games dreamed that he was being conveyed in a four-horse chariot. The next morning he went to an interpreter of dreams, who told him, "You will gain the victory; for this is what the horses' speed and power signifies." Then the same man went to Antiphon; but he said, "You will necessarily be defeated: or do you not understand that there were four running in front of you?" And here is another runner: [. . .]. He reported to an interpreter that he had dreamed that he had been transformed into an eagle, and that man said, "You have gained the victory: for no bird flies more powerfully than that bird of yours." To the same man Antiphon said, "You fool, do you not see that you have been defeated? That bird of yours is always the very last one, because it pursues other birds and drives them before it."

b (≠ DK) Diogenes of Oenoanda, Epicurean inscription

. . . [Col. II] who was planning to compete at Olympia, that he would be left behind. For, he [i.e. probably: Chrysippus or Antipater] says, that man [i.e. that runner] said when he consulted Antiphon that he had dreamed that he was pursuing an eagle. And he [i.e. Antiphon] told him on the spot . . . [Col. III] when he was asked, he said that the god had not said outright to the runner that he would be left behind, and that the eagle was not a problem. If he had not indicated him with the help of Antiphon, so that . . .

Divination (D78)

D78 (B81a) Melamp. Περὶ παλμῶν μαντική 18–19

ὀφθαλμὸς δεξιὸς ἐὰν ἄλληται, κατὰ Φημονόην καὶ
Αἰγυπτίους καὶ Ἀντιφῶντα ἐχθροὺς ὑποχειρίους ἕξει·
ἄγει δὲ καὶ ἀποδήμους. ὀφθαλμοῦ δεξιοῦ τὸ ἄνω βλέ-
φαρον ἐὰν ἄλληται, ἐπίκτησιν πάντως δηλοῖ, κατὰ δὲ
Ἀντιφῶντα πρᾶξιν καὶ ὑγείαν, δούλῳ ἐπιβουλήν,
χήρᾳ ἀποδημίαν.

*Isolated Words Attributed to Antiphon but Not
Attributable to a Specific Treatise (D79–D82)
Crafts (D79–D80)*

D79 (B40) Pollux *Onom.* 7.169

Ἀντιφῶν βάψιν χαλκοῦ καὶ σιδήρου.

D80 (B41) Pollux *Onom.* 7.189

[. . .] βιομήχανοι ὡς Ἀντιφῶν.

Weights and Measures (D81)

D81

a (B42) Pollux *Onom.* 9.53

ἡ μὲν γὰρ Ἀντιφῶντος ταλάντωσις τὸ βάρος δηλοῖ.

Divination (D78)

D78 (B81a) Melampus, *On Divination by Vibrations*

If the right eye quivers, according to Phemonoe, the Egyptians, and Antiphon you will have your enemies in your power; it also guides travelers abroad. If the upper lid of the right eye quivers, this signifies profit in general, and according to Antiphon success and health, for a slave a conspiracy, for a widow travel abroad.

Isolated Words Attributed to Antiphon but Not Attributable to a Specific Treatise (D79–D82)
Crafts (D79–D80)

D79 (B40) Pollux, *Onomasticon*

Antiphon: **'dipping'** of bronze and iron.

D80 (B41) Pollux, *Onomasticon*

[. . .] **'people who are good at contriving a living,'** as Antiphon.

Cf. **D39**

Weights and Measures (D81)

D81

a (B42) Pollux, *Onomasticon*

For Antiphon's **'weighing'** means the weight.

b (F42b Pendrick) Hesych. T.61

ταλαντώσει· σταθμήσει, στήσει.

Another Isolated Word (D82)

D82 (B16) Anecd. Gr. 1.171.15 Bachmann

ἀφήκοντος· Ἀντιφῶν ἀντὶ τοῦ διήκοντος.

Appendix: Xenophon's Representation
of Antiphon (D83–D84)

D83 (< A3) Xen. *Mem.* 1.6.1–4, 10–15

ἄξιον δ' αὐτοῦ καὶ ἃ πρὸς Ἀντιφῶντα τὸν σοφιστὴν
διελέχθη μὴ παραλιπεῖν. ὁ γὰρ Ἀντιφῶν ποτε βουλό-
μενος τοὺς συνουσιαστὰς αὐτοῦ παρελέσθαι προσελ-
θὼν τῷ Σωκράτει παρόντων αὐτῶν ἔλεξε τάδε· [2] "ὦ
Σώκρατες, ἐγὼ μὲν ᾤμην τοὺς φιλοσοφοῦντας εὐδαι-
μονεστέρους χρῆναι γίγνεσθαι· σὺ δέ μοι δοκεῖς τἀναντία τῆς φιλοσοφίας ἀπολελαυκέναι. ζῇς γοῦν οὕτως ὡς οὐδ' ἂν εἷς δοῦλος ὑπὸ δεσπότῃ διαιτώμενος
μείνειε· σῖτά τε σιτεῖ καὶ ποτὰ πίνεις τὰ φαυλότατα,
καὶ ἱμάτιον ἠμφίεσαι οὐ μόνον φαῦλον, ἀλλὰ τὸ αὐτὸ
θέρους τε καὶ χειμῶνος, ἀνυπόδητός τε καὶ ἀχίτων
διατελεῖς. [3] καὶ μὴν χρήματά γε οὐ λαμβάνεις, ἃ καὶ
κτωμένους εὐφραίνει καὶ κεκτημένους ἐλευθεριώτερόν
τε καὶ ἥδιον ποιεῖ ζῆν. εἰ οὖν ὥσπερ καὶ τῶν ἄλλων
ἔργων οἱ διδάσκαλοι τοὺς μαθητὰς μιμητὰς ἑαυτῶν

b (≠ DK) Hesychius, *Lexicon*

'by weighing': by measuring the weight, by placing it on the scales.

Another Isolated Word (D82)

D82 (B16) *Anecdota Graeca*

'arriving at': Antiphon instead of 'extending to.'

*Appendix: Xenophon's Representation
of Antiphon (D83–D84)*

D83 (< A3) Xenophon, *Memorabilia*

The discussion he [i.e. Socrates] had with Antiphon the sophist also deserves not to be omitted. For one day Antiphon, wanting to detach Socrates' companions from him, came to Socrates while they were present and spoke as follows: [2] "Socrates, I for one used to think that those who practice philosophy must become happier. But you yourself seem to have obtained the opposite from philosophy. For at any rate you live in such a way as not even a single slave spending his life under a master would endure: you eat and drink the cheapest food and drink; and not only is the cloak you wear cheap but it is also the same one, summer and winter; and you never have shoes or a shirt on. [3] And yet you do not accept money, which is what makes people happy when they acquire it and lets them live more freely and pleasantly when they possess it. If then, just as teachers of other subjects make their disciples imitators of themselves, so you too are going to

ἀποδεικνύουσιν, οὕτω καὶ σὺ τοὺς συνόντας διαθή-
σεις, νόμιζε κακοδαιμονίας διδάσκαλος εἶναι." [4] καὶ
ὁ Σωκράτης πρὸς ταῦτα εἶπε· "δοκεῖς μοι, ὦ Ἀντιφῶν,
ὑπειληφέναι με οὕτως ἀνιαρῶς ζῆν, ὥστε πέπεισμαι
σὲ μᾶλλον ἀποθανεῖν ἂν ἑλέσθαι ἢ ζῆν ὥσπερ ἐγώ.
ἴθι οὖν ἐπισκεψώμεθα τί χαλεπὸν ᾔσθησαι τοῦ ἐμοῦ
βίου. [. . .] [10] ἔοικας, ὦ Ἀντιφῶν, τὴν εὐδαιμονίαν
οἰομένῳ τρυφὴν καὶ πολυτέλειαν εἶναι· ἐγὼ δ' ἐνόμιζον
τὸ μὲν μηδενὸς δεῖσθαι θεῖον εἶναι, τὸ δ' ὡς ἐλαχί-
στων ἐγγυτάτω τοῦ θείου, καὶ τὸ μὲν θεῖον κράτιστον,
τὸ δ' ἐγγυτάτω τοῦ θείου ἐγγυτάτω τοῦ κρατίστου."
[11] πάλιν δέ ποτε ὁ Ἀντιφῶν διαλεγόμενος τῷ Σωκράτει εἶπεν· "ὦ Σώκρατες, ἐγώ τοί σε δίκαιον μὲν
νομίζω, σοφὸν δὲ οὐδ' ὁπωστιοῦν· δοκεῖς δέ μοι καὶ
αὐτὸς τοῦτο γιγνώσκειν· οὐδένα γοῦν τῆς συνουσίας
ἀργύριον πράττῃ. καίτοι τό γε ἱμάτιον ἢ τὴν οἰκίαν
ἢ ἄλλο τι ὧν κέκτησαι νομίζων ἀργυρίου ἄξιον εἶναι
οὐδενὶ ἂν μὴ ὅτι προῖκα δοίης, ἀλλ' οὐδ' ἔλαττον τῆς
ἀξίας λαβών. [12] δῆλον δὴ ὅτι εἰ καὶ τὴν συνουσίαν
ᾤου τινὸς ἀξίαν εἶναι, καὶ ταύτης ἂν οὐκ ἔλαττον τῆς
ἀξίας ἀργύριον ἐπράττου. δίκαιος μὲν οὖν ἂν εἴης, ὅτι
οὐκ ἐξαπατᾷς ἐπὶ πλεονεξίᾳ, σοφὸς δὲ οὐκ ἄν, μηδενός γε ἄξια ἐπιστάμενος." [13] ὁ δὲ Σωκράτης πρὸς
ταῦτα εἶπεν· "ὦ Ἀντιφῶν, [. . .] ὅστις [. . .] ὃν ἂν γνῷ
εὐφυῆ ὄντα διδάσκων ὅ τι ἂν ἔχῃ ἀγαθὸν φίλον ποιεῖται, τοῦτον νομίζομεν, ἃ τῷ καλῷ κἀγαθῷ πολίτῃ
προσήκει, ταῦτα ποιεῖν. [. . .]"
[15] καὶ πάλιν ποτὲ τοῦ Ἀντιφῶντος ἐρομένου αὐτόν,

have the same effect upon your own companions, then acknowledge that you are a teacher of misfortune." [4] And Socrates replied, "You seem to me, Antiphon, to suppose that I live so wretchedly that I am convinced that you would prefer to die rather than to live as I do. Come, then, let us consider what you perceive to be difficult in my life. [. . .] [10] You, Antiphon, are like someone who thinks that happiness consists of luxury and expense; but I have always thought that to be in need of nothing is what is divine, and that to be in need of as few things as possible is the closest thing to what is divine, and that what is divine is the thing that is best, and that what is closest to what is divine is what is closest to what is best."

[11] And on another occasion, when Antiphon was discussing with Socrates, he said, "Socrates, I myself consider you to be just, but not at all wise; and I think that you yourself know this. At least you do not charge any money for your company. And yet your cloak, your house, or any of your other possessions that you think is worth money, you would not give them to anyone for free, nor would you be willing to sell it for less than it is worth. [12] It is quite clear that if you thought that your company was worth something, you would not charge less money for it than it is worth. So while you might well be just, since you do not deceive people for the sake of your own advantage, you would not be wise, since what you know is worth nothing." [13] And Socrates replied, "Antiphon, [. . .] whoever makes someone he knows to have a good natural disposition his friend and teaches him whatever good he might possess, we think that this man is doing what is fitting for a fine and noble citizen. [. . .]"

[15] And on another occasion, when Antiphon asked him

πῶς ἄλλους μὲν ἡγοῖτο πολιτικοὺς ποιεῖν, αὐτὸς δ᾽
οὐ πράττει τὰ πολιτικά, εἴπερ ἐπίσταιτο· "ποτέρως δ᾽
ἄν," ἔφη, "ὦ Ἀντιφῶν, μᾶλλον τὰ πολιτικὰ πράττοιμι,
εἰ μόνος αὐτὰ πράττοιμι ἢ εἰ ἐπιμελοίμην τοῦ ὡς
πλείστους ἱκανοὺς εἶναι πράττειν αὐτά;"

D84 (< A4) Athen. *Deipn.* 15.15 673F

[. . .] σφετερισάμενος καὶ ταῦτα ἐπέγραψέν τι βιβλίον
Περὶ τοῦ παρὰ Ξενοφῶντι ἐν τοῖς Ἀπομνημονεύμασιν
Ἀντιφῶντος, οὐδὲν ἴδιον προσεξευρών.

how he could make other men good at politics when he did not engage in politics himself, if indeed he knew how to do so, he replied, "Antiphon, would I be engaging in politics more if I were to engage in it alone or if I took care that as many men as possible were competent at engaging in it?"

D84 (< A4) Athenaeus, *Deipnosophists*

[. . .] he [i.e. Hephaestion] took over these [scil. statements by Adrastus about Antiphon the tragedian] and wrote a book *On the Antiphon in Xenophon's Memorabilia* without adding anything of his own that he had discovered himself.

ANTIPHON [87 DK]

R

The Identity of the Orator and the Sophist in the Lexicographical Tradition: An Example (R1)

R1 (cf. B14, B63) Harpocr. Δ.42

διάθεσις· ἀντὶ τοῦ πρᾶσις Ἰσοκράτης Βουσίριδι [Isoc. 11.14]. ἀντὶ δὲ τοῦ ἀποδεδόμεθα "διεθέμεθα" εἶπεν Ἀντιφῶν ἐν τῷ Πρὸς τὴν Καλλίου ἔνδειξιν [Frag. 17 Blass], καὶ ἀντὶ τοῦ διοίκησις ὁ αὐτὸς ἐν τῷ Περὶ ὁμονοίας "ἀλλὰ εἰδότες τὴν διάθεσιν ἀκούουσιν." Φρύνιχος Τραγῳδοῖς "τῇ διαθέσει τῶν ἐπῶν" φησί. καὶ γὰρ τὸ ῥῆμα διαθέσθαι λέγουσιν ἐπὶ τοῦ διοικῆσαι· Ἀντιφῶν Ἀληθείας α'· "γυμνωθεῖσα δὲ ἀφορμῆς πολλὰ ἂν καὶ καλὰ κακῶς διαθεῖτο."

Antiphon as Rhetorician and Orator (R2–R9)
His Place in the History of Rhetoric (R2–R6)

R2 (≠ DK) Quintil. *Inst. or.* 3.1.11

Antiphon [. . .] et orationem primus omnium scripsit, et

ANTIPHON

R

R1 (cf. B14, B63) Harpocration, *Lexicon of the Ten Orators*

'organization': instead of 'sale', Isocrates in *Busiris*. Instead of 'we have given,' Antiphon in his *Against the Accusation by Callias* said, "we have organized"; and instead of 'arrangement,' the same man in his *On Concord:* **"but, knowing the organization, they listen"** [= D41a]. Phrynichus in his *Tragic Actors* says, "by the organization of the words." For they use the verb 'to organize' for 'to arrange.' Antiphon, Book 1 of *Truth:* **"stripped of resources** (*aphormê*) **it** [i.e. thought?] **would organize badly many fine things"** [= D14].

R2 (≠ DK) Quintilian, *Training in Oratory*

Antiphon [. . .] was the first of all to write a speech but

101

nihilo minus artem et ipse composuit et pro se dixisse optime est creditus.

R3 (< A2) Hermog. *Ideis* 2.11 (401.3–5 Rabe)

[. . . = **R8**] ἐπεὶ καὶ πρῶτος λέγεται τοῦτο μετελθεῖν τὸ εἶδος καὶ ὅλως εὑρετὴς καὶ ἀρχηγὸς γενέσθαι τοῦ τύπου τοῦ πολιτικοῦ [. . . = **P4**].

R4 (≠ DK) Philostr. *Vit. soph.* 1.15, p. 15.27–32 Kayser

ῥητορικὴν δὲ τὸν Ἀντιφῶντα οἱ μὲν οὐκ οὖσαν εὑρεῖν, οἱ δ' εὑρημένην αὐξῆσαι, γενέσθαι τε αὐτὸν οἱ μὲν αὐτομαθῶς σοφόν, οἱ δὲ ἐκ πατρός. πατέρα γὰρ εἶναι δὴ αὐτῷ Σώφιλον διδάσκαλον ῥητορικῶν λόγων, ὃς ἄλλους τε τῶν ἐν δυνάμει καὶ τὸν τοῦ Κλεινίου ἐπαίδευσεν.

R5 (≠ DK) Clem. Alex. *Strom.* 1.79.3

φασὶ δὲ καὶ τοὺς κατὰ διατριβὴν λόγους καὶ τὰ ῥητορικὰ ἰδιώματα εὑρεῖν καὶ μισθοῦ συνηγορῆσαι πρῶτον δικανικὸν λόγον εἰς ἔκδοσιν γραψάμενον Ἀντιφῶντα ⟨Σω⟩φίλου[1] Ῥαμνούσιον [. . . cf. **P3**].

[1] φίλου ms., corr. Potter

R6 (≠ DK) Ps.-Plut. *Vit. X Orat.* 832C–D, E

καί τινας λόγους τοῖς δεομένοις τῶν πολιτῶν συν-

nonetheless he both composed a technical manual himself, and is thought to have spoken excellently in his own defense [cf. **P15**].

R3 (< A2) Hermogenes, *On Types of Style*

[...] since he is said to have been the first to have practiced this genre and in general to have been the inventor and founder of the political kind [scil. of oratory] [...].

R4 (≠ DK) Philostratus, *Lives of the Sophists*

Some people say that Antiphon discovered rhetoric and that it did not exist before him, others that it had already been discovered but that he developed it further; some people say that he became expert on his own, others thanks to his father. For his father was Sophilus, a teacher of rhetorical speeches who taught the sons of powerful people, including Clinias' [i.e. Alcibiades].

R5 (≠ DK) Clement of Alexandria, *Stromata*

They say that Antiphon of Rhamnous, the son of Sophilus, invented speeches for study and the styles specific to oratory, and that he was the first to deliver publicly a judicial speech for a fee after having written it for publication [...].

R6 (≠ DK) Ps.-Plutarch, *Lives of the Ten Orators*

And he wrote some speeches for contests in the law courts

ἔγραφεν εἰς τοὺς ἐν τοῖς δικαστηρίοις ἀγῶνας πρῶτος
ἐπὶ τοῦτο τραπείς, ὥσπερ τινές φασιν· τῶν γοῦν πρὸ
αὐτοῦ γενομένων οὐδενὸς φέρεται δικανικὸς λόγος,
ἀλλ' οὐδὲ τῶν κατ' αὐτόν, διὰ τὸ μηδέπω ἐν ἔθει τοῦ
συγγράφειν εἶναι [. . .]. πρῶτος δὲ καὶ ῥητορικὰς τέχνας ἐξήνεγκε [. . .].

Judgments on His Style (R7–R9)

R7 (B44a) Philostr. *Vit. soph.* 1.15, p. 17.22–28 Kayser

λόγοι δ' αὐτοῦ δικανικοὶ μὲν πλείους, ἐν οἷς ἡ δεινό-
της καὶ πᾶν τὸ ἐκ τέχνης ἔγκειται, σοφιστικοὶ δὲ καὶ
ἕτεροι μέν, σοφιστικώτατος δὲ ὁ ὑπὲρ τῆς ὁμονοίας,
ἐν ᾧ γνωμολογίαι τε λαμπραὶ καὶ φιλόσοφοι σεμνή
τε ἀπαγγελία καὶ ἐπηνθισμένη ποιητικοῖς ὀνόμασι
καὶ τὰ ἀποτάδην ἑρμηνευόμενα παραπλήσια τῶν πε-
δίων τοῖς λείοις.

R8 (cf. A2) Hermog. *Ideis* 2.11 (400.22–401.2, 6–23
Rabe)

ὁ τοίνυν Ῥαμνούσιος Ἀντιφῶν, οὗπερ οἱ φονικοὶ
φέρονται, πολιτικὸς μὲν καὶ κατὰ τὸ σαφὲς καὶ κατὰ
τὸ ἀληθινὸν καὶ τὸ ἄλλως ἠθικόν, ὥστε καὶ πιθανός,
ἧττον δὲ ἅπαντα ταῦτα ἢ κατὰ τοὺς ἄλλους· [. . . =
R3] μεγέθει δὲ χρῆται μὲν οὐκ ὀλίγῳ, καλῶς δέ πως
συνυφασμένῳ καὶ οὐ κατὰ τὸν Ὑπερίδην διεστηκότι
τῶν ἄλλων οὐδ' αὖ κατὰ τὸν Αἰσχίνην σοφιστικῷ,

for the use of his fellow citizens who needed them, being the first person to have turned to this, as some people say; at least there is no judicial speech extant composed by any of his predecessors, nor of his contemporaries either, since it was not yet the custom to write them down [. . .]. And he was the first person to publish technical manuals of rhetoric [. . .].

Judgments on His Style (R7–R9)

R7 (B44a) Philostratus, *Lives of the Sophists*

There exist many judicial discourses of his, which display great skill and everything that derives from art. Others are sophistic, and the most sophistic of all is the one *On Concord*, where there are maxims that are brilliant and philosophical, a mode of style that is lofty and embellished by poetic diction, and lengthy expositions similar to level plains.

R8 (cf. A2) Hermogenes, *On Types of Style*

The Antiphon from Rhamnous, whose homicide speeches are extant, is a political speaker with regard to clarity, sincerity, and other aspects of ethical character, so that he is also believable, but he is inferior in regard to all this than are the other ones [i.e. the Attic orators]. [. . .] He employs an amplitude that is not inconsiderable, but is woven finely [scil. into the tissue of the speech] and is not, as in Hyperides, separated from the rest nor, as in Aeschines, sophis-

καίτοι τῆς λέξεως αὐτῷ πολλαχοῦ διηρμένης. ἐπι-
μελής γε μὴν οὕτως ὡς μὴ εἶναι προσκορής, γοργὸς
δὲ μετρίως ἐστὶ καὶ δεινὸς ὡσαύτως. ὁ δ' ἕτερος Ἀντιφῶν, οὗπερ οἱ τῆς Ἀληθείας εἰσὶ λεγόμενοι λόγοι,
πολιτικὸς μὲν ἥκιστά ἐστι, σεμνὸς δὲ καὶ ὑπέρογκος
τοῖς τε ἄλλοις καὶ τῷ δι' ἀποφάνσεων περαίνειν τὸ
πᾶν, ὃ δὴ τοῦ ἀξιωματικοῦ τε λόγου ἐστὶ καὶ πρὸς
μέγεθος ὁρῶντος, ὑψηλὸς δὲ τῇ λέξει καὶ τραχύς,
ὥστε καὶ μὴ πόρρω σκληρότητος εἶναι. καὶ περιβάλ-
λει δὲ χωρὶς εὐκρινείας, διὸ καὶ συγχεῖ τὸν λόγον καὶ
ἔστιν ἀσαφὴς τὰ πολλά. καὶ ἐπιμελὴς δὲ κατὰ τὴν
συνθήκην καὶ ταῖς παρισώσεσι χαίρων. οὐ μὴν ἤθους
γέ τι οὐδ' ἀληθινοῦ τύπου μέτεστι τῷ ἀνδρί, φαίην δ'
ἂν ὡς οὐδὲ δεινότητος πλὴν τῆς φαινομένης μέν, οὐ
μὴν οὔσης γε ὡς ἀληθῶς.

R9 (≠ DK) Ps.-Plut. *Vit. X Orat.* 832E

ἔστι δ' ἐν τοῖς λόγοις ἀκριβὴς καὶ πιθανὸς καὶ δεινὸς
περὶ τὴν εὕρεσιν καὶ ἐν τοῖς ἀπόροις τεχνικὸς καὶ
ἐπιχειρῶν ἐξ ἀδήλου καὶ ἐπὶ τοὺς νόμους καὶ[1] τὰ πάθη
τρέπων τοὺς λόγους τοῦ εὐπρεποῦς μάλιστα στοχα-
ζόμενος.

[1] καὶ ‹οὐ› Gernet

tic, even though his style is often lofty. He takes care not to be tedious, he is moderately vehement and forceful in the same way. The other Antiphon, who is the author of the discourses called *Of Truth,* is not in the least political, but is lofty and very weighty, especially because he proceeds entirely by means of declarative statements, which is something characteristic of a dignified discourse that aims for grandeur. His diction is sublime and rugged, to the point of not being far from harshness. And he amplifies without clarity; and this is why his discourse becomes confused and is often obscure. He is careful with regard to composition and is fond of balanced clauses. But the man has nothing of a determinate character or sincerity, and, I would say, not even of forcefulness, except for what is apparent but is not so in reality.

R9 (≠ DK) Ps.-Plutarch, *Lives of the Ten Orators*

In his speeches he is precise and persuasive, very forceful in invention and skillful in dealing with difficulties, venturesome when the matter is unclear, and he directs his speeches toward the laws and the passions, aiming above all at decorum.

See also **THRAS. D8**

His Fame as an Interpreter of Dreams (R10–R12)

R10 (B79) Cic. *Div.* 1.20.39

de quibus disputans Chrysippus multis et minutis somniis colligendis facit idem quod Antipater ea conquirens quae Antiphontis interpretatione explicata declarant illa quidem acumen interpretis [. . .].

R11 (B81) Sen. *Contr.* 2.1.33

Otho Iunius pater [. . .] edidit quidem quattuor libros Colorum, quos belle Gallio noster 'Antiphontis libros' vocabat, tantum in illis somniorum est.

R12 (> A7) Luc. *V. hist.* 2.33

ἐν μέσῃ δὲ τῇ ἀγορᾷ πηγή τίς ἐστιν, ἣν καλοῦσι Καρεῶτιν· καὶ πλησίον ναοὶ δύο Ἀπάτης καὶ Ἀλη-θείας· ἔνθα καὶ τὸ ἄδυτόν ἐστιν αὐτοῖς καὶ τὸ μαν-τεῖον, οὗ προειστήκει προφητεύων Ἀντιφῶν ὁ τῶν ὀνείρων ὑποκριτὴς ταύτης παρὰ τοῦ Ὕπνου λαχὼν τῆς τιμῆς.

His Fame as a Soothsayer (R13)

R13 (T11a Pendrick) Ps.-Call. *Hist. Alex.* rec. vet. 11.1–4, p. 11.6–17, 20–21

μετ' ὀλίγας δὲ παντελῶς ἡμέρας ἔν τινι συμφύτῳ τόπῳ τῶν βασιλείων καθεζομένου τοῦ Φιλίππου, παν-

His Fame as an Interpreter of Dreams (R10–R12)

R10 (B79) Cicero, *On Divination*

When Chrysippus discusses these [scil. dreams], he does the same thing as Antipater: he collects many trivial dreams and tries to find the ones that manifest the interpreter's intelligence when they are explained by means of Antiphon's interpretation [. . .].

R11 (B81) Seneca the Elder, *Controversies*

Junius Otho senior [. . .] published four books of 'colors' [i.e. arguments presenting the facts of a case under a favorable color], which our friend Gallio wittily called 'the books of Antiphon,' so full of dreams were they.

R12 (> A7) Lucian, *True Histories*

In the middle of the marketplace [scil. in the City of Dreams] there is a spring that they call Careotis. And nearby are two temples, of Deceit and of Truth. There too are their sacred precinct and oracle; in front of this stood Antiphon, the interpreter of dreams, prophesying, since he had received this office from Sleep.

His Fame as a Soothsayer (R13)

R13 (≠ DK) Ps.-Callisthenes, *History of Alexander the Great*

Some days later, while Philip [scil. of Macedon] was sitting in a thickly wooded area of the palace, with all kinds of

τοίων ὀρνέων παρ' αὐτοῦ τρεφομένων καὶ ἐν τῷ χωρίῳ
νεμομένων, πρὸς τὴν ἡσυχίαν ἐν φιλολόγοις βιβλίοις
γενομένου αὐτοῦ ὄρνις ἥμερος νεοττὸς[1] εἰς τοὺς κόλ-
πους αὐτοῦ ἀλλομένη ἔτεκεν ᾠόν, ὃ κατακυλισθὲν ἐπὶ
τῆς γῆς ἐρράγη. ἀφ' οὗ ἐξεπήδησε μικρὸν δρακόντιον·
κυκλεῦσαν δὲ τὸ ᾠόν, ὅθεν ἐξῆλθε, καὶ εἰσελθεῖν βου-
λόμενον, πρὶν βαλεῖν ἔσω τὴν κεφαλὴν ἐτελεύτησεν.
τούτου γεναμένου ταραχθεὶς οὐ μετρίως ὁ Φίλιππος
μετεπέμψατο τὸν κατὰ ἐκεῖνον τὸν καιρὸν ἐπίσημον
σημειολύτην Ἀντιφῶντα καὶ ὑφηγεῖται αὐτῷ τὸ γενόμενον. ὁ δὲ πρὸς τοῦτο εἶπεν· "υἱός σοι ἔσται, ὃς βα-
σιλεύσει καὶ περιελεύσεται τὸν ὅλον κόσμον, τῇ ἰδίᾳ
δυνάμει πάντας ὑποτάσσων· οὗτος δὲ εἰς τὰ ἴδια
συστρέφων ὀλιγοχρόνιος τελευτήσει [. . .]." οὗτος μὲν
οὖν ἐπιλύσας τὸ σημεῖον δωνατισθεὶς ἐξῄει.

[1] νεοττός Müller: νόθος mss.

Reactions to Antiphon's Attempt to Square
the Circle (R14–R16)
Two Interpretations Deriving Probably from
Eudemus (R14–R15)

R14 (< B13) Them. *In Phys.*, p. 4.3–8, Schenkl

[. . .] ὃς ἐγγράφων τρίγωνον ἰσόπλευρον εἰς τὸν κύκλον καὶ ἐφ' ἑκάστης τῶν πλευρῶν ἕτερον ἰσοσκελὲς
συνιστὰς πρὸς τῇ περιφερείᾳ τοῦ κύκλου καὶ τοῦτο
ἐφεξῆς ποιῶν ᾤετό ποτε ἐφαρμόσειν τοῦ τελευταίου
τριγώνου τὴν πλευρὰν εὐθεῖαν οὖσαν τῇ περιφερείᾳ.

birds that he kept and that were feeding in that place, a tame young bird jumped into his lap, while he was spending some time at leisure among his scholarly books, and laid an egg, which rolled down onto the ground and broke open. From it leaped forth a small snake, which coiled itself around the egg out of which it had come and wanted to go back into it, but which died before it could put its head inside. Philip was very troubled by this incident and sent for the soothsayer Antiphon, who was very celebrated at that time, and he reported to him what had happened. And he replied, "You will have a son who will be a king and will travel about the whole world, subjecting all men to his own power. But while he is returning to his own country he will die while he is still young. [. . .]." And thus, after he had deciphered the omen, Antiphon received gifts and departed.[1]

[1] This fictional anecdote presupposes that Antiphon the soothsayer was active in the middle of the fourth century BC.

Reactions to Antiphon's Attempt to Square the Circle (R14–R16)
Two Interpretations Deriving Probably from Eudemus (R14–R15)

R14 (< B13) Themistius, *Paraphrase of Aristotle's* Physics

[. . .] by inscribing an equilateral triangle in a circle, constructing on each of its sides another isosceles triangle touching the circumference of the circle, and doing this in succession, he [i.e. Antiphon] thought that at some time the side of the final triangle, though being straight,

111

τοῦτο δὲ[1] τὴν ἐπ᾽ ἄπειρον τομὴν ἀναιροῦντος, ἣν ὑπό-
θεσιν ὁ γεωμέτρης λαμβάνει.

[1] δὲ ἦν ⟨τοῦ⟩ Diels

R15 (< B13) Simpl. *In Phys.*, pp. 54.20–55.11

[. . . = **D36b**] ὁ δὲ Ἀντιφῶν γράψας κύκλον ἐνέγραψέ
τι χωρίον εἰς αὐτὸν πολύγωνον τῶν ἐγγράφεσθαι δυναμένων. ἔστω δὲ εἰ τύχοι τετράγωνον τὸ ἐγγεγραμ-
μένον. ἔπειτα ἑκάστην τῶν τοῦ τετραγώνου πλευρῶν
δίχα τέμνων ἀπὸ τῆς τομῆς ἐπὶ τὰς περιφερείας[1] πρὸς
ὀρθὰς ἦγε γραμμάς, αἳ δηλονότι δίχα ἔτεμνον ἑκά-
στη τὸ καθ᾽ αὑτὴν τμῆμα τοῦ κύκλου. ἔπειτα ἀπὸ[2] τῆς
τομῆς ἐπεζεύγνυεν ἐπὶ τὰ πέρατα τῶν γραμμῶν τοῦ
τετραγώνου εὐθείας, ὡς γίνεσθαι τέτταρα τρίγωνα τὰ
ἀπὸ τῶν εὐθειῶν, τὸ δὲ ὅλον σχῆμα τὸ ἐγγεγραμμέ-
νον ὀκτάγωνον. καὶ οὕτως πάλιν κατὰ τὴν αὐτὴν μέθ-
οδον, ἑκάστην τῶν τοῦ ὀκταγώνου πλευρῶν δίχα τέμνων ἀπὸ τῆς τομῆς ἐπὶ τὴν περιφέρειαν πρὸς ὀρθὰς
ἄγων καὶ ἐπιζευγνὺς ἀπὸ τῶν σημείων, καθ᾽ ἃ αἱ
πρὸς ὀρθὰς ἀχθεῖσαι ἐφήπτοντο τῶν περιφερειῶν,
εὐθείας ἐπὶ τὰ πέρατα τῶν διῃρημένων εὐθειῶν, ἑκκαι-
δεκάγωνον ἐποίει τὸ ἐγγραφόμενον. καὶ κατὰ τὸν αὐτὸν πάλιν λόγον τέμνων τὰς πλευρὰς τοῦ ἑκκαιδεκα-
γώνου τοῦ ἐγγεγραμμένου καὶ ἐπιζευγνὺς εὐθείας καὶ

[1] τὴν περιφέρειαν Torstrik
[2] ἀπὸ Ald.: ἐπὶ DE[b]F

would coincide with the circumference. But this belongs to someone who violates divisibility to infinity, which the geometer takes as an assumption.

R15 (< B13) Simplicius, *Commentary on Aristotle's Physics*

[. . .] Antiphon drew a circle and then inscribed within it one of the polygons that can be inscribed in it. Let the inscribed figure be for example a square. Then, dividing each of the sides of the square in half, he drew perpendicular lines from the point of division to the circumference; clearly each one divided in half its corresponding arc of the circle. Then from the point of division [scil. on the circumference] he connected straight lines to the end points of the sides of the square so that four triangles would be produced from the straight lines and the whole inscribed figure would be an octagon. And so again according to the same procedure: by dividing in half each of the sides of the octagon, drawing perpendicular lines from the point of division to the circumference and connecting straight lines from the points at which the perpendicular lines that had been drawn touched the circumference, to the end points of the divided sides [scil. of the octagon], he made the inscribed figure a sixteen-sided polygon. And again according to the same method: by dividing the sides of the inscribed sixteen-sided polygon, connecting straight lines, and doubling the inscribed polygon, and repeating

διπλασιάζων τὸ ἐγγραφόμενον πολύγωνον καὶ τοῦτο
ἀεὶ ποιῶν ᾤετό³ ποτε δαπανωμένου τοῦ ἐπιπέδου ἐγ-
γραφήσεσθαί τι πολύγωνον τούτῳ τῷ τρόπῳ ἐν τῷ
κύκλῳ, οὗ αἱ πλευραὶ διὰ σμικρότητα ἐφαρμόσουσι
τῇ τοῦ κύκλου περιφερείᾳ. παντὶ δὲ πολυγώνῳ ἴσον
τετράγωνον δυνάμενοι θέσθαι, ὡς ἐν τοῖς Στοιχείοις
[Eucl. 2.14] παρελάβομεν, διὰ τὸ ἴσον ὑποκεῖσθαι τὸ
πολύγωνον τῷ κύκλῳ ἐφαρμόζον αὐτῷ, ἐσόμεθα καὶ
κύκλῳ ἴσον τιθέντες τετράγωνον.

³ ᾤετό coni. Diels: ὥστε vel ὡς τό mss.

A Discussion about the Nature of the
Error in Antiphon's Reasoning (R16)

R16

a (B13) Arist. *Phys.* 1.2 185a14–17

ἅμα δ' οὐδὲ λύειν ἅπαντα προσήκει, ἀλλ' ἢ ὅσα ἐκ

this in succession, he thought that at some point, the area [scil. of the circle] being exhausted, in this way there would be inscribed within the circle some kind of polygon, whose sides, because of their smallness, would coincide with the circumference of the circle. But since we are able to construct a square equal to any polygon, as we have learned in the *Elements* [scil. of Euclid], because the polygon that coincides with the circle is assumed to be equal to it we shall have constructed a square that is also equal to a circle.[1]

[1] This description, like those found in other testimonia (F13c–l Pendrick), probably reflects Antiphon's method in global terms, but the details doubtless derive from reconstructions.

A Discussion about the Nature of the
Error in Antiphon's Reasoning (R16)

R16

a (B13) Aristotle, *Physics*

At the same time, it is not necessary to solve all difficulties

τῶν ἀρχῶν τις ἐπιδεικνὺς ψεύδεται, ὅσα δὲ μή, οὔ,
οἷον τὸν τετραγωνισμὸν τὸν μὲν διὰ τῶν τμημάτων
γεωμετρικοῦ διαλῦσαι, τὸν δὲ Ἀντιφῶντος οὐ γεωμετρικοῦ.

b (B13) Simpl. *In Phys.*, p. 54.12–16

τὸν γὰρ τετραγωνισμὸν τοῦ κύκλου πολλῶν ζητούν-
των (τοῦτο δὲ ἦν τὸ κύκλῳ ἴσον τετράγωνον θέσθαι)
καὶ Ἀντιφῶν ἐνόμισεν εὑρίσκειν καὶ Ἱπποκράτης ὁ
Χῖος ψευσθέντες. ἀλλὰ τὸ μὲν Ἀντιφῶντος ψεῦδος διὰ
τὸ μὴ ἀπὸ γεωμετρικῶν ἀρχῶν ὡρμῆσθαι [. . .] οὐκ
ἔστι γεωμετρικοῦ λύειν [. . .].

c (< F13e Pendrick) Simpl. *In Phys.*, p. 55.12–24

καὶ δῆλον ὅτι ἡ συναγωγὴ παρὰ τὰς γεωμετρικὰς
ἀρχὰς γέγονεν οὐχ ὡς ὁ Ἀλέξανδρός φησιν, ὅτι ὑποτίθεται μὲν ὁ γεωμέτρης τὸ τὸν κύκλον τῆς εὐθείας
κατὰ σημεῖον ἅπτεσθαι ὡς ἀρχήν, ὁ δὲ Ἀντιφῶν
ἀναιρεῖ τοῦτο. οὐ γὰρ ὑποτίθεται ὁ γεωμέτρης τοῦτο,
ἀλλ᾽ ἀποδείκνυσιν αὐτὸ ἐν τῷ τρίτῳ[1] βιβλίῳ [cf. Eucl.
3.2 et 3.16]. ἄμεινον οὖν λέγειν ἀρχὴν εἶναι τὸ ἀδύνατον εἶναι εὐθεῖαν ἐφαρμόσαι περιφερείᾳ, ἀλλ᾽ ἡ μὲν
ἐκτὸς κατὰ ἓν σημεῖον ἐφάψεται τοῦ κύκλου, ἡ δὲ
ἐντὸς κατὰ δύο μόνον καὶ οὐ πλείω, καὶ ἡ ἐπαφὴ κατὰ
σημεῖον γίνεται. καὶ μέντοι τέμνων ἀεὶ τὸ μεταξὺ τῆς

[1] τρίτῳ Diels: ιγ DF: ὀγδόῳ Eᵇ

either, but only those that someone falsely demonstrates
on the basis of the principles—the others, not: for example, it is up to the geometer to refute the squaring [scil. of
the circle] by means of segments, but it is not up to the
geometer [scil. to refute] that of Antiphon.

b (B13) Simplicius, *Commentary on Aristotle's* Physics

Many people were looking for how to square the circle
(this is the construction of a square equal to a circle), but
both Antiphon and Hippocrates of Chios thought they had
discovered it—mistakenly. But it is not up to the geometer
to refute the fallacy of Antiphon since it does not arise
from geometrical principles [. . .] [cf. **D36**].

c (≠ DK) Simplicius, *Commentary on Aristotle's* Physics

And it is clear that the conclusion goes against the principles of geometry, but not, as Alexander says, because the
geometer assumes as a principle that a circle touches a
straight line at a point, and that Antiphon violates this. For
the geometer does not assume this, but he demonstrates
it in the third book [scil. of Euclid's *Elements:* it is a consequence of 3.2 and 3.16 with the corollary]. So it is better
to say that the principle is that it is impossible to make a
straight line coincide with an arc of a circle, but that an
external line will touch the circle in one point, while an
internal one will do so in two points and not in more, and
that the contact takes place at a point. And if he divides in

εὐθείας καὶ τῆς τοῦ κύκλου περιφερείας ἐπίπεδον οὐ
δαπανήσει αὐτὸ οὐδὲ καταλήψεταί ποτε τὴν τοῦ
κύκλου περιφέρειαν, εἴπερ ἐπ᾽ ἄπειρόν ἐστι διαιρετὸν
τὸ ἐπίπεδον. εἰ δὲ καταλαμβάνει, ἀνήρηταί τις ἀρχὴ
γεωμετρικὴ ἡ λέγουσα ἐπ᾽ ἄπειρον εἶναι τὰ μεγέθη
διαιρετά. καὶ ταύτην καὶ ὁ Εὔδημος τὴν ἀρχὴν ἀναι-
ρεῖσθαί φησιν [Frag. 140 Wehrli, p. 159] ὑπὸ τοῦ Ἀντιφῶντος.

A Christian Polemic (R17)

R17 (< B12) Orig. *Cels.* 4.25

[. . .] Ἀντιφῶν ἄλλος ῥήτωρ νομιζόμενος εἶναι καὶ τὴν
πρόνοιαν ἀναιρῶν ἐν τοῖς ἐπιγεγραμμένοις Περὶ ἀληθείας [. . .] οὐδὲν ἧττόν εἰσιν οὗτοι σκώληκες ἐν βορ-
βόρου γωνίᾳ τοῦ τῆς ἀμαθίας καὶ ἀγνοίας καλινδού-
μενοι.

succession the plane surface between the straight line and the circumference of the circle, he will nonetheless not exhaust it and he will never reach the circumference of the circle, since the area is divisible to infinity. And if he does reach it, a geometric principle, which says that magnitudes are divisible to infinity, has been violated. And it is this principle that Eudemus too says has been violated by Antiphon.

A Christian Polemic (R17)

R16 (< B12) Origen, *Against Celsus*

[. . .] Antiphon, who is thought to be another orator [scil. besides Demosthenes], and who abolishes providence in his books entitled *On Truth* [. . .]: these people are not less [scil. than any other evil people] worms rolling around in a corner of the mire of stupidity and ignorance.

38. LYCOPHRON [LYC.]

Aside from an (often suspected) allusion in the second Pseudo-Platonic letter (**P1**) to Lycophron's presence at the court of Dionysius II, nothing whatsoever is known about Lycophron beyond the information provided by Aristotle—Alexander of Aphrodisias seems to have no other basis, for the explanations he provides for a passage in the *Sophistic Refutations* (**D5b**), than his own hypotheses. Aristotle, who mentions Lycophron six times, calls him a 'sophist.' Some modern scholars, on the basis of his definition of law (**D3**), have considered him an important forerunner of social contract theory; Aristotle's own interest in him appears to have been directed above all to his definitions, his innovative use of language, and his rhetorical techniques. To judge from the few surviving traces, he seems to have been a lesser Gorgias.

BIBLIOGRAPHY

R. G. Mulgan. "Lycophron and Greek Theories of Social Contract," *Journal of the History of Ideas* 40 (1979): 121–28.

See also the titles listed in the General Introduction to Chapters 31–42.

LYCOPHRON

OUTLINE OF THE CHAPTER

P

LYCOPHRON [83 DK]

P

Lycophron at the Court of
Dionysius II in Sicily? (P1)

P1 (≠ DK) Ps.-Plat. *Epist.* 2 314d1–5

ἐγὼ δὲ καὶ περὶ Λυκόφρονος καὶ τῶν ἄλλων τῶν παρὰ
σοὶ ὄντων λέγω καὶ πάλαι καὶ νῦν τὸν αὐτὸν λόγον,
ὅτι πρὸς τὸ διαλεχθῆναι καὶ φύσει καὶ τῇ μεθόδῳ τῶν
λόγων πάμπολυ διαφέρεις αὐτῶν [. . .].

LYCOPHRON

Lycophron at the Court of
Dionysius II in Sicily? (P1)

P1 (≠ DK) Ps.-Plato, *Letter* 2

But, with regard to both Lycophron and the other men who are with you, I have been saying for a long time the same thing, and I say it again now: that you [i.e. Dionysius] are far superior to them in the art of discussion, both by your natural talent and by your mode of argumentation [. . .].[1]

[1] According to this indication, Lycophron would have lived in the first part of the fourth century BC. But this testimonium has often been considered suspect.

LYCOPHRON [83 DK]

D

A Radical Solution to the Problem of
Multiple Predication (D1)

D1 (< A2) Arist. *Phys.* 1.2 185b25–31

ἐθορυβοῦντο δὲ καὶ οἱ ὕστεροι τῶν ἀρχαίων ὅπως μὴ
ἅμα γένηται αὐτοῖς τὸ αὐτὸ ἓν καὶ πολλά. διὸ οἱ μὲν
τὸ ἔστι ἀφεῖλον, ὥσπερ Λυκόφρων, [. . .] ἵνα μή ποτε
τὸ ἔστι προσάπτοντες πολλὰ εἶναι ποιῶσι τὸ ἕν.[1]

[1] τὸ ἕν Λ, add. E[1]: τὸ ὄν S

Three Definitions (D2–D4)
Definition of Knowledge (D2)

D2 (< A1) Arist. *Metaph.* H6 1045b9–11

οἱ δὲ συνουσίαν,[1] ὥσπερ Λυκόφρων φησὶν εἶναι τὴν
ἐπιστήμην τοῦ ἐπίστασθαι καὶ ψυχῆς.

[1] ψυχῆς post συνουσίαν hab. mss., del. Bonitz

LYCOPHRON

D

A Radical Solution to the Problem of Multiple Predication (D1)

D1 (< A2) Aristotle, *Physics*

Among the ancient thinkers, those who were later [scil. than Parmenides and Melissus] were also troubled by the question of knowing how to avoid that the same thing be at the same time one and many for them. That is why some of them suppressed the word 'is,' like Lycophron, [. . .] in order not to make the one be many by adding the word 'is.'

See also **PROT. R26**

Three Definitions (D2–D4)
Definition of Knowledge (D2)

D2 (< A1) Aristotle, *Metaphysics*

Some people [scil. speak, in order to explain how the terms of a definition are united,] of **'coexistence,'** as Lycophron says that **knowledge** (*epistêmê*) **is** [scil. the coexistence] **of the act of knowing** (*epistasthai*) **and the soul.**

125

Definition of Law (D3)

D3 (< A3) Arist. *Pol.* 3.9 1280b8–12

γίνεται [. . .] ὁ νόμος συνθήκη καί, καθάπερ ἔφη Λυκόφρων ὁ σοφιστής, ἐγγυητὴς ἀλλήλοις τῶν δι-
καίων, ἀλλ᾽ οὐχ οἷος ποιεῖν ἀγαθοὺς καὶ δικαίους
τοὺς πολίτας.

Definition of Nobility (D4)

D4 (A4) Arist. *Nob.* Frag. 91 (p. 92.5–10 Rose) = Stob.
4.29.24

λέγω δὲ τοῦτο, πότερον τῶν τιμίων ἐστὶ καὶ σπου-
δαίων ἤ, καθάπερ Λυκόφρων ὁ σοφιστὴς ἔγραψε, κε-
νόν[1] τι πάμπαν. ἐκεῖνος γὰρ ἀντιπαραβάλλων ἑτέροις
ἀγαθοῖς αὐτήν "εὐγενείας μὲν οὖν" φησίν[2] "ἀφανὲς
τὸ κάλλος, ἐν λόγῳ δὲ τὸ σεμνόν," ὡς πρὸς δόξαν
οὖσαν τὴν αἵρεσιν αὐτῆς, κατὰ δ᾽ ἀλήθειαν οὐθὲν δια-
φέροντας τοὺς ἀγενεῖς τῶν εὐγενῶν.

[1] καινὸν mss., corr. Jacobs
[2] εὐγενείας . . . φησίν Jacobs: εὐγένεια . . . ἧς mss.

Definition of Law (D3)

D3 (< A3) Aristotle, *Politics*

Law becomes [. . .] a [scil. mere] contract and, as Lycophron the sophist said, **'the guarantor for each other of
what is just,'** but not capable of making the citizens good
and just.

Definition of Nobility (D4)

D4 (A4) Aristotle, Fragment *On Nobility*

I mean this: whether it [i.e. nobility] belongs to the things
that are honorable and worth taking seriously, or whether,
as Lycophron the sophist wrote, it is something entirely
empty. For that man, comparing it to other good things,
said, **"the beauty of nobility is invisible, dignity exists
in speech,"** on the idea that the preference accorded to
it is based on opinion, while according to the truth those
people who are not noble do not differ in any way from
the ones who are noble.

Rhetorical Issues (D5–D6)
A Loophole (D5)

D5

a (A6) Arist. *SE* 15 174b30–33

ἐπιχειρητέον δ᾽ ἐνίοτε καὶ πρὸς ἄλλα τοῦ εἰρημένου, ἐκεῖνο ἐκλαβόντας, ἐὰν μὴ πρὸς τὸ κείμενον ἔχῃ τις ἐπιχειρεῖν· ὅπερ ὁ Λυκόφρων ἐποίησε προβληθέντος λύραν ἐγκωμιάζειν.

b (> A6) Alex. *In SE*, pp. 118.30–119.3

καὶ ὁ σοφιστὴς Λυκόφρων τοὺς λυρικοὺς ἐπαινῶν ἐπὶ τὴν λύραν μετήνεγκε τὸν ἔπαινον· ἢ μᾶλλον ἐπειδὴ ὑπό τινων ἠναγκάζετο ἐπαινέσαι τὴν λύραν, εἶτα μὴ λόγων εὐπόρει πολλῶν, μικρόν τι ἐπαινέσας τὴν αἰσθητὴν ταύτην λύραν ἐπὶ τὴν οὐράνιον ἀνηνέχθη· ἔστι γὰρ ἐν οὐρανῷ ἄστρον τι ἐξ ἄστρων πολλῶν συγκείμενον λύρα ὀνομαζόμενον, εἰς ἣν πολλοὺς καλοὺς καὶ ἀγαθοὺς λόγους ἐξεῦρεν.

Rhetorical Issues (D5–D6)
A Loophole (D5)

D5

a (A6) Aristotle, *Sophistic Refutations*

Sometimes one must undertake something different from what has been said, interpreting this [scil. in a certain way], if one is not able to undertake what has been laid down—this is what Lycophron did when the proposal was made to deliver an encomium on the lyre.

b (> A6) Alexander of Aphrodisias, *Commentary on Aristotle's* Sophistic Refutations

And while the sophist Lycophron was praising the lyric poets, he transferred his praise to the lyre; or rather, when he was obliged by certain people to praise the lyre but did not have available much to say about it, first he briefly praised the perceptible lyre that we know and then he moved upward to the lyre in the heavens. For in the heavens there is a constellation made up of a number of stars called 'the Lyre,' concerning which he found many fine and excellent things to say.[1]

[1] The double explanation suggests that these are simple hypotheses and that no other information about the incident mentioned was available.

The Use of Compound and Rare Terms (D6)

D6 (A5) Arist. *Rhet.* 3.3 1405b34–37, 1406a7–8

τὰ δὲ ψυχρὰ ἐν τέτταρσι γίνεται κατὰ τὴν λέξιν, ἔν τε τοῖς διπλοῖς ὀνόμασιν, οἷον Λυκόφρων τὸν πολυπρόσωπον οὐρανὸν τῆς μεγαλοκορύφου[1] γῆς καὶ ἀκτὴν δὲ στενόπορον [. . .]· τὸ χρῆσθαι γλώτταις, οἷον Λυκόφρων Ξέρξην τὸν πέλωρον ἄνδρα καὶ Σκίρων σίνις ἀνήρ [. . .].

---

[1] μεγαλοκορύφου mss.: μελανοκ-anon.

The Use of Compound and Rare Terms (D6)

D6 (A5) Aristotle, *Rhetoric*

Frigidity in style is produced in four ways: by compound terms, as in Lycophron **'the many-faced heavens of the great-summitted earth'** and **'narrow-passaged promontory'** [. . .]; by the use of rare terms, as in Lycophron **'Xerxes, the monstrous** (*pelôros*) **man'** and **'Sciron, a ravaging** (*sinis*) **man'** [. . .].[1]

---

[1] Both terms are otherwise exclusively poetic. *pelôros* is not usually applied to human beings; *sinis* is usually not an adjective but a substantive.

39. XENIADES [XENI.]

Our only source for the philosophical views of Xeniades of Corinth is Sextus Empiricus, who mentions him seven times; one of these passages (**D1**) provides a summary of his four principal theses and what is probably a report (unless it is merely a reconstruction) of Xeniades' argument for one of them. The nature of his ontological theses and his epistemological nihilism are the only evidence for counting Xeniades among the 'sophists'; they seem to be linked less closely to Gorgias (with whom he has often been connected) than to Protagoras' epistemological doctrine. It is probably for this reason that he attracted Democritus' attention (cf. **ATOM. P25**).

Scholars disagree about whether this Xeniades of Corinth is to be identified with a Xeniades of Corinth, mentioned by Diogenes Laertius (6.30, 36, 74), who bought Diogenes the Cynic as a slave; the chronology makes this unlikely, even if we assign our Xeniades a relatively late date (the beginning of the fourth century BC).

BIBLIOGRAPHY

Studies

J. Brunschwig. "Democritus and Xeniades," in V. Caston and D. W. Graham, eds., *Presocratic Philosophy. Essays in Honour of Alexander Mourelatos* (Aldershot, 2002), pp. 159–67.

See also the titles listed in the General Introduction to Chapters 31–42.

OUTLINE OF THE CHAPTER

D

Sextus Empiricus' Report on Xeniades' Theses (D1)

R

A Rapprochement between Xeniades and Xenophanes (R1)
A Contrast with Protagoras (R2)
A Skeptical Criticism of Xeniades (R3)

XENIADES [81 DK]

D

Sextus Empiricus' Report on
Xeniades' Theses (D1)

D1 (> 81., 68 B163) Sext. Emp. *Adv. Math.* 7.53

Ξενιάδης δὲ ὁ Κορίνθιος, οὗ καὶ Δημόκριτος μέμνηται, πάντ᾽ εἰπὼν ψευδῆ καὶ πᾶσαν φαντασίαν καὶ δόξαν ψεύδεσθαι καὶ ἐκ τοῦ μὴ ὄντος πᾶν τὸ γινόμενον γίνεσθαι καὶ εἰς τὸ μὴ ὂν πᾶν τὸ φθειρόμενον φθείρεσθαι [. . . = **R1**]. τὸ δ᾽ ὅτι πάντα ἐστὶ ψευδῆ καὶ διὰ τοῦτο ἀκατάληπτα, δείκνυται ἐκ τῆς τῶν αἰσθήσεων διαβολῆς· εἰ γὰρ τὸ ἐπαναβεβηκὸς κριτήριον πάντων τῶν πραγμάτων ἐστὶ ψευδές, ἐξ ἀνάγκης καὶ πάντα ἐστὶ ψευδῆ. τὸ δέ γε ἐπαναβεβηκὸς κριτήριον πάντων τῶν πραγμάτων εἰσὶν αἱ αἰσθήσεις, καὶ δείκνυνται ψευδεῖς· πάντα ἄρα τὰ πράγματά ἐστι ψευδῆ.

XENIADES

D

Sextus Empiricus' Report on Xeniades' Theses (D1)

D1 (> 81., 68 B163) Sextus Empiricus, *Against the Logicians*

Xeniades of Corinth, whom Democritus mentions [cf. **ATOM. P25**], and who asserted that all things are false, that every representation and opinion is false, that everything that comes to be comes to be out of what is not, and that everything that perishes perishes into what is not [. . .]. And it is demonstrated on the basis of slandering the senses that all things are false and for this reason cannot be known: for if the highest criterion of all things is false, then of necessity all things too are false. Now the highest criterion of all things are the perceptions, and it is demonstrated that they are false; therefore all things are false.

XENIADES [81 DK]

R

A Rapprochement between Xeniades and Xenophanes (R1)

R1 (> 81.) Sext. Emp. *Adv. Math.* 7.53

Ξενιάδης δὲ ὁ Κορίνθιος [. . . = **D1**] δυνάμει τῆς αὐτῆς ἔχεται τῷ Ξενοφάνει στάσεως. μὴ ὄντος γάρ τινος ἀληθοῦς κατὰ διαφορὰν τοῦ ψεύδους, ἀλλὰ πάντων ψευδῶν ὄντων καὶ διὰ τοῦτο ἀκαταλήπτων, οὐδὲ δια-κριτικόν τι τούτων ἔσται κριτήριον.

A Contrast with Protagoras (R2)

R2 (≠ DK) Sext. Emp. *Adv. Math.* 7.388

εἰ γὰρ κριτήριον ἀπολειπτέον[1] τὴν φαντασίαν, ἤτοι πᾶσαν ἀληθῆ φαντασίαν λεκτέον εἶναι, καθὼς ἔλεγεν

---

[1] ἀπολειπτέον N: ἀποληπτέον LEϚ

XENIADES

R

A Rapprochement between Xeniades and Xenophanes (R1)

R1 (> 81.) Sextus Empiricus, *Against the Logicians*

Xeniades of Corinth [. . .] occupies potentially the same position as Xenophanes. For if nothing true exists that would be different from what is false, but all things are false and for this reason cannot be known, there will not exist either any criterion that could distinguish among them [cf. **XEN. R21b**].

A Contrast with Protagoras (R2)

R2 (≠ DK) Sextus Empiricus, *Against the Logicians*

For if one admits that the representation (*phantasia*) is the criterion, then one must say either that every representa-

ὁ Πρωταγόρας, ἢ πᾶσαν ψευδῆ, ὡς ἔφασκε Ξενιάδης
ὁ Κορίνθιος [. . .].

A Skeptical Criticism of Xeniades (R3)

R3 (≠ DK) Sext. Emp. *Adv. Math.* 7.399

εἰ γὰρ πᾶσαι αἱ φαντασίαι εἰσὶ ψευδεῖς καὶ οὐδέν
ἐστιν ἀληθές, ἀληθές ἐστι τὸ 'οὐδέν ἐστιν ἀληθές.' εἰ
ἄρα μηδέν ἐστιν ἀληθές, ἔστιν ἀληθές· καὶ οὕτως εἰς
τοὐναντίον τῇ προθέσει περιήχθησαν οἱ περὶ τὸν Ξε-
νιάδην, λέγοντες πάσας τὰς φαντασίας εἶναι ψευδεῖς
καὶ μηδὲν ὅλως ἐν τοῖς οὖσιν ὑπάρχειν ἀληθές.

tion is true, as Protagoras said, or else that every one is false, as Xeniades of Corinth asserted [. . .].

A Skeptical Criticism of Xeniades (R3)

R3 (≠ DK) Sextus Empiricus, *Against the Logicians*

For if all representations (*phantasiai*) are false and nothing is true, the proposition 'nothing is true' is true: if therefore nothing is true, there is something true. And in this way Xeniades and his followers are led by reversal to affirm the contrary of their thesis, when they say that all representations are false and that there is nothing true at all among the things that are.

40. THE ANONYMOUS OF IAMBLICHUS [ANON. IAMBL.]

In one section of his *Protrepticus*, the Neoplatonist philosopher Iamblichus presents a series of paragraphs on the subjects of how one can achieve excellence (*aretê*), how one's own excellence can be made to benefit other people, and why one should practice temperance and respect for the laws and justice. In 1889 Friedrich Blass identified these paragraphs as an extract, almost entirely continuous (setting aside transitions added by Iamblichus), from a treatise on ethics and politics from the time of the Peloponnesian War. Since then scholars have attributed them to a number of possible authors, including Antiphon, Antisthenes, Critias, Protagoras, or one of his followers. But even if some suggestions are more plausible than others, any such attribution is destined to remain arbitrary in the absence of any decisive evidence. And even the traditional dating of the text to the fifth century and its identification as belonging to the 'sophistic' movement are not certain; indeed, recently the proposal has been made to date it as late as the fourth century BC on the basis of certain affinities with Xenophon's writings.

For this text and its translation, we have adopted the following conventions:

(1.) = reference to the numbering in DK

[. . .] = lines of the text of Iamblichus that are omitted here

[1] = indications taken from the text of DK

BIBLIOGRAPHY

Editions and Translations

F. Blass. *De Antiphonte sophista Iamblichi auctore* (Progr. Kiel, 1889).

D. Musti (trans., intro., comm. M. Mari). *Anonimo di Giamblico: La pace e il benessere. Idee sull'economia, la società, la morale* (Milan, 2003).

Studies

A. T. Cole, Jr. "The Anonymus Iamblichi and His Place in Greek Political Theory," *Harvard Studies in Classical Philology* 65 (1962): 127–63.

J. de Romilly. "Sur un écrit anonyme ancien et ses rapports avec Thucydide," *Journal des Savants* (1980): 19–34.

See also the titles listed in the General Introduction to Chapters 31–42.

THE ANONYMOUS OF
IAMBLICHUS [89 DK]

(> DK) Anon. in Iambl. *Protr.*

[Excellence derives from a combination
of natural disposition and training]
p. 95.13–24 Pistelli

(1.) [. . .] [1] ὅ τι ἄν τις ἐθέλῃ ἐξεργάσασθαι εἰς τέλος
τὸ βέλτιστον, ἐάν τε σοφίαν ἐάν τε ἀνδρείαν ἐάν τε
εὐγλωσσίαν ἐάν τε ἀρετὴν ἢ τὴν σύμπασαν ἢ μέρος
τι αὐτῆς, ἐκ τῶνδε οἷόν τε εἶναι κατεργάσασθαι. [2]
φῦναι μὲν πρῶτον δεῖν, καὶ τοῦτο μὲν τῇ τύχῃ ἀπο-
δεδόσθαι, τὰ δὲ ἐπ᾽ αὐτῷ ἤδη τῷ ἀνθρώπῳ τάδε εἶναι,
ἐπιθυμητὴν γενέσθαι τῶν καλῶν καὶ ἀγαθῶν φιλόπο-
νόν τε καὶ πρωιαίτατα μανθάνοντα καὶ πολὺν χρόνον
αὐτοῖς συνδιατελοῦντα. [3] εἰ δέ τι ἀπέσται τούτων καὶ
ἕν, οὐχ οἷόν τέ ἐστιν οὐδὲ[1] ἐς τέλος τὸ ἄκρον ἐξεργάσασθαι, ἔχοντος δὲ ἅπαντα ταῦτα, ἀνυπέρβλητον γίγνεται τοῦτο, ὅ τι ἂν ἀσκῇ τις τῶν ἀνθρώπων. [. . .]

---

[1] οὐδὲν Kaibel

142

THE ANONYMOUS OF
IAMBLICHUS

(> DK) Anonymous, in Iamblichus, *Protreptic*

[Excellence derives from a combination
of natural disposition and training]

(1.) [. . .] [1] whatever one wishes to bring to perfection in
the finest terms possible—whether wisdom, manly valor,
eloquence, or virtue, either as a whole or in some part of
it—one can achieve this in the following way. [2] First one
must have a certain natural disposition, and while this has
been assigned by chance, the following things are already
within a person's own power: to become desirous of fine
and good things and to become industrious, learning these
things as early as possible and also continuing to spend a
long time with them. [3] If any of these [scil. factors] is
absent, even if only one of them, it is not possible to bring
to perfection what is highest either; but if one possesses
all of these, then whatever a person works at turns out to
be unsurpassable. [. . .]

[This combination is most effective when
it is practiced over a long period of time]
pp. 96.1–97.8

(2.) [. . .] [1] ἐξ οὗ ἄν τις βούληται δόξαν παρὰ τοῖς
ἀνθρώποις λαβεῖν καὶ τοιοῦτος φαίνεσθαι οἷος ἂν ᾖ,
αὐτίκα δεῖ νέον τε ἄρξασθαι καὶ ἐπιχρῆσθαι αὐτῷ
ὁμαλῶς ἀεὶ καὶ μὴ ἄλλοτε ἄλλως. [2] συγχρονισθὲν
μὲν γὰρ ἕκαστον τούτων καὶ αὐτίκα τε ἀρξάμενον καὶ
συναυξηθὲν εἰς τέλος λαμβάνει βέβαιον τὴν δόξαν
καὶ τὸ κλέος διὰ τάδε, ὅτι πιστεύεταί τε ἤδη ἀνενδοι-
άστως, καὶ ὁ φθόνος τῶν ἀνθρώπων οὐ προσγίγνεται,
δι᾽ ὃν τὰ μὲν οὐκ αὔξουσιν οὐδ᾽ εὐλόγως μηνύουσι,
τὰ δὲ καταψεύδονται μεμφόμενοι παρὰ τὸ δίκαιον. [3]
οὐ γὰρ ἡδὺ τοῖς ἀνθρώποις ἄλλον τινὰ τιμᾶν (αὐτοὶ
γὰρ στερίσκεσθαί τινος ἡγοῦνται), χειρωθέντες δὲ
ὑπὸ τῆς ἀνάγκης αὐτῆς καὶ κατὰ σμικρὸν ἐκ πολλοῦ
ἐπαχθέντες ἐπαινέται καὶ ἄκοντες ὅμως γίγνονται· [4]
ἅμα δὲ καὶ οὐκ ἀμφιβάλλουσιν, εἴτε[1] ἄρα τοιοῦτος
ἄνθρωπός ἐστιν οἷος φαίνεται, ἢ ἐνεδρεύει καὶ θηρεύε-
ται τὴν δόξαν ἐπὶ ἀπάτῃ, καὶ ἃ ποιεῖ, ταῦτα καλλω-
πίζεται ὑπαγόμενος τοὺς ἀνθρώπους· ἐν ἐκείνῳ δὲ τῷ
τρόπῳ, ᾧ ἐγὼ προεῖπον, ἀσκηθεῖσα ἡ ἀρετὴ πίστιν
ἐμποιεῖ περὶ ἑαυτῆς καὶ εὔκλειαν. [5] ἑαλωκότες γὰρ
ἤδη κατὰ τὸ ἰσχυρὸν οἱ ἄνθρωποι οὔτε τῷ φθόνῳ ἔτι
δύνανται χρῆσθαι οὔτε ἀπατᾶσθαι ἔτι οἴονται. [6] ἔτι
δὲ καὶ ὁ χρόνος συνὼν μὲν ἑκάστῳ ἔργῳ καὶ πρά-

---

[1] εἰ Diels

[This combination is most effective when
it is practiced over a long period of time]
(2.) [. . .] [1] from the moment that one forms the desire
to obtain renown among men and to show oneself to be
the sort of man one is, one must begin straightaway while
young and one must practice it always in the same way and
not in different ways at different times. [2] For when each
of these [scil. good] things has lasted a long time and has
begun straightaway and has grown to fulfillment, he ob-
tains a secure renown and fame for the following reasons:
because by now he is trusted without hesitation, and the
envy of humans does not adhere to him—envy, on account
of which people do not extol certain things or speak in
praise of them, and speak falsely about other things, criti-
cizing them unjustly. [3] For it does not provide pleasure
to people to assign honor to another person (for they suppose that they themselves are being deprived of something); but if they are defeated by necessity itself and have
been influenced little by little over a long time, they become praisers, even if unwillingly. [4] At the same time,
they do not doubt whether a person really is then just as
he appears to be, or is setting a trap and hunting for
renown by means of deceit, or [scil. suspect] that whatever
he does he is only putting on a show and misleading
people. But if virtue is practiced in the way I just mentioned, it produces trust in itself and a good reputation.
[5] For when people have already been strongly won over,
they are no longer capable of feeling envy and they do
not think any longer that they are being deceived. [6]
Moreover, a long duration of time too, when it accompanies each deed and action, at length provides confirma-

γματι πολὺς καὶ διὰ μακροῦ κρατύνει τὸ ἀσκούμενον,
ὁ δὲ ὀλίγος χρόνος οὐ δύναται τοῦτο ἀπεργάζεσθαι.
[7] καὶ τέχνην μὲν ἄν τις τὴν κατὰ λόγους πυθόμενος
καὶ μαθὼν οὐ χείρων τοῦ διδάσκοντος ἂν γένοιτο ἐν
ὀλίγῳ χρόνῳ, ἀρετὴ δὲ ἥτις ἐξ ἔργων πολλῶν συνίσταται, ταύτην γε² οὐχ οἷόν τε ὀψὲ ἀρξαμένῳ οὔτε³
ὀλιγοχρονίως ἐπὶ τέλος ἀγαγεῖν, ἀλλὰ συντραφῆναί
τε αὐτῇ δεῖ καὶ συναυξηθῆναι τῶν μὲν εἰργόμενον
κακῶν καὶ λόγων καὶ ἠθῶν, τὰ δ᾽ ἐπιτηδεύοντα καὶ
κατεργαζόμενον σὺν πολλῷ χρόνῳ καὶ ἐπιμελείᾳ. [8]
ἅμα δέ τις καὶ τῇ ἐξ ὀλίγου χρόνου εὐδοξίᾳ προσγίγνεται βλάβη τοιάδε· τοὺς γὰρ ἐξαπιναίως καὶ ἐξ
ὀλίγου χρόνου ἢ πλουσίους ἢ σοφοὺς ἢ ἀγαθοὺς ἢ
ἀνδρείους γενομένους οὐκ ἀποδέχονται ἡδέως οἱ ἄνθρωποι. [. . .]

² δὲ ms., corr. Kiessling: δὴ Pistelli   ³ οὐδὲ Pistelli

[Excellence must be applied to good ends]
p. 97.16–24

(3.) [. . .] [1] ὅταν τις ὀρεχθείς τινος τούτων¹ κατεργα-
σάμενος ἔχῃ αὐτὸ εἰς τέλος, ἐάν τε εὐγλωσσίαν ἐάν
τε σοφίαν ἐάν τε ἰσχύν, τούτῳ εἰς ἀγαθὰ καὶ νόμιμα
καταχρῆσθαι δεῖ· εἰ δὲ εἰς ἄδικά τε καὶ ἄνομα χρήσεται τις τῷ ὑπάρχοντι ἀγαθῷ, πάντων κάκιστον εἶναι τὸ τοιοῦτον καὶ ἀπεῖναι κρεῖσσον αὐτὸ ἢ παρεῖ-
ναι· [2] καὶ ὥσπερ ἀγαθὸς τελέως ὁ τούτων τι ἔχων
γίγνεται εἰς τὰ ἀγαθὰ αὐτοῖς καταχρώμενος, οὕτω
πάλιν πάγκακος τελέως ὁ εἰς τὰ πονηρὰ χρώμενος.

tion for what one is devoting one's efforts to, whereas a short period of time is not able to accomplish this. [7] And in the case of an art, it is possible for someone who learns and is taught the art of speeches to become as good as his teacher in a short time; but it is not possible to bring virtue, which is made up of a large number of deeds, to perfection if someone begins late, or to do so in a short time, but one must be raised together with it and must grow together with it, avoiding both wicked words and wicked habits, and instead practicing and achieving ones of the other kind over a long time and with diligence. [8] At the same time, there is a drawback adhering to a good reputation acquired in a short time, namely that people do not accept with pleasure those who, suddenly and in a short time, have become either wealthy or wise or good or valorous. [. . .]

[Excellence must be applied to good ends]
(3.) [. . .] [1] whenever someone desiring one of these [scil. good] things, has obtained it by his labor, and possesses it to perfection, whether it is eloquence, wisdom, or strength, he must use it for good and lawful ends; but if anyone uses what is good for unjust and unlawful ends, this sort of thing is the worst of all, and it is better that it be absent rather than present. [2] And just as someone who possesses one of these [scil. good things] shows himself to be a perfectly good man if he uses it for good ends, so too in turn he shows himself to be a perfectly wicked one if he uses it for evil ends.

---

1 τοῦτο ms., corr. Töpfer: secl. Blass

[The greatest excellence is what
benefits the most people]
pp. 97.25–98.11

[3] τόν τε αὖ ἀρετῆς ὀρεγόμενον τῆς συμπάσης σκε-
πτέον εἶναι, ἐκ τίνος ἂν λόγου ἢ ἔργου ἄριστος εἴη·
τοιοῦτος δ᾽ ἂν εἴη ὁ πλείστοις ὠφέλιμος ὤν. [4] εἰ μέν
τις χρήματα διδοὺς εὐεργετήσει τοὺς πλησίον, ἀναγ-
κασθήσεται κακὸς εἶναι πάλιν αὖ συλλέγων τὰ χρή-
ματα· ἔπειτα οὐκ ἂν οὕτω ἄφθονα συναγάγοι ὥστε μὴ
ἐπιλείπειν διδόντα καὶ δωρούμενον· εἶτα αὕτη αὖθις
δευτέρα κακία προσγίγνεται μετὰ τὴν συναγωγὴν
τῶν χρημάτων, ἐὰν ἐκ πλουσίου πένης γένηται καὶ ἐκ
κεκτημένου μηδὲν ἔχων. [5] καὶ προσέτι δωρούμενος
πῶς ἂν ἔχοι τὴν δόσιν ἀνέκλειπτον;[1] πῶς ἂν οὖν δή
τις μὴ χρήματα νέμων ἀλλὰ ἄλλῳ δή τινι τρόπῳ εὐ-
ποιητικὸς ἂν εἴη ἀνθρώπων, καὶ ταῦτα μὴ σὺν κακίᾳ
ἀλλὰ σὺν ἀρετῇ; [6] ὧδε οὖν ἔσται τοῦτο, εἰ τοῖς
νόμοις τε καὶ τῷ δικαίῳ ἐπικουροίη· τοῦτο γὰρ τάς τε
πόλεις καὶ τοὺς ἀνθρώπους τὸ συνοικίζον καὶ τὸ
συνέχον.[2] [. . .]

[1] καὶ . . . ἀνέκλειπτον post ἀρετῇ; infra hab. ms., transp.
nos   [2] post συνέχον hab. ms. εἶναι, secl. Wilamowitz

[One must practice temperance,
especially regarding money]
pp. 98.17–99.15

(4.) [. . .] [1] ἐγκρατέστατόν γε δεῖ εἶναι πάντα ἄνδρα
διαφερόντως· τοιοῦτος δ᾽ ἂν μάλιστα, εἴ τις[1] τῶν χρη-

148

[The greatest excellence is what
benefits the most people]

[3] One must now consider on the basis of what speech or what deed the man who desires the whole of virtue could become best. Such a man would be the one who is beneficial to the most people. [4] For if someone does a good deed to his neighbors by giving them money, he will be obliged to be wicked again in turn when he collects the money; and then, it would not be possible for him to accumulate resources in such abundance that he would not end up being in need if he made gifts and presents; then again, here is a second drawback that comes about from accumulating money, if, after having been rich, one becomes poor, and, after having been affluent, one possesses nothing. [5] And furthermore, if he gives presents, how could he continue to do so without interruption? How then could someone do a good deed to people not by distributing money but in some other way, and do this not with wickedness but with virtue? [6] That will happen in the following way: if he comes to the aid of the laws and of justice. For this is what brings together cities and people and holds them together. [. . .]

[One must practice temperance,
especially regarding money]

(4.) [. . .] [1] it is necessary that every man be surpassingly temperate. That person would most of all be a man of this

---

¹ μάλιστα εἴη, εἰ Diels: μάλιστα εἴη, εἴ τις Kiessling

μάτων κρείσσων εἴη, πρὸς ἃ πάντες διαφθείρονται,
καὶ τῆς ψυχῆς ἀφειδὴς ἐπὶ τοῖς δικαίοις ἐσπουδακὼς
καὶ τὴν ἀρετὴν μεταδιώκων· πρὸς ταῦτα γὰρ δύο οἱ
πλεῖστοι ἀκρατεῖς εἰσι. [2] διὰ τοιοῦτον δέ τι ταῦτα
πάσχουσιν· φιλοψυχοῦσι μέν, ὅτι τοῦτο ἡ ζωή ἐστιν,
ἡ ψυχή·[2] ταύτης οὖν φείδονται καὶ ποθοῦσιν αὐτὴν
διὰ φιλίαν τῆς ζωῆς καὶ συνήθειαν ᾗ συντρέφονται·
φιλοχρηματοῦσι δὲ τῶνδε εἵνεκα, ἅπερ φοβεῖ αὐτούς.
[3] τί δ᾿ ἐστὶ ταῦτα; αἱ νόσοι, τὸ γῆρας, αἱ ἐξαπιναῖοι
ζημίαι, οὐ τὰς ἐκ τῶν νόμων λέγω ζημίας (ταύτας μὲν
γὰρ καὶ εὐλαβηθῆναι ἔστι καὶ φυλάξασθαι), ἀλλὰ
τὰς τοιαύτας, πυρκαϊάς, θανάτους οἰκετῶν, τετραπόδων, ἄλλας αὖ συμφοράς, αἳ περίκεινται αἱ μὲν τοῖς
σώμασιν, αἱ δὲ ταῖς ψυχαῖς, αἱ δὲ τοῖς χρήμασι. [4]
τούτων δὴ οὖν ἕνεκα πάντων, ὅπως ἐς ταῦτα ἔχωσι
χρῆσθαι τοῖς χρήμασι, πᾶς ἀνὴρ τοῦ πλούτου ὀρέγε-
ται. [5] καὶ ἄλλ᾿ ἄττα δέ ἐστιν ἅπερ οὐχ ἧσσον ἢ τὰ
προειρημένα ἐξορμᾷ τοὺς ἀνθρώπους ἐπὶ τὸν χρημα-
τισμόν, αἱ πρὸς ἀλλήλους φιλοτιμίαι καὶ οἱ ζῆλοι καὶ
αἱ δυναστεῖαι, δι᾿ ἃς τὰ χρήματα περὶ πολλοῦ ποιοῦνται, ὅτι συμβάλλεται εἰς τὰ τοιαῦτα. [6] ὅστις δέ
ἐστιν ἀνὴρ ἀληθῶς ἀγαθός, οὗτος οὐκ ἀλλοτρίῳ κόσμῳ περικειμένῳ τὴν δόξαν θηρᾶται, ἀλλὰ τῇ αὑτοῦ
ἀρετῇ. [. . .]

[2] ἢ ζωή ἐστιν ἢ ψυχή ms., corr. Diels: ταὐτὸ ἡ ζωή ἐστι
τῇ ψυχῇ Kiessling: alii alia

sort if he were superior to money, which is what corrupts all men, and if, without caring about his life, he bestowed his pains on things that are just and pursued virtue. For these are the two areas in which most men lack temperance. [2] It is for the following reason that they suffer this. On the one hand they are pusillanimous [*philopsukhein*, literally 'they love their souls'], because this is what their life is, namely their soul [*psukhê*]; hence they care about this and they feel a great desire for it because of their love for life and because of their familiarity with what they were raised with. And on the other hand they love money because they fear the following things. [3] What are these? Diseases, old age, sudden adversities—I do not mean adversities from the laws (for one can take precautions against these and guard against them), but instead ones of the following sort: house fires, the deaths of members of one's household, of animals, and again other misfortunes, some of which concern bodies, others souls, and others money. [4] It is because of all these things that every man desires wealth, so that he can use his money against these eventualities. [5] And there are some other reasons that, no less than the ones I have mentioned, drive people to moneymaking: rivalries with each other, jealousies, political powers, because of which they attach great importance to money, because it makes a contribution in situations of this sort. [6] But whoever is a truly good man seeks a renown not by means of an ornament that does not belong to him but by means of his own virtue. [. . .]

[Arguments against pusillanimity]
p. 99.19–28

(5.) [1] [. . .] ὅτι, εἰ μὲν ὑπῆρχε τῷ ἀνθρώπῳ εἰ μὴ ὑπ'
ἄλλου ἀποθάνοι ἀγήρῳ τε εἶναι καὶ ἀθανάτῳ τὸν λοιπὸν χρόνον, συγγνώμη ἂν[1] πολλὴ τῷ φειδομένῳ τῆς
ψυχῆς· [2] ἐπεὶ δὲ ὑπάρχει τῷ βίῳ μηκυνομένῳ τό τε
γῆρας κάκιον ὂν ἀνθρώποις καὶ μὴ ἀθάνατον εἶναι,
καὶ[2] ἀμαθία ἤδη ἐστὶ[3] μεγάλη καὶ συνήθεια πονηρῶν
λόγων τε καὶ ἐπιθυμημάτων, ταύτην περιποιεῖν ἐπὶ
δυσκλείᾳ, ἀλλὰ μὴ ἀθάνατόν ‹τι›[4] ἀντ' αὐτῆς λείπεσθαι,[5] ἀντὶ θνητῆς οὔσης εὐλογίαν ἀέναον καὶ ἀεὶ
ζῶσαν. [. . .]

---

[1] ἂν ‹ἦν› Blass   [2] post καὶ hab. ms. ἡ, del. Pistelli]
[3] an δή ἐστι scribendum?   [4] ‹τι› nos
[5] λείπεσθαι ‹κλέος› Wilamowitz

[Respect for the laws and justice]
pp. 100.5–101.6

(6.) [1] [. . .] οὐκ ἐπὶ πλεονεξίαν ὁρμᾶν δεῖ, οὐδὲ τὸ
κράτος τὸ ἐπὶ τῇ πλεονεξίᾳ ἡγεῖσθαι ἀρετὴν εἶναι, τὸ
δὲ τῶν νόμων ὑπακούειν δειλίαν·[1] πονηροτάτη γὰρ
αὕτη ἡ διάνοιά ἐστι, καὶ ἐξ αὐτῆς πάντα τἀναντία
τοῖς ἀγαθοῖς γίνεται, κακία τε καὶ βλάβη. εἰ γὰρ
ἔφυσαν μὲν οἱ ἄνθρωποι ἀδύνατοι καθ' ἕνα ζῆν, συν-
ῆλθον δὲ πρὸς ἀλλήλους τῇ ἀνάγκῃ εἴκοντες, πᾶσα
δὲ ἡ ζωὴ αὐτοῖς εὕρηται καὶ τὰ τεχνήματα πρὸς
αὐτήν, σὺν ἀλλήλοις δὲ εἶναι αὐτοὺς κἂν[2] ἀνομίᾳ δι-
αιτᾶσθαι οὐχ οἷόν τε (μείζω γὰρ αὐτοῖς ζημίαν[3] οὕτω

THE ANONYMOUS OF IAMBLICHUS

[Arguments against pusillanimity]
(5.) [1] [. . .] if it befell the man who cared about his life,
unless he was killed by someone else, to be ageless and
deathless for the rest of time, then he would be easily
forgiven. [2] But since what befalls a life that is prolonged
is old age, which is worse for people, and not to be deathless, it is truly both a great foolishness and the effect of
habituation to wicked words and desires to preserve this
[scil. life] at the cost of a bad reputation, and not to leave
behind in its place something deathless, a renown that is
everlasting and always alive instead of one that is mortal.
[. . .]

[Respect for the laws and justice]
(6.) [. . .] [1] one must not be greedy to have more, nor
think that power founded upon greed is virtue while obe-
dience to the laws is cowardice. For this is the most evil
idea of all, and it is the source of all the things that are the
contrary of good ones: viz., iniquity and harm. For if by
nature people have been born unable to live alone, and
came together with one another yielding to constraint, and
discovered all the means of life and the technical resources
to achieve it, and if it is also not possible for them to live
with one another and to spend their lives without laws (for
a greater tribulation happens to them in this way than

---

1 δεῖ λίαν ms., corr. Arcerius   2 καὶ ms., corr. Diels
3 ζημίαν ⟨ἂν⟩ Diels

153

γίγνεσθαι ἐκείνης τῆς κατὰ ἕνα διαίτης), διὰ ταύτας
τοίνυν τὰς ἀνάγκας τόν τε νόμον καὶ τὸ δίκαιον ἐμ-
βασιλεύειν τοῖς ἀνθρώποις καὶ οὐδαμῇ μεταστῆναι
ἂν αὐτά· φύσει γὰρ ἰσχυρᾷ[4] ἐνδεδέσθαι ταῦτα. [2] εἰ
μὲν δὴ γένοιτό τις ἐξ ἀρχῆς φύσιν τοιάνδε ἔχων,
ἄτρωτος τὸν χρῶτα ἄνοσός τε καὶ ἀπαθὴς καὶ ὑπερ-
φυὴς καὶ ἀδαμάντινος τό τε σῶμα καὶ τὴν ψυχήν, τῷ
τοιούτῳ ἴσως ἄν τις ἀρκεῖν ἐνόμισε τὸ ἐπὶ τῇ πλεονεξίᾳ κράτος (τὸν γὰρ τοιοῦτον τῷ νόμῳ μὴ ὑποδύνοντα
δύνασθαι ἀθῷον εἶναι), οὐ μὴν ὀρθῶς οὗτος οἴεται· [3]
εἰ γὰρ καὶ τοιοῦτός τις εἴη, ὡς οὐκ ἂν γένοιτο, τοῖς
μὲν νόμοις συμμαχῶν καὶ τῷ δικαίῳ καὶ ταῦτα κρα-
τύνων καὶ τῇ ἰσχύι χρώμενος ἐπὶ ταῦτά τε καὶ τὰ
τούτοις ἐπικουροῦντα, οὕτω μὲν ἂν σῴζοιτο ὁ τοιοῦτος,
ἄλλως δὲ οὐκ ἂν διαμένοι· [4] δοκεῖν γὰρ ἂν τοὺς
ἅπαντας ἀνθρώπους τῷ τοιούτῳ φύντι πολεμίους
κατασταθέντας διὰ τὴν ἑαυτῶν εὐνομίαν, καὶ τὸ πλῆ-
θος ἢ τέχνῃ ἢ δυνάμει ὑπερβαλέσθαι ἂν καὶ περι-
γενέσθαι τοῦ τοιούτου ἀνδρός. [5] οὕτω φαίνεται καὶ
αὐτὸ τὸ κράτος, ὅπερ δὴ κράτος ἐστί, διά τε τοῦ
νόμου καὶ διὰ τὴν δίκην σῳζόμενον. [. . .]

---

[4] ἰσχυρὰ ms., corr. Blass et iam MT

[Positive consequences of respect for the laws]
pp. 101.17–102.24

(< 7.) [. . .] [1] πίστις μὲν πρώτη ἐγγίγνεται ἐκ τῆς
εὐνομίας μεγάλα ὠφελοῦσα τοὺς ἀνθρώπους τοὺς

from living alone)—because of all these constraints, law and justice rule over people and could not be altered in any way. For these [scil. law and justice] are bound together by a strong nature. [2] Indeed, if someone were born possessing from the beginning such a nature as to be invulnerable in his flesh, immune to illness and suffering, extraordinarily large, and indestructible in body and soul, one might perhaps think that, for someone like that, power founded upon greed might be sufficient: for a man like that could live in impunity without submitting to the law. And yet to think like this is incorrect. [3] For even if someone like this, such as could never come about, actually existed, it would only be by allying himself with the laws and justice, and fortifying these, using his strength for the benefit of them and of what comes to their aid, that someone like this could preserve himself; otherwise he could not survive. [4] For all men would decide to make themselves the enemies of the man who had this nature, because of their respect for the laws: and their multitude, either by skill or by strength, would surpass such a man and would prevail over him. [5] In this way it is evident that even force itself, as force, is preserved by law and justice. [. . .]

[Positive consequences of respect for the laws]
(< 7.) [. . .] [1] Trust is the first thing that comes about from respect for the laws; it greatly benefits all people, and it

σύμπαντας, καὶ τῶν μεγάλων ἀγαθῶν τοῦτό ἐστι·
κοινὰ γὰρ τὰ χρήματα γίγνεται ἐξ αὐτῆς, καὶ οὕτω
μὲν ἐὰν καὶ ὀλίγα ᾖ ἐξαρκεῖ ὅμως κυκλούμενα, ἄνευ
δὲ ταύτης οὐδ' ἂν πολλὰ ᾖ ἐξαρκεῖ. [2] καὶ αἱ τύχαι
δὲ αἱ εἰς τὰ χρήματα καὶ τὸν βίον, αἵ τε ἀγαθαὶ καὶ
μή, ἐκ τῆς εὐνομίας τοῖς ἀνθρώποις προσφορώτατα
κυβερνῶνται· τούς τε γὰρ εὐτυχοῦντας ἀσφαλεῖ αὐτῇ
χρῆσθαι καὶ ἀνεπιβουλεύτῳ, τούς τε αὖ δυστυχοῦν-
τας ἐπικουρεῖσθαι ἐκ τῶν εὐτυχούντων διὰ τὴν ἐπιμι-
ξίαν τε καὶ πίστιν, ἅπερ ἐκ τῆς εὐνομίας γίγνεται. [3]
τόν τε αὖ χρόνον τοῖς ἀνθρώποις διὰ τὴν εὐνομίαν εἰς
μὲν τὰ πράγματα ἀργὸν γίγνεσθαι, εἰς δὲ τὰ ἔργα
τῆς ζωῆς ἐργάσιμον. [4] φροντίδος δὲ τῆς μὲν ἀηδε-
στάτης ἀπηλλάχθαι τοὺς ἀνθρώπους ἐν τῇ εὐνομίᾳ,
τῇ δὲ ἡδίστῃ συνεῖναι· πραγμάτων μὲν γὰρ φροντίδα
ἀηδεστάτην εἶναι, ἔργων δὲ ἡδίστην. [5] εἴς τε αὖ τὸν
ὕπνον ἰοῦσιν, ὅπερ ἀνάπαυμα κακῶν ἐστιν ἀνθρώποις, ἀφόβους μὲν καὶ ἄλυπα μεριμνῶντας ἔρχεσθαι
εἰς αὐτόν, γιγνομένους δὲ ἀπ'[1] αὐτοῦ ἕτερα τοιαῦτα
πάσχειν, καὶ μὴ ἐμφόβους ἐξάπινα καθίστασθαι,
οὕτω δ'[2] ἐκ μεταλλαγῆς ἡδίστης τὸ[3] γνωστὴν τὴν
ἡμέραν εἶναι προσδέχεσθαι, ἀλλὰ ἡδέως[4] φροντίδας
μὲν ἀλύπους περὶ τὰ ἔργα τῆς ζωῆς ποιουμένους,
τοὺς πόνους δὲ τῇ ἀντιλήψει ἀγαθῶν ἐλπίσιν εὐπί-
στοις καὶ εὐπροσδοκήτοις ἀνακουφίζοντας, ὧν πάν-

---

[1] ἐπ' ms., corr. Wilamowitz   [2] οὐδ' ms., corr. Töpfer: ὧδε
δὲ Vitelli   [3] τοῦ ms., corr. Vitelli   [4] ἀδεῶς Wilamowitz

belongs among the great good things. For because of this, resources are shared in common, and in this way, even if they are scarce, nonetheless they suffice because they circulate, while, without this, they would not suffice even if they were abundant. [2] And the most suitable way for people to navigate the uncertainties of fortune that affect money and life, both those that are favorable and those that are not, is for them to base themselves on respect for the laws: for those people who have good fortune enjoy it in safety and freedom from intrigues, while on the contrary those who have bad fortune receive assistance from the fortunate ones on the basis of the interconnection and trust that come about from respect for the laws. [3] Again, thanks to respect for the laws, people's time is freed from legal matters and can be devoted to the activities of their own life. [4] When the laws are respected, men are relieved of the most disagreeable kinds of thoughts and spend their time on the most agreeable ones: for thinking about legal matters is most disagreeable, but thinking about one's own activities is most agreeable. [5] Again, when they go to sleep, which for people is a repose from evils, they do so without fear and painful thoughts; and when they wake up they feel the same way, and they are not suddenly filled with fear, nor in this way, after a most agreeable respite, do they wait for the day to make itself known, but agreeably thinking painless thoughts about the activities of their life, they lessen their troubles by thinking instead about good things, with confident and optimistic hopes. For all these things, respect for the laws is the

τῶν τὴν εὐνομίαν αἰτίαν εἶναι. [6] καὶ τὸ κακὰ μέγιστα τοῖς ἀνθρώποις πορίζον, πόλεμον ἐπιφερόμενον
εἰς καταστροφὴν καὶ δούλωσιν, καὶ τοῦτο ἀνομοῦσι
μὲν μᾶλλον ἐπέρχεσθαι, εὐνομουμένοις δ᾽ ἧσσον. [7]
καὶ ἄλλα δὲ πολλά ἐστιν ἐν τῇ εὐνομίᾳ ἀγαθά, ἅπερ
ἐπικουρήματα τῇ ζωῇ καὶ παραψυχὴ τῶν χαλεπῶν ἐξ
αὐτῆς γίγνεται.

[Negative consequences of lack of respect for the laws]
p. 102.26–104.16

[. . .] [8] ἄσχολοι μὲν πρῶτον οἱ ἄνθρωποι πρὸς τὰ
ἔργα γίγνονται καὶ ἐπιμελοῦνται τοῦ ἀηδεστάτου,
πραγμάτων ἀλλ᾽ οὐκ ἔργων, τά τε χρήματα δι᾽
ἀπιστίαν καὶ ἀμιξίαν ἀποθησαυρίζουσιν ἀλλ᾽ οὐ κοι-
νοῦνται, καὶ οὕτως σπάνια γίγνεται, ἐὰν καὶ πολλὰ ᾖ.
[9] αἵ τε τύχαι αἱ φλαῦραι ‹. . .›[1] καὶ αἱ ἀγαθαὶ εἰς
τἀναντία ὑπηρετοῦσιν· ἥ τε γὰρ εὐτυχία οὐκ ἀσφαλής
ἐστιν ἐν τῇ ἀνομίᾳ ἀλλ᾽ ἐπιβουλεύεται, ἥ τε δυστυχία
οὐκ ἀπωθεῖται ἀλλὰ κρατύνεται διὰ τὴν ἀπιστίαν καὶ
ἀμιξίαν. [10] ὅ τε πόλεμος ἔξωθεν μᾶλλον ἐπάγεται
καὶ ἡ οἰκεία στάσις ἀπὸ τῆς αὐτῆς αἰτίας, καὶ ἐὰν μὴ
πρόσθεν γίγνηται, τότε συμβαίνει· ἔν τε πράγμασι[2]
συμβαίνει καθεστάναι[3] ἀεὶ διὰ ἐπιβουλὰς τὰς ἐξ ἀλλήλων, δι᾽ ἅσπερ εὐλαβουμένους τε διατελεῖν καὶ
ἀντεπιβουλεύοντας ἀλλήλοις.

[1] lac. pos. nos, e.g. ‹ἔτι βαρύτεραι γίγνονται›vel ‹οὐ (ἀνα-)
κουφίζονται›vel ‹οὐκ ἐπανορθοῦνται›   [2] πράγματι ms.,
corr. Cobet   [3] καθιστάναι ms., corr. Cobet

cause. [6] And what is responsible for the greatest evils for people, war, which leads to subjugation and enslavement, this too happens more to people who do not respect the laws, less to those who respect them. [7] And in respect for the laws there are many other good things that provide assistance to life and consolation for the difficulties that come from it.

[Negative consequences of lack of respect for the laws] [. . .] [8] first, people do not have time for their own activities and busy themselves with what is most disagreeable, legal matters and not their own activities, and they hoard their money out of a lack of trust and interconnection and do not share it in common, and in this way it becomes scarce, even if it is abundant. [9] Adverse fortunes <e.g. become even worse> and good ones serve contrary ends: for good fortune is not safe when the laws are not respected, but instead is the object of intrigues, while misfortune is not expelled, but instead is exacerbated by lack of trust and interconnection. [10] War is introduced all the more from abroad, and internal dissension too, for the same reason, and if it did not come about earlier, it happens then: it happens that people are always involved in legal matters because of intrigues devised by each other, because of which they spend all their time on their guard and devising intrigues against each other in return.

[11] καὶ οὔτε ἐγρηγορόσιν ἡδείας τὰς φροντίδας εἶναι
οὔτε ἐς τὸν ὕπνον ἀπερχομένοις ἡδεῖαν τὴν ὑποδοχὴν
ἀλλὰ ἐνδείματον, τήν τε ἀνέγερσιν ἔμφοβον καὶ πτο-
οῦσαν τὸν ἄνθρωπον ἐπὶ μνήμας κακῶν ἐξαπιναίους
ἄγειν· ἅπερ ἐκ τῆς ἀνομίας ταῦτά τε καὶ τὰ ἄλλα
κακὰ τὰ προειρημένα ἅπαντα ἀποβαίνει.

[12] γίνεται δὲ καὶ ἡ τυραννίς, κακὸν τοσοῦτόν τε καὶ
τοιοῦτον, οὐκ ἐξ ἄλλου τινὸς ἢ ἀνομίας. οἴονται δέ
τινες τῶν ἀνθρώπων, ὅσοι μὴ ὀρθῶς συμβάλλονται,
τύραννον ἐξ ἄλλου τινὸς καθίστασθαι καὶ τοὺς ἀνθρώπους στερίσκεσθαι τῆς ἐλευθερίας οὐκ αὐτοὺς
αἰτίους ὄντας, ἀλλὰ βιασθέντας ὑπὸ τοῦ καταστα-
θέντος τυράννου, οὐκ ὀρθῶς ταῦτα λογιζόμενοι· [13]
ὅστις γὰρ ἡγεῖται βασιλέα ἢ τύραννον ἐξ ἄλλου τινὸς γίγνεσθαι ἢ ἐξ ἀνομίας τε καὶ πλεονεξίας, μωρός
ἐστιν. ἐπειδὰν γὰρ ἅπαντες ἐπὶ κακίαν τράπωνται,
τότε τοῦτο γίγνεται· οὐ γὰρ οἷόν τε ἀνθρώπους ἄνευ
νόμων καὶ δίκης ζῆν. [14] ὅταν οὖν ταῦτα τὰ δύο ἐκ
τοῦ πλήθους ἐκλίπῃ, ὅ τε νόμος καὶ ἡ δίκη, τότε ἤδη
εἰς ἕνα ἀποχωρεῖν τὴν ἐπιτροπίαν τούτων καὶ φυλα-
κήν. πῶς γὰρ ἂν ἄλλως εἰς ἕνα μοναρχία περισταίη,
εἰ μὴ τοῦ νόμου ἐξωσθέντος τοῦ τῷ πλήθει συμφέρον-
τος; [15] δεῖ γὰρ τὸν ἄνδρα τοῦτον, ὃς τὴν δίκην κατα-
λύει[4] καὶ τὸν νόμον τὸν πᾶσι κοινὸν καὶ συμφέροντα
ἀφαιρήσεται, ἀδαμάντινον γενέσθαι, εἰ μέλλει συλή-
σειν ταῦτα παρὰ τοῦ πλήθους τῶν ἀνθρώπων εἷς ὢν
παρὰ πολλῶν· [16] σάρκινος δὲ καὶ ὅμοιος τοῖς λοι-
ποῖς γενόμενος ταῦτα μὲν οὐκ ἂν δυνηθείη ποιῆσαι,

[11] And neither when they awaken are their thoughts agreeable, nor when they go to sleep is their expectation agreeable, but fearful, and their frightened and terrifying awakening brings a man to sudden memories of evils. These things, and the other evils I mentioned earlier, all derive from lack of respect for the laws.

[12] And tyranny, which is so great an evil and one of such a kind, comes about for no other reason than from lack of respect for the laws. Some people—those who reason incorrectly—think that a tyrant comes to power for some other reason and that people are deprived of their freedom without their being responsible themselves, but because they have been coerced by the tyrant who has come to power. But to reason like this is incorrect. [13] For whoever supposes that a king or tyrant comes to power for any other reason than from lack of respect for the laws and from greed is a fool. For when everyone turns to iniquity, then this is what happens; for it is not possible for people to live without laws and justice. [14] So when these two things, law and justice, are lacking for the multitude of the people, then the power of decision over them and their custody pass over to a single man. For otherwise how could a monarchy devolve upon a single man, unless the law, which is beneficial to the multitude, has been expelled? [15] This man, who overthrows justice and will abolish the law, which is shared in common and is beneficial for all, must of necessity be made of steel, if, being only one man, he is planning to deprive of these things the multitude of people, though they are many. [16] But if he were made of flesh and were similar to the rest of man-

---

⁴ καταλύσει Kiessling

τἀναντία⁵ δὲ ἐκλελοιπότα καθιστὰς μοναρχήσειεν ἄν·
διὸ καὶ γιγνόμενον τοῦτο ἐνίους τῶν ἀνθρώπων λαν-
θάνει.
[17] εἰ τοίνυν τοσούτων μὲν αἰτία κακῶν ἐστιν ἀνομία,
τοσοῦτον δὲ ἀγαθὸν⁶ εὐνομία, οὐκ ἄλλως ἔνεστι τυ-
χεῖν εὐδαιμονίας εἰ μή τις νόμον ἡγεμόνα προστή-
σαιτο τοῦ οἰκείου βίου. [. . .]

5 συλῆσαι, τοὐναντίον Vitelli: ποιῆσαι τὰ πάτρια vel ποιῆσαι τοὐναντίον ‹τὰ πάτρια› Diels
6 τοσούτων δὲ ἀγαθῶν ex Ciz. Kiessling

kind, he would not be able to do this; [scil. only] if he made the opposition cease to exist, could he become a monarch. And this is why some people do not notice that this is happening.

[17] If then lack of respect for the laws is the cause of so many evils, and if respect for the laws is such a great good, then it is not possible to achieve happiness in any other way than by establishing law as the guide for one's own life.[1] [. . .]

---

[1] Diels does not include this sentence at the beginning of section 17; Untersteiner adds a few more lines.

41. *PAIRS OF ARGUMENTS (DISSOI LOGOI)* (DISS.)

The manuscripts that transmit the works of Sextus Empiricus append at their end a further text for which they do not indicate either the title or the author. It was first published in 1570 by Henri Étienne, under the arbitrary title Διαλέξεις (*Arguments*), as an appendix to his edition of Diogenes Laertius; the name by which modern scholars refer to this text, Δισσοὶ Λόγοι (*Pairs of Discourses* or *Arguments*), is not so much a title (and is certainly not its author's intended title) as rather a description of its contents, derived from the opening words of the text (which are repeated three times in what follows). The treatise does in fact begin with a series of four opposing arguments presenting two contrasting positions on the same issue indicated by titles—whether good and bad, seemly and unseemly, just and unjust, true and false are identical with one another or not; occasionally the author expresses a preference for one position or the other. But then, after a lacuna of indeterminable extent, the text goes on to deal with a variety of heterogeneous topics—insanity and sanity, wisdom and foolishness, whether wisdom and virtue (*aretê*) can be taught and learned, whether political offices should be assigned by lot, whether someone who knows the art of speeches can speak on all subjects, and how to exercise one's memory—in five further sections that do not all propose contrasting arguments and that are not furnished with titles. Shortly after the beginning of the ninth section, the manuscripts indicate that the text breaks off. The treatise is written for the most part in a Doric dialect; its date is unknown, but on the fragile basis of a reference to the end of the Peloponnesian War it is usually assigned to sometime between the last decades of the fifth and the first decades of the fourth centuries BC. A number of subjects discussed in Plato's dialogues, especially the *Gorgias* and the *Protagoras,* can be recognized, particularly in the final sections.

The reader should note that, whereas elsewhere in our edition we have indicated by boldface the words that we consider to be exact verbal citations from the works of the early Greek philosophers, considerations of appearance have led us in the present chapter to use plain characters for this text, which has reached us *in extenso* by direct transmission via medieval manuscripts.

BIBLIOGRAPHY

Edition

T. M. Robinson. *Contrasting Arguments. An Edition of the Dissoi Logoi* (New York, 1979).

See also the titles listed in the General Introduction to Chapters 31–42.

Δισσοὶ λόγοι (vel Διαλέξεις)
[90 DK]

1. Περὶ ἀγαθῶ καὶ κακῶ

[1] δισσοὶ λόγοι λέγονται ἐν τῇ Ἑλλάδι ὑπὸ τῶν φιλοσοφούντων περὶ τῶ ἀγαθῶ καὶ τῶ κακῶ. τοὶ μὲν γὰρ λέγοντι ὡς ἄλλο μέν ἐστι τὸ ἀγαθόν, ἄλλο δὲ τὸ κακόν· τοὶ δέ ὡς τὸ αὐτό ἐστι, καὶ τοῖς μὲν ἀγαθὸν εἴη, τοῖς δὲ κακόν, καὶ τῷ αὐτῷ ἀνθρώπῳ τοτὲ μὲν ἀγαθόν, τοτὲ δὲ κακόν. [2] ἐγὼ δὲ καὶ αὐτὸς τοῖσδε ποτιτίθεμαι. σκέψομαι δὲ ἐκ τῶ ἀνθρωπίνω βίω, ᾧ[1] ἐπιμελὲς βρώσιός τε καὶ πόσιος καὶ ἀφροδισίων· ταῦτα γὰρ ἀσθενοῦντι μὲν κακόν, ὑγιαίνοντι δὲ καὶ δεομένῳ ἀγαθόν. [3] καὶ ἀκρασία τοίνυν τούτων τοῖς μὲν ἀκρατέσι κακόν, τοῖς δὲ πωλεῦντι ταῦτα καὶ μισθαρνέοντι ἀγαθόν. νόσος τοίνυν τοῖς μὲν ἀσθενεῦντι κακόν, τοῖς δὲ ἰατροῖς ἀγαθόν. ὁ τοίνυν θάνατος τοῖς μὲν ἀποθανοῦσι κακόν, τοῖς δ' ἐνταφιοπώλαις καὶ τυμβοποιοῖς ἀγαθόν. [4] γεωργία τε καλῶς ἐξενείκασα τὼς καρπὼς τοῖς μὲν γεωργοῖς ἀγαθόν, τοῖς δὲ ἐμπόροις κακόν. τὰς τοίνυν ὁλκάδας συντρίβεσθαι καὶ παραθραύεσθαι τῷ μὲν ναυκλήρῳ κακόν, τοῖς δὲ

PAIRS OF ARGUMENTS
(DISSOI LOGOI)

1. On Good and Bad

[1] A pair of arguments is stated in Greece by those who philosophize about good and bad. For some people say that the good is one thing, the bad another; but other people say that they are the same thing, and that for some people it is good, for others bad, and for the same person at one time good and at another time bad. [2] As for me, I agree with these latter. I shall consider this question in terms of human life, which is concerned for food, drink, and sex; for these things are bad for a sick person but good for a healthy one who needs them. [3] And so intemperance (*akrasia*) in these matters is bad for intemperate people (*akrateis*), but it is good for those who sell them and profit from them. So illness is bad for sick people, but it is good for doctors. So death is bad for those who die, but it is good for undertakers and gravediggers. [4] Farming that produces crops in abundance is good for the farmers, but it is bad for merchants. So when trading vessels are staved in and smashed this is bad for the ship owner,

---

1 ὦν mss., corr. Wilamowitz

ναυπαγοῖς ἀγαθόν. [5] ἔτι ⟨δὲ⟩² τὸν σίδαρον κατέσθε-
σθαι καὶ ἀμβλύνεσθαι καὶ συντρίβεσθαι τοῖς μὲν
ἄλλοις κακόν, τῷ δὲ χαλκῇ ἀγαθόν. καὶ μὰν τὸν
κέραμον παραθραύεσθαι τοῖς μὲν ἄλλοις κακόν, τοῖς
δὲ κεραμεῦσιν ἀγαθόν. τὰ δὲ ὑποδήματα κατατρίβε-
σθαι καὶ διαρρήγνυσθαι τοῖς μὲν ἄλλοις κακόν, τῷ
δὲ σκυτῇ ἀγαθόν. [6] ἐν τοίνυν τοῖς ἀγῶσι τοῖς γυμνι-
κοῖς³ καὶ τοῖς μωσικοῖς καὶ τοῖς πολεμικοῖς· αὐτίκα ἐν
τῷ γυμνικῷ, τῷ σταδιοδρόμῳ ἁ νίκα τῷ μὲν νικῶντι
ἀγαθόν, τοῖς δὲ ἡσσαμένοις κακόν. [7] καττωὐτὸ⁴ δὲ
καὶ τοὶ παλαισταὶ καὶ πύκται καὶ τοὶ ἄλλοι πάντες
μωσικοί· αὐτίκα ἁ κιθαρῳδία⁵ τῷ μὲν νικῶντι ἀγαθόν,
τοῖς δὲ ἡσσαμένοις κακόν. [8] ἔν τε τῷ πολέμῳ (καὶ
τὰ νεώτατα⁶ πρῶτον ἐρῶ) ἁ τῶν⁷ Λακεδαιμονίων νίκα,
ἂν⁸ ἐνίκων Ἀθηναίως καὶ τὼς συμμάχως, Λακεδαιμονίοις μὲν ἀγαθόν, Ἀθηναίοις δὲ καὶ τοῖς συμμάχοις
κακόν· ἅ τε νίκα, ἂν τοὶ Ἕλλανες τὸν Πέρσαν ἐνίκα-
σαν, τοῖς μὲν Ἕλλασιν ἀγαθόν, τοῖς δὲ βαρβάροις
κακόν. [9] ἁ τοίνυν τοῦ Ἰλίου αἵρεσις τοῖς μὲν Ἀχαι-
οῖς ἀγαθόν, τοῖς δὲ Τρωσὶ κακόν. καδδὲ ταὐτὸν καὶ
τὰ τῶν Θηβαίων καὶ τὰ τῶν Ἀργείων πάθη. [10] καὶ
ἁ τῶν Κενταύρων καὶ Λαπιθᾶν μάχα τοῖς μὲν Λαπί-
θαις ἀγαθόν, τοῖς δὲ Κενταύροις κακόν. καὶ μὰν καὶ
ἁ τῶν θεῶν καὶ Γιγάντων λεγομένα μάχα καὶ νίκα
τοῖς μὲν θεοῖς ἀγαθόν, τοῖς δὲ Γίγασι κακόν.

² ⟨δὲ⟩ Vossianus   ³ γυμναστικοῖς mss., corr. Blass
⁴ καὶ τοῦτο mss., corr. Matthew de Varis

but it is good for the shipbuilders. [5] Furthermore, when an iron tool rusts, loses its edge, and is broken, this is bad for other people, but it is good for the blacksmith. And certainly when a clay pot is smashed this is bad for other people, but it is good for the potters. When sandals are worn out and split apart this is bad for other people, but it is good for the cobbler. [6] And so in competitions, athletic, musical, and military ones: for example in the athletic one, the victory is good for the runner in the stadium race who wins, but it is bad for the losers. [7] The same holds for the wrestlers and boxers and for all the musicians: for example singing to the cithara is good for the winner, but it is bad for the losers. [8] And in war (I shall speak first about the most recent events), the victory of the Spartans that they won over the Athenians and their allies was good for the Spartans, but it was bad for the Athenians and their allies. And the victory that the Greeks won over the Persian was good for the Greeks, but it was bad for the barbarians. [9] So the capture of Troy was good for the Achaeans, but it was bad for the Trojans. And the same holds for what happened to the Thebans and the Argives. [10] And the battle of the Centaurs and Lapiths was good for the Lapiths, but it was bad for the Centaurs. And certainly the battle that is reported between the gods and the Giants and the victory was good for the gods, but it was bad for the Giants.

---

⁵ ἁ κιθαρῳδία mss. (ὁ κιθαρῳδός P1 P2): ἁ κιθαρῳδίας Diels: ⟨ἁ νίκα⟩ ἁ κιθαρῳδίας Kranz   ⁶ τὰ νεώτατα Koen: τᾷ νεότατι mss. (τὰ P2, νεώτατοι M S): τὰ νεωστὶ North

⁷ ἁ τῶν Koen: αὐτῶν mss.

⁸ ἁ̂ν Weber: ἐν ἁ̂ mss.

[11] ἄλλος δὲ λόγος λέγεται, ὡς ἄλλο μὲν τἀγαθὸν
εἴη, ἄλλο δὲ τὸ κακόν, διαφέρον ὥσπερ καὶ τὤνυμα,
οὕτω καὶ τὸ πρᾶγμα. ἐγὼ δὲ καὶ αὐτὸς τοῦτον διαι-
ρεῦμαι τὸν τρόπον· δοκῶ γὰρ οὐδὲ διάδαλον⁹ ἦμεν,
ποῖον ἀγαθὸν καὶ ποῖον κακόν, αἰ τὸ αὐτὸ καὶ μὴ
ἄλλο ἑκάτερον εἴη· καὶ γὰρ θαυμαστόν κ' εἴη. [12]
οἶμαι δὲ οὐδέ κ' αὐτὸν ἔχεν ἀποκρίνασθαι, αἴ τις¹⁰
ἔροιτο τὸν ταῦτα λέγοντα· "εἶπον δή μοι, ἤδη τύ τι
τοὶ γονέες ἀγαθὸν ἐποίησαν;"¹¹ φαίη κα· "καὶ πολλὰ
καὶ μεγάλα." "τὺ ἄρα κακὰ καὶ μεγάλα καὶ πολλὰ
τούτοις ὀφείλεις, αἴπερ τωὐτόν ἐστι τὸ ἀγαθὸν τῷ
κακῷ." [13]—"τί δέ, τὼς συγγενέας ἤδη τι ἀγαθὸν
ἐποίησας;¹² τὼς ἄρα συγγενέας κακὸν ἐποίεις. τί δέ,
τὼς ἐχθρὼς ἤδη κακῶς¹³ ἐποίησας; καὶ πολλὰ καὶ με-
γάλα¹⁴ ἄρα ἀγαθὰ ἐποίησας." [14] "ἄγε δή μοι καὶ
τόδε ἀπόκριναι· ἄλλο τι ἢ τὼς πτωχὼς οἰκτίρεις, ὅτι
πολλὰ καὶ μεγάλα ⟨κακὰ⟩¹⁵ ἔχοντι, ⟨καὶ⟩¹⁶ πάλιν εὐ-
δαιμονίζεις, ὅτι πολλὰ καὶ ἀγαθὰ πράσσοντι, αἴπερ
τωὐτὸ κακὸν καὶ ἀγαθόν;" [15] τὸν δὲ βασιλῆ τὸν μέγαν οὐδὲν κωλύει ὁμοίως διακεῖσθαι τοῖς πτωχοῖς. τὰ
γὰρ πολλὰ καὶ μεγάλα ἀγαθὰ αὐτῷ πολλὰ κακὰ καὶ
μεγάλα ἐστίν, αἴ γα¹⁷ τωὐτόν ἐστιν ἀγαθὸν καὶ κακόν.
καὶ τάδε μὲν περὶ τῶ παντὸς εἰρήσθω. [16] εἶμι δὲ καὶ
καθ' ἕκαστον ἀρξάμενος ἀπὸ τῶ ἐσθίεν καὶ πίνεν καὶ

---

⁹ διάδαλόν ⟨κ'⟩ Blass
¹⁰ post τις hab. mss. αὐτὸν (αὐτὸν αὐτόν P6 V2), del. Diels

[11] Another argument is stated, that the good is one thing, the bad another, which differs, just as in the name, so too in the thing (*pragma*). As for me, I explain the distinction in the following way: for I think that one could not even distinguish what kind of thing is good and what kind of thing is bad, if both of them were the same and not different; and this would be astonishing. [12] I think that the man who affirms this would not even be able to answer, if someone asked him, "Tell me, did your parents already do you any good?" He would say, "Yes, a great deal." "Then you owe them much that is bad, if indeed the good is the same thing as the bad." [13] "Well then, have you ever done your relatives any good? Then you have been doing your relatives ill. Well then, have you ever done your enemies ill? Then you have done them a great deal of good." [14] "Come now and answer me this: do you not pity beggars, because they suffer many bad things; ‹and› inversely you consider them happy, because they have many good things, if indeed bad and good are the same?" [15] Nothing prevents the Great King [scil. of Persia] from being in the same condition as beggars. For his many great good things are for him many great bad things, if good and bad are the same. And let these arguments be made about everything. [16] I shall consider each case, beginning with

---

¹¹ τύ τι τοὶ γονέες ἀγαθὸν ἐποίησαν W. Schulze: τι τοὺς (τὼς P1 P2 P4 P6 V2) γονέας ἀγαθὸν ἐποίησας Robinson

¹² ἐποίησας;" ‹"καὶ πολλὰ καὶ μεγάλα."› Diels

¹³ κακῶς mss. (κακὸν P1 P2)   ¹⁴ μεγάλα mss. (μέγιστα P1 P2): μεγάλα." "μέγιστα Diels   ¹⁵ μεγάλα ‹κακὰ› Matth. de Varis: κακὰ Diels   ¹⁶ ‹καὶ› Schanz

¹⁷ αἴκα mss., corr. Diels

171

ἀφροδισιάζεν. ταῦτα[18] γὰρ τοῖς ἀσθενεῦντι ‹ποιὲν κακόν, καὶ πάλιν›[19] ταῦτα ποιὲν ἀγαθόν ἐστιν αὐτοῖς,[20]
αἵπερ τωὐτόν ἐστιν ἀγαθὸν καὶ κακόν· καὶ τοῖς νοσέ-
οντι κακόν ἐστι τὸ νοσεῖν καὶ ἀγαθόν, αἵπερ τωὐτόν
ἐστι τὸ ἀγαθὸν τῷ κακῷ. [17] καδδὲ τόδε καὶ τἆλλα
πάντα, τὰ ἐν τῷ ἔμπροσθεν λόγῳ εἴρηται. καὶ οὐ
λέγω τί ἐστι τὸ ἀγαθόν, ἀλλὰ τοῦτο πειρῶμαι διδά-
σκειν, ὡς οὐ τωὐτὸν εἴη κακὸν καὶ ἀγαθόν,[21] ἀλλ᾽
‹ἄλλο›[22] ἑκάτερον.

18 ταῦτα Mullach: τοῦτο mss.: τωὐτὸ Orelli
19 ‹ποιὲν κακόν, καὶ πάλιν› Blass   20 αὐτοῖς del. Trieber
21 τὸ κακὸν καὶ τἀγαθόν Diels   22 ‹ἄλλο› Blass

2. Περὶ καλοῦ καὶ αἰσχροῦ

[1] λέγονται δὲ καὶ περὶ τῶ καλῶ καὶ[1] αἰσχρῶ δισσοὶ
λόγοι. τοὶ μὲν γάρ φαντι ἄλλο μὲν ἦμεν τὸ καλόν,
ἄλλο δὲ τὸ αἰσχρόν, διαφέρον, ὥσπερ καὶ τὤνυμα,
οὕτω καὶ τὸ σῶμα· τοὶ δὲ τωὐτὸ καλὸν καὶ αἰσχρόν.
[2] κἀγὼ πειρασεῦμαι τόνδε τὸν τρόπον ἐξαγεύμενος.
αὐτίκα γὰρ παιδὶ[2] ὡραίῳ ἐραστᾷ μὲν χρηστῷ[3] χαρί-
ζεσθαι καλόν, μὴ ἐραστᾷ δὲ καλῷ[4] αἰσχρόν. [3] καὶ
τὰς γυναῖκας λοῦσθαι ἔνδοι[5] καλόν, ἐν παλαίστρᾳ δὲ
αἰσχρόν (ἀλλὰ τοῖς ἀνδράσιν ἐν παλαίστρᾳ καὶ ἐν
γυμνασίῳ καλόν). [4] καὶ συνίμεν τῷ ἀνδρὶ ἐν ἀσυχίᾳ

1 καὶ ‹τῶ› Trieber   2 παιδίῳ mss., corr. Blass
3 χρηστῷ del. Wilamowitz   4 καλῷ del. Diels post
Wilamowitz, alii alia   5 ἔνδοι Vahlen: ἔνιοι P1 P2: ἔνδον cett.

eating, drinking, and sex. For those who are sick these things are <bad to do, and inversely> to do them is good for them, if indeed good and bad are the same thing. And for those who are sick it is bad to be sick, and good, if indeed the good is the same thing as the bad. [17] And the same holds for all the other cases too that I mentioned in the preceding argument. And I am not saying what the good is, but I am trying to teach the following: that bad and good are not the same thing, but each one is <different> [scil. from the other].

2. On Seemly (*kalon*) and Unseemly (*aischron*)[1]

[1] We have maintained the translation of *kalon* as 'seemly' and of *aiskhron* as 'unseemly' throughout, even though in certain cases 'beautiful' and 'ugly' would have been more appropriate in English.

[1] About the seemly and unseemly too a pair of arguments is stated. For some people say that the seemly is one thing, the unseemly another, which differs, just as in the name, so too in the reality named (*sôma*); but other people say that seemly and unseemly are the same. [2] And as for me, I shall try to explain in the following way. For example, it is seemly for a boy in the bloom of youth to give pleasure to a fine lover, but unseemly to do so to one who is not a seemly lover. [3] And it is seemly for women to wash themselves at home, but unseemly in a palaestra (but it is seemly for men in a palaestra or gymnasium). [4] And it is seemly to have sex with her husband when they are alone,

μὲν καλόν, ὅπου τοίχοις κρυφθήσεται· ἔξω δὲ αἰσχρόν, ὅπου τις ὄψεται. [5] καὶ τῷ μὲν ἑαυτᾶς συνίμεν
ἀνδρὶ καλόν, ἀλλοτρίῳ δὲ αἴσχιστον.[6] καὶ τῷ γ᾽ ἀνδρὶ
τᾷ μὲν ἑαυτῶ γυναικὶ συνίμεν καλόν, ἀλλοτρίᾳ δὲ αἰσχρόν. [6] καὶ κοσμεῖσθαι καὶ ψιμυθίῳ χρίεσθαι καὶ
χρυσία περιάπτεσθαι, τῷ μὲν ἀνδρὶ αἰσχρόν, τᾷ δὲ
γυναικὶ καλόν. [7] καὶ τὼς μὲν φίλως εὖ ποιὲν καλόν,
τὼς δὲ ἐχθρὼς αἰσχρόν. καὶ τὼς μὲν πολεμίως φεύγεν
αἰσχρόν, τὼς δὲ ἐν σταδίῳ ἀγωνιστὰς[7] καλόν. [8] καὶ
τὼς μὲν φίλως καὶ τὼς πολίτας φονεύεν αἰσχρόν, τὼς
δὲ πολεμίως καλόν. καὶ τάδε μὲν περὶ πάντων.

[9] εἶμι δ᾽ <ἐφ᾽>[8] ἃ ταὶ πόλιές τε αἰσχρὰ ἄγηνται
καὶ τὰ ἔθνεα. αὐτίκα Λακεδαιμονίοις τὰς κόρας
γυμνάζεσθαι <καὶ>[9] ἀχειριδώτως καὶ ἀχίτωνας παρέρ-
πεν καλόν, Ἴωσι δὲ αἰσχρόν· [10] καὶ[10] τὼς παῖδας μὴ
μανθάνειν μωσικὰ καὶ γράμματα καλόν, Ἴωσι δ᾽ αἰσχρὸν μὴ ἐπίστασθαι ταῦτα πάντα. [11] Θεσσαλοῖσι
δὲ καλὸν τὼς ἵππως ἐκ τᾶς ἀγέλας λαβόντι αὐτῷ[11]
δαμάσαι καὶ τὼς ὀρέας, βῶν τε λαβόντι αὐτῷ σφάξαι
καὶ ἐκδεῖραι καὶ κατακόψαι· ἐν Σικελίᾳ δὲ αἰσχρὸν
καὶ δώλων ἔργα. [12] Μακεδόσι δὲ καλὸν δοκεῖ ἦμεν
τὰς κόρας, πρὶν ἀνδρὶ γάμασθαι, ἐρᾶσθαι καὶ ἀνδρὶ
συγγίνεσθαι, ἐπεὶ δέ κα γάμηται,[12] αἰσχρόν· Ἕλλασι
δ᾽ ἄμφω αἰσχρόν. [13] τοῖς δὲ Θραξὶ κόσμος τὰς

[6] αἴσχιστον F2 P1 P3 R V1 (ex αἰσχρόν Z, in mg. V2): αἰσχρόν cett.   [7] ἀνταγωνιστὰς Orelli
[8] <ἐφ᾽> Stephanus   [9] <καὶ> Blass

where it will be concealed by walls, but unseemly outside, where someone will see. [5] And it is seemly to have sex with her own husband, but most unseemly of all with another woman's husband; and it is seemly for a man to have sex with his own wife, but unseemly with another man's wife. [6] And to adorn oneself, apply makeup, and wear gold jewelry is unseemly for a man, but seemly for a woman. [7] And it is seemly to do good to one's friends, but unseemly to one's enemies. And to run away from one's enemies in war is unseemly, but from one's competitors in the stadium is seemly. [8] And to kill one's friends and fellow citizens is unseemly, but one's enemies in war is seemly. And this can be said about all subjects.

[9] I shall proceed <to> the things that cities and peoples consider unseemly. For example, for the Spartans it is seemly that girls engage in athletics <and> appear in public without sleeves or tunics, but for the Ionians it is unseemly; [10] and it is seemly that their [i.e. the Spartans'] children not learn music and letters, but for the Ionians it is unseemly not to know all these things. [11] For the Thessalians it is seemly that a man select horses and mules from a herd and break them in himself, and that he take a cow and slaughter it himself, skin it, and chop it up, but in Sicily this is unseemly and is the work of slaves. [12] The Macedonians think that it is seemly that girls fall in love and have sex with a man before they get married, but unseemly when they are married; but for the Greeks both are unseemly. [13] For the Thracians it is an adorn-

---

10 καὶ ⟨τοῖς μὲν⟩ Diels
11 αὐτὼς mss., corr. Blass
12 καὶ γαμεῖται mss., corr. Blass

κόρας στίζεσθαι· τοῖς δ᾽ ἄλλοις τιμωρία[13] τὰ στίγ-
ματα τοῖς ἀδικέοντι. τοὶ δὲ Σκύθαι καλὸν νομίζοντι,
ὃς ἄνδρα <κα>[14] κατακανὼν[15] ἐκδείρας τὰν κεφαλὰν τὸ
μὲν κόμιον πρὸ τοῦ ἵππου φορῇ, τὸ δ᾽ ὀστέον χρυσώ-
σας καὶ[16] ἀργυρώσας πίνῃ ἐξ αὐτοῦ καὶ σπένδῃ τοῖς
θεοῖς· ἐν δὲ τοῖς Ἕλλασιν οὐδέ κ᾽ ἐς τὰν αὐτὰν οἰκίαν
συνεισελθεῖν βούλοιτό[17] τις τοιαῦτα[18] ποιήσαντι.
[14] Μασσαγέται δὲ τὼς γονέας κατακόψαντες κατ-
έσθοντι, καὶ τάφος κάλλιστος δοκεῖ ἦμεν ἐν τοῖς
τέκνοις τεθάφθαι· ἐν δὲ τᾷ Ἑλλάδι αἴ τις ταῦτα ποιή-
σαι,[19] ἐξελαθεὶς ἐκ τῆς Ἑλλάδος κακῶς κα[20] ἀποθάνοι
ὡς αἰσχρὰ καὶ δεινὰ ποιέων. [15] τοὶ δὲ Πέρσαι
κοσμεῖσθαί τε ὥσπερ τὰς γυναῖκας καὶ τὼς ἄνδρας
καλὸν νομίζοντι καὶ τᾷ θυγατρὶ καὶ τᾷ ματρὶ καὶ τᾷ
ἀδελφᾷ συνίμεν· τοὶ δὲ Ἕλλανες καὶ αἰσχρὰ καὶ
παράνομα. [16] Λυδοῖς τοίνυν τὰς κόρας πορνευθείσας
καὶ ἀργύριον ἐνεργάσασθαι καὶ οὕτως γάμασθαι
καλὸν δοκεῖ ἦμεν, ἐν δὲ τοῖς Ἕλλασιν οὐδείς κα θέλοι
γᾶμαι. [17] Αἰγύπτιοί τε οὐ ταὐτὰ νομίζοντι καλὰ τοῖς
ἄλλοις· τῇδε μὲν γὰρ γυναῖκας ὑφαίνειν καὶ[21] ἐργάζεσθαι καλόν, ἀλλὰ τηνεῖ τὼς ἄνδρας, τὰς δὲ γυναῖκας
πράσσεν, ἅπερ τῇδε τοὶ ἄνδρες· τὸν παλὸν δεύειν ταῖς
χερσί, τὸν δὲ σῖτον τοῖς ποσί, τήνοις καλόν, ἀλλ᾽
ἀμὶν τὸ ἐναντίον. [18] οἶμαι δ᾽, ἄν[22] τις τὰ καλὰ[23] ἐς ἓν

[13] τιμωρίαν mss., corr. Weber   [14] <κα> Robinson
[15] κατακανὼν Blass: κατακτανὼν P2: κατκτανὼν P1: κανὼν
ZL: κτανὼν BRN   [16] ἢ Wilamowitz: <ἢ> καὶ Diels

ment that girls are tattooed, but for everyone else tattoos are a punishment for those who have committed a crime. The Scythians consider it seemly that whoever kills a man cut off his scalp and set it on the front of his horse, and after having covered the skull with a layer of gold and silver to drink from it and to use it to give libations to the gods; but among the Greeks no one would wish even to go into the same house with anyone who did these things. [14] The Massagetes chop their parents up and eat them, and the most seemly burial is thought by them to be if they are buried inside their children; but in Greece if anyone did this he would be driven out of Greece and would die a terrible death for having done unseemly and terrible things. [15] The Persians consider it seemly that men too be adorned like women and have sex with their daughter, mother, and sister; but the Greeks, that this is both unseemly and illegal. [16] So the Lydians think that it is seemly that girls make money by prostituting themselves and then get married in this way, but among the Greeks no one would be willing to marry a girl like that. [17] And Egyptians do not consider the same things to be seemly as other people do: for here it is seemly that women weave and do manual labor, but there it is the men, and the women do what men do here; to moisten clay with the hands and dough with the feet is seemly for them, but the opposite is the case for us. [18] I think that if someone

---

17 βούλοιτ' ἄν mss., corr. Blass   18 τῷ ταῦτα Diels
19 ποιήσῃ uel ποιήσῃ mss. (ποιήσας P2), corr. Blass
20 κακὰ mss., corr. Blass   21 καὶ ⟨ἔρια⟩Valckenaer
22 αἴ Wilamowitz   23 αἰσχρὰ . . . καλὰ (infra ante λαβέν) North

κελεύοι συνενεῖκαι πάντας ἀνθρώπως, ἃ ἕκαστοι νομίζοντι, καὶ πάλιν ἐξ ἀθρόων τούτων[24] τὰ αἰσχρὰ λαβέν, ἃ ἕκαστοι ἄγηνται, οὐδὲν[25] <κα> καλλειφθῆμεν,[26]
ἀλλὰ πάντας πάντα διαλαβέν. οὐ γὰρ πάντες ταὐτὰ
νομίζοντι. [19] παρεξοῦμαι δὲ καὶ ποίημά τι [TrGF
Adesp. F26]·

κ̀αὶ γὰρ τὸν ἄλλον ὧδε θνητοῖσιν νόμον
ὄψῃ διαιρῶν· οὐδὲν ἦν[27] πάντῃ καλόν,
οὐδ᾿ αἰσχρόν, ἀλλὰ ταῦτ᾿[28] ἐποίησεν λαβών
ὁ καιρὸς αἰσχρὰ καὶ διαλλάξας καλά.

[20] ὡς δὲ τὸ σύνολον εἶπαι, πάντα καιρῷ μὲν καλά
ἐντι, ἐν ἀκαιρίᾳ δ᾿ αἰσχρά.

τί ὦν διεπραξάμην; ἔφαν ἀποδείξειν ταὐτὰ αἰσχρὰ
καὶ καλὰ ἐόντα, καὶ ἀπέδειξα ἐν τούτοις πᾶσι.

[21] λέγεται δὲ καὶ περὶ τῶ αἰσχρῶ καὶ[29] καλῶ, ὡς
ἄλλο ἑκάτερον εἴη. ἐπεὶ αἴ τις ἐρωτάσαι τὼς λέγοντας
ὡς τὸ αὐτὸ πρᾶγμα αἰσχρὸν καὶ καλόν ἐστιν, αἴ ποκά
τι αὐτοῖς καλὸν ἔργασται,[30] αἰσχρὸν ὁμολογησοῦντι,
αἴπερ τωὐτὸν καὶ τὸ αἰσχρὸν καὶ τὸ καλόν. [22] καὶ
αἴ τινά γα καλὸν οἴδαντι ἄνδρα, τοῦτον καὶ αἰσχρὸν
τὸν αὐτόν· καὶ αἴ τινά γα λευκόν, καὶ μέλανα τοῦτον
τὸν αὐτόν. καὶ <αἰ>[31] καλόν γ᾿ ἐστὶ τὼς θεὼς σέβε-

---

[24] τούτων Weber: τοι mss.   [25] οὐδὲ ἕν Diels

[26] <κα> καλλειφθῆμεν Weber: καλλειφθῆμεν P1, καλυφθεῖ-
μεν R, καλυφθῆμεν cett.: κα λειφθῆμεν Matth. de Varis

[27] ἂν mss., corr. Nauck   [28] ταῦτ᾿ Valckenaer: ταῦτ᾿ mss.:
πάντ᾿ Wilamowitz   [29] καὶ <τῶ> Blass

ordered everyone to gather together the things that each one considered to be seemly and then to take away from the heaps those things that each one considered to be unseemly, nothing would be left, but everything would be divided up by everyone. For all people do not think the same things. [19] I shall also cite some verses:[1]

> For you will see, if you distinguish, a different law
> For mortals, like this: nothing is seemly in every regard,
> Nor unseemly, but the right occasion (*kairos*) takes the same things
> And makes them unseemly and, changing them, seemly.

[20] To say this in general: all things are seemly when it is the right occasion and unseemly when it is not the right occasion.

What, therefore, have I accomplished? I said that I would show that the same things are unseemly and seemly, and I have shown this in all these cases.

[21] It is also said about the unseemly and seemly that each one is different [scil. from the other]. For if someone were to ask those people who say that the same thing is both unseemly and seemly whether they have ever done anything seemly, they would admit [scil. that it was] unseemly, if both the unseemly and the seemly are the same thing. [22] And if they know some man who is seemly, this same man is unseemly too; and if they know any man who is white, this same man is black too. And if it is seemly to

---

[1] From an unknown tragic poet.

30 ἔργασται ⟨καὶ⟩ Wilamowitz   31 ⟨αἱ⟩ Robinson

179

σθαι, καὶ αἰσχρὸν ἄρα[32] τὼς θεὼς σέβεσθαι, αἴπερ τωὐτὸν αἰσχρὸν καὶ καλόν ἐστι.

[23] καὶ τάδε μὲν περὶ ἁπάντων εἰρήσθω μοι· τρέψομαι δὲ ἐπὶ τὸν λόγον αὐτῶν, ὃν λέγοντι. [24] αἱ γὰρ τὰν γυναῖκα καλόν ἐστι κοσμεῖσθαι, τὰν γυναῖκα[33] αἰσχρὸν κοσμεῖσθαι, αἴπερ τωὐτὸν αἰσχρὸν καὶ καλόν· καὶ τἆλλα κατὰ τωὐτόν. [25] ἐν Λακεδαίμονί ἐστι καλὸν τὰς παῖδας γυμνάζεσθαι, ἐν Λακεδαίμονί ἐστιν αἰσχρὸν τὰς παῖδας γυμνάζεσθαι, καὶ τἆλλα οὕτως. [26] λέγοντι δέ, ὡς αἴ τινες τὰ αἰσχρὰ ἐκ τῶν ἐθνέων πάντοθεν συνενείκαιεν, ἔπειτα συγκαλέσαντες[34] κελεύοιεν, ἅ τις καλὰ νομίζοι, λαμβάνεν, πάντα κα[35] ἐν καλῷ ἀπενειχθῆμεν. ἐγὼ θαυμάζω, αἰ τὰ αἰσχρὰ συνενεχθέντα καλὰ ἐσεῖται, καὶ οὐχ οἷάπερ ἦνθεν. [27] αἰ γοῦν ἵππως ἢ βῶς ἢ ὄις ἢ ἀνθρώπως ἄγαγον, οὐκ ἄλλο τί κα ἀπᾶγον· ἐπεὶ οὐδ᾽ αἰ χρυσὸν ἤνεικαν, χαλκόν ἀπήνεικαν,[36] οὐδ᾽ ἂν[37] ἀργύριον[38] ἤνεικαν, μόλιβδόν κα ἀπέφερον. [28] ἀντὶ δ᾽ ἄρα τῶν αἰσχρῶν καλὰ ἀπάγοντι;[39] φέρε δή, αἰ ἄρα τις αἰσχρὸν[40] ἄγαγε,[41] τοῦτον αὖ <κα>[42] καλὸν ἀπάγαγε·[43] ποιητὰς δὲ μάρτυρας ἐπάγονται, <οἳ>[44] ποτὶ ἁδονάν, οὐ ποτὶ ἀλάθειαν ποιεῦντι.

---

[32] ἄρα vel ἄρ mss.: αὖ Wilamowitz

[33] γυναῖκα <καὶ> Diels   [34] συγκαλεύσαντες vel συγκαλεσοῦντες mss., corr. Schanz   [35] καὶ mss., corr. Orelli

[36] ἀπήνεικαν del. Wilamowitz   [37] οὐδ᾽ ἂν P1 P2: οὐδὲ cett.: οὐδ᾽ αἰ Weber   [38] ἄργυρον Blass

[39] ἀπάγαγοντι mss., corr. Wilamowitz

worship the gods, then again [scil. it is] unseemly to worship the gods, if unseemly and seemly are the same thing.

[23] And let these things be said by me about all cases. I shall turn to the argument that they state. [24] For if it is seemly that a woman adorn herself, it is unseemly that a woman adorn herself, if indeed unseemly and seemly are the same thing. And the same applies to all the other cases. [25] In Sparta it is seemly that girls engage in athletics, in Sparta it is unseemly that girls engage in athletics; and in the same way for all the other cases. [26] They say that if some people brought together unseemly things from peoples everywhere, then summoned them and ordered them to take away what each person considered seemly, everything would be taken away, as belonging to what is seemly. As for me, I am astonished that things that were unseemly when they were brought together become seemly, and do not remain as they were when they arrived. [27] At least if they had brought horses, cows, sheep, or people, they would not have taken away something different; for if they had brought gold, they would not have taken away bronze either, and if they had brought silver, they would not have carried off lead. [28] So do they take away seemly things instead of unseemly ones? Come then, if someone brought something unseemly, would he lead it away again as seemly? They introduce poets as witnesses, ⟨but these⟩ compose for the sake of pleasure, not for the sake of truth.

---

40 αἰσχρὸν ⟨ἄνδρα⟩ Diels

41 ἀπάγαγε mss., corr. Mullach

42 αὖ ⟨κα⟩ Robinson: δ' ἂν F2 P1 P4 P6 F: ἂν cett.: δ' αὖ ⟨κα⟩ Diels: 43 ἀπᾶγε Diels   44 ⟨οἱ⟩ Orelli

3. Περὶ δικαίου καὶ ἀδίκου

[1] δισσοὶ δὲ λόγοι λέγονται καὶ περὶ τῶ δικαίω καὶ τῶ ἀδίκω. καὶ τοὶ μὲν ἄλλο ἦμεν τὸ δίκαιον, ἄλλο δὲ τὸ ἄδικον· τοὶ δὲ τωὐτὸ δίκαιον καὶ ἄδικον· καὶ ἐγὼ τούτῳ πειρασοῦμαι τιμωρέν. [2] καὶ πρῶτον μὲν ψεύδεσθαι ὡς δίκαιόν ἐστι λεξῶ καὶ ἐξαπατᾶν. τὼς μὲν πολεμίως ταῦτα ποιὲν[1] αἰσχρὸν καὶ πονηρὸν ἂν ἐξείποιεν,[2] τὼς δὲ φιλτάτως οὔ, αὐτίκα τὼς γονέας· αἱ γὰρ δέοι τὸν πατέρα ἢ τὰν ματέρα φάρμακον πιὲν καὶ[3] φαγέν, καὶ μὴ θέλοι, οὐ δίκαιόν ἐστι καὶ ἐν τῷ ῥοφήματι καὶ ἐν τῷ ποτῷ δόμεν καὶ μὴ φάμεν ἐνῆμεν; [3] οὐκῶν[4] ἤδη ψεύδεσθαι καὶ ἐξαπατᾶν τὼς γονέας καὶ κλέπτεν μὰν τὰ τῶν φίλων καὶ βιῆσθαι τὼς φιλτάτως δίκαιον. [4] αὐτίκα αἴ τις λυπηθείς τι τῶν οἰκηίων καὶ ἀχθεσθεὶς μέλλοι αὐτὸν[5] διαφθείρεν ἢ ξίφει ἢ σχοινίῳ ἢ ἄλλῳ τινί, δίκαιόν ἐστι ταῦτα κλέψαι, αἱ δύναιτο, αἱ δὲ ὑστερίξαι καὶ ἔχοντα καταλάβοι, ἀφελέσθαι βίᾳ. [5] ἀνδραποδίξασθαι δὲ πῶς οὐ δίκαιον τὼς πολεμίως,[6] αἴ τις δύναιτο ἑλὼν πόλιν ὅλαν ἀποδόσθαι; τοιχωρυχὲν δὲ τὰ τῶν πολιτῶν κοινὰ οἰκήματα δίκαιον φαίνεται. αἱ γὰρ ὁ πατὴρ ἐπὶ θανάτῳ, κατεστασιασμένος ὑπὸ τῶν ἐχθρῶν, δεδεμένος εἴη, ἆρα οὐ δίκαιον διορύξαντα κλέψαι καὶ σῶσαι τὸν πατέρα; [6] ἐπιορκὲν δέ· αἴ τις ὑπὸ τῶν πολεμίων

---

[1] ταῦτα ⟨μὴ⟩ ποιὲν Blass: ταῦτα ποιὲν ⟨καλὸν καὶ δίκαιον, τὼς δὲ φίλως⟩ Diels   [2] ἐξείποιεν· ⟨πῶς δὲ τὼς πολεμίως,⟩ Diels   [3] ἢ Diels

3. On Just and Unjust

[1] A pair of arguments is stated about the just and the unjust too. And some people [scil. state] that the just is one thing, the unjust another; but other people, that just and unjust are the same thing. And as for me, I shall try to support the latter. [2] And first I shall maintain that it is just to tell lies and to deceive. For they [i.e. the first group] would assert that to do this to enemies in war is unseemly and wicked, but not to those who are dearest, for example, to one's parents: for if one's father or mother were supposed to drink and eat some medicine but refused to do so, is it not just to put it into their porridge or drink and to deny that it is in it? [3] Therefore already to tell lies and deceive one's parents, and certainly to steal what belongs to one's friends and to inflict violence upon those who are dearest, is just. [4] For example, if some member of the household, in a state of grief and distress, were about to kill himself with a sword or rope or something else, it is just to steal it if one can, and if one arrives too late and catches him holding it, to take it away by violence. [5] And how is it not just to enslave one's enemies in war, if one can sell into slavery a whole city after having captured it? And to break in to the public buildings of one's fellow citizens is evidently just. For if one's father has been overthrown by his political enemies and is in prison on a death penalty, is it not just to break in so as to steal one's father away and save him? [6] And perjury: if some-

---

4 οὐκῶν Matth. de Varis: οὔκων uel οὔκουν mss.: οὐκοῦν Mullach: οὐκῶν ⟨δίκαιον⟩ Diels

5 αὐτὸν mss., corr. Stephanus

6 πολεμίως ⟨καὶ⟩ Diels

λαφθεὶς ὑποδέξαιτο ὀμνύων ἦ μὰν ἀφεθεὶς τὰν πόλιν
προδώσεν, ἆρα οὗτος δίκαιά <κα>[7] ποιῆσαι εὐορκή-
σας; [7] ἐγὼ μὲν γὰρ οὐ δοκῶ, ἀλλὰ μᾶλλον τὰν
πόλιν καὶ τὼς φίλως καὶ τὰ ἱερὰ σῶσαι <τὰ>[8] πα-
τρῷα ἐπιορκήσας. ἤδη ἄρα δίκαιον καὶ τὸ ἐπιορκεῖν.
καὶ τὸ ἱεροσυλέν· [8] τὰ μὲν ἴδια τῶν πόλεων ἐῶ· τὰ
δὲ κοινὰ τᾶς Ἑλλάδος, τὰ ἐκ Δελφῶν καὶ τὰ ἐξ Ὀλυμ-
πίας, μέλλοντος τῷ βαρβάρῳ τὰν Ἑλλάδα λαβεῖν[9]
καὶ τὰς σωτηρίας ἐν χρήμασιν ἐούσας, οὐ δίκαιον
λαβεῖν[10] καὶ χρῆσθαι ἐς τὸν πόλεμον; [9] φονεύεν
δὲ τὼς φιλτάτως δίκαιον· ἐπεὶ καὶ Ὀρέστας καὶ
Ἀλκμαίων· καὶ ὁ θεὸς ἔχρησε δίκαια αὐτῶ[11] ποιῆσαι.

[10] ἐπὶ δὲ τὰς τέχνας τρέψομαι καὶ τὰ τῶν[12] ποιη-
τῶν. ἐν γὰρ τραγῳδοποιίᾳ καὶ ζωγραφίᾳ ὅστις <κα>[13]
πλεῖστα ἐξαπατῇ ὅμοια τοῖς ἀληθινοῖς ποιέων, οὗτος
ἄριστος. [11] θέλω δὲ καὶ ποιημάτων[14] παλαιοτέρων
μαρτύριον ἐπαγαγέσθαι. Κλεοβουλίνης [Frag. 2 West]·

ἄνδρ' εἶδον κλέπτοντα καὶ ἐξαπατῶντα βιαίως,[15]
καὶ τὸ βίᾳ ῥέξαι τοῦτο δικαιότατον.

[12] ἦν πάλαι ταῦτα· Αἰσχύλου δὲ ταῦτα [Frag. 301,
302 Radt]·

ἀπάτης δικαίας οὐκ ἀποστατεῖ θεός·[16]
ψευδῶν δὲ καιρὸν ἔσθ' ὅπου[17] τιμῇ θεός.

7 <κα> Matthaei   8 <τὰ> Matth. de Varis: <κα> Matthaei:
<κα τὰ> Diels: <ἀν τὰ> Robinson   9 λαβεῖν Diels: λαβὲν
vel λαβὲν mss.   10 λαβὲν Fabricius
11 αὐτῶ Blass: αὐτῶ vel αὐτῷ ms.: αὐτὼς Stephanus

DISSOI LOGOI

one who has been captured by enemies in war promises
on oath that if he is freed he will certainly betray his city,
<would> he be acting justly if he kept his oath? [7] For as
for me, I think he should not [scil. do this], but instead
should save his city, his friends, and his ancestral temples
by perjuring himself. So it is already just to commit perjury as well. And to rob temples: [8] I omit the ones at-
tached to the various cities; but as for the ones belonging
in common to Greece, those in Delphi and Olympia: when
the barbarian was about to conquer Greece and safety lay
in money, was it not just to take them and use them for the
war? [9] And to murder one's dearest is just. For both
Orestes and Alcmaeon [scil. did this]: and the god pro-
claimed that what they both did was just.

[10] I shall turn to the arts and to the works of the
poets. For in tragedy and painting, whoever deceives the
most by making things similar to true ones is the best one.
[11] I wish to introduce the testimony of more ancient
poems too. From Cleobulina:

A man I saw stealing and deceiving by force,
    And to do this by force was most just.

[12] These lines were ancient. The following ones are
from Aeschylus:

From just deceit a god does not stand aloof:
Sometimes a god honors the right occasion for lies.

---

¹² ταῦτα mss., corr. Diels   ¹³ <κα> Blass
¹⁴ ποιήματα τῶν mss., corr. Diels   ¹⁵ βία· ὡς mss.,
corr. Matth. de Varis   ¹⁶ <καὶ> post θεός Diels ut separet
duos versus singulos   ¹⁷ ὅποι mss., corr. Hermann

185

[13] λέγεται δὲ καὶ τῷδε ἀντίος λόγος, ὡς ἄλλο τὸ
δίκαιον καὶ τὸ ἄδικόν ἐστιν, διαφέρον ὥσπερ καὶ τώ-
νυμα, οὕτω καὶ τὸ πρᾶγμα. ἐπεὶ αἴ τις ἐρωτάσαι τὼς
λέγοντας, ὡς τὸ αὐτό ἐστιν ἄδικον καὶ δίκαιον, αἰ
ἤδη[18] τι δίκαιον περὶ τὼς γονέας ἔπραξαν, ὁμολογησοῦντι.[19] καὶ ἄδικον ἄρα· τὸ γὰρ αὐτὸ ἄδικον καὶ
δίκαιον ὁμολογέοντι ἦμεν. [14] φέρε ἄλλο δή·[20] αἴ τινα
γινώσκει[21] δίκαιον ἄνδρα, καὶ ἄδικον ἄρα τὸν αὐτόν,
καὶ μέγαν τοίνυν καὶ μικρὸν κατὰ τωὐτόν. καίτοι[22]
πολλὰ ἀδικήσας ἀποθανέτω, ἀποθανέτω[23] ⟨πολλὰ καὶ
δίκαια δια⟩πραξάμενος.[24] [15] καὶ περὶ μὲν τούτων
ἅλις. εἶμι δὲ ἐφ᾽ ἃ λέγοντες ἀξιόοντι τὸ αὐτὸ καὶ
δίκαιον καὶ ἄδικον ἀποδεικνύεν. [16] τὸ γὰρ κλέπτεν
τὰ τῶν πολεμίων δίκαιον, καὶ ἄδικον ἀποδεικνύεν
τοῦτ᾽ αὐτό, αἴ κ᾽ ἀληθὴς ὁ τήνων λόγος, καὶ τἆλλα
καττωὐτό. [17] τέχνας δὲ ἐπάγονται, ἐν αἷς οὐκ ἔστι
τὸ δίκαιον καὶ τὸ ἄδικον. καὶ τοὶ ποιηταὶ οὗτοι[25] ποτ᾽
ἀλάθειαν, ἀλλὰ ποτὶ τὰς ἀδονὰς τῶν ἀνθρώπων τὰ
ποιήματα ποιέοντι.

---

[18] αἴ κα δή mss., corr. Wilamowitz

[19] ὁμολογοῦντι mss. (ὁμολογοσοῦντι P1), corr. Matth. de
Varis   [20] ἄλλον δὲ mss., corr. Diels

[21] γινώσκεις Diels

[22] καί τοι mss., corr. Blass: καί τοι ⟨ὁ⟩ Diels: καὶ ⟨αἰ⟩ λέ-
γοιτο Kranz

[23] ἀποθανέτω bis C P6 V2 Y1 Y2, semel cett.

[24] ⟨πολλὰ καὶ δίκαια δια⟩πραξάμενος Blass, alii alia

[25] οὗτο vel οὗτό mss., corr. Blass

[13] An opposing argument is stated to this one too: that the just and the unjust are different, differing just as in the name, so too in the thing named (*pragma*). For if someone were to ask those who say that unjust and just are the same thing whether they had ever yet acted justly regarding their parents, they would say yes. But then, unjustly: for they admit that unjust and just are the same thing. [14] Come then, another case: if one knows some man who is just, then therefore this same man is unjust too; and so too certainly large and small, by the same argument. So let him be killed for having performed many acts of injustice—let him be killed for having performed ‹ many acts of justice ›. [15] And that is enough about these cases. I shall proceed to what those people say who claim that they prove that the same thing is both just and unjust. [16] For [scil. one can assert] that to steal what belongs to enemies in war is just and also that to prove that this same thing is unjust, if their argument is true, and so too in all the other cases. [17] And they introduce the arts, in which the just and the unjust do not exist. And the poets certainly do not compose their poems for the sake of truth, but for the sake of people's pleasure.

4. Περὶ ἀλαθείας καὶ ψεύδεος

[1] λέγονται δὲ καὶ περὶ τῶ ψεύδεος καὶ τῶ ἀλαθέος[1]
δισσοὶ λόγοι, ὧν ὁ μέν φατι ἄλλον μὲν τὸν ψεύσταν
ἦμεν λόγον, ἄλλον δὲ τὸν ἀλαθῆ· τοὶ δὲ τὸν αὐτὸν αὖ.
[2] κἀγὼ τόνδε λέγω· πρῶτον μέν, ὅτι τοῖς αὐτοῖς
ὀνόμασι λέγονται· ἔπειτα δέ, ὅταν λόγος ῥηθῇ, αἱ μὲν
ὥς <κα>[2] λέγηται ὁ λόγος, οὕτω γεγένηται,[3] ἀλαθὴς ὁ
λόγος, αἱ δὲ μὴ γεγένηται,[4] ψευδὴς ὁ αὐτὸς λόγος. [3]
αὐτίκα κατηγορεῖ ἱεροσυλίαν τω· αἴ γ'[5] ἐγένετο τὦργον, ἀλαθὴς ὁ λόγος· αἱ δὲ μὴ ἐγένετο, ψεύστας. καὶ
τῶ ἀπολογουμένω ὥς γε ὁ[6] λόγος. καὶ τά γε δικαστήρια τὸν αὐτὸν λόγον καὶ ψεύσταν καὶ ἀλαθῆ κρίνοντι. [4] ἔπει τοι καὶ[7] ἑξῆς καθήμενοι αἱ λέγοιμεν[8]
"μύστας[9] εἰμί," τὸ αὐτὸ μὲν πάντες ἐροῦμεν, ἀλαθὴς
δὲ μόνος ἐγώ, ἐπεὶ καὶ εἰμί. [5] δᾶλον ὦν ὅτι ὁ αὐτὸς
λόγος, ὅταν μὲν αὐτῷ παρῇ τὸ ψεῦδος, ψεύστας ἐστίν,
ὅταν δὲ τὸ ἀλαθές, ἀλαθής (ὥσπερ καὶ ἄνθρωπος τὸ
αὐτό, καὶ παῖς καὶ νεανίσκος καὶ ἀνὴρ καὶ γέρων,
ἐστίν).

[6] λέγεται δὲ καὶ ὡς ἄλλος εἴη ὁ ψεύστας λόγος,
ἄλλος δὲ ὁ ἀλαθής, διαφέρων τὦνυμα <ὥσπερ καὶ τὸ
πρᾶγμα>·[10] αἱ γάρ τις ἐρωτάσαι τὼς λέγοντας, ὡς ὁ
αὐτὸς λόγος εἴη ψεύστας καὶ ἀλαθής, ὃν αὐτοὶ λέ-

---

1 ἀλαθείας mss. (ἀλαθείας P3 P4), corr. Diels
2 <κα> Blass   3 γένηται mss. (<γε>γένηται P4 in mg.),
corr. Blass   4 γένηται mss., corr. Blass
5 αἴκ' mss., corr. Diels   6 ὦυτὸς Wilamowitz

4. On True and False

[1] About the true and the false too a pair of arguments is stated, of which the one says that the false speech is one thing, the true one another; while others in turn say that they are the same. [2] And as for me, I maintain the latter: first, because these are stated with the same words; and then, whenever a speech is spoken, if things turn out just as the speech has asserted, the speech is true, whereas if they do not turn out like that, the same speech is false. [3] For example, a man accuses someone of robbing temples: if this deed happened, then his speech is true; if it did not happen, it is false. And the same argument applies to the speech of the defendant. And the law courts judge the same speech to be both false and true. [4] For surely if, sitting in a row, we were to say, "I have been initiated into the mysteries," we would all be saying the same thing, but I would be the only one to be telling the truth, since I also happen to be [scil. an initiate]. [5] So it is clear that the same speech, when it is accompanied by falsehood, is false, but when it is the truth [scil. that accompanies it], it is true (just as a human being too is the same person, as a boy, a youth, an adult man, and an old man).

[6] But it is also said that a false speech is one thing, a true one another, and that they differ in the name ⟨just as in the thing named⟩. For if someone were to ask those people who say that the same speech is false and true,

---

⁷ ἔπειτα τοὶ Diels   ⁸ λέγοιμι mss. (λέγοιμεν P4 post corr., λέγοι μὲν Y1 Y2), corr. North   ⁹ Μίμας Stephanus: Μίλτας Bergk: alii alia   ¹⁰ ⟨ὥσπερ καὶ τὸ πρᾶγμα⟩ Diels, alii alia

189

γοντι, πότερός ἐστιν· αἱ μὲν "ψεύστας," δᾶλον ὅτι δύο
εἴη· αἱ δ' "ἀλαθής" ἀποκρίναιτο,[11] καὶ ψεύστας ὁ αὐτὸς οὗτος. καὶ ⟨αἱ⟩ ἀλαθές τί[12] ποκα εἶπεν ἢ ἐξεμαρ-
τύρησε, καὶ ψευδῆ ἄρα τὰ αὐτὰ ταῦτα. καὶ αἴ τινα
ἄνδρα ἀλαθῆ οἶδε, καὶ ψεύσταν τὸν αὐτόν. [7] ἐκ δὲ
τῶ λόγω λέγοντι ταῦτα, ὅτι γενομένω μὲν τῶ πράγματος ἀλαθῆ τὸν λόγον,[13] ἀγενήτω δὲ ψεύσταν.
οὔκων διαφέρει ⟨αὐτῶν τὤνυμα, ἀλλὰ τὸ πρᾶγμα.
ἐρωτάσαι δὲ κά τις⟩[14] [8] αὖθις τὼς δικαστάς, ὅ τι
κρίνοιντο[15] (οὐ γὰρ πάρεντι τοῖς πράγμασιν)· [9] ὁμολογέοντι δὲ καὶ αὐτοί, ᾧ μὲν τὸ ψεῦδος ἀναμέμεικται,
ψεύσταν ἦμεν, ᾧ δὲ τὸ ἀλαθές, ἀλαθῆ. τοῦτο δὲ ὅλον
διαφέρει . . .[16]

[11] ἀποκρίναιτο del. Schanz   [12] ⟨αἱ⟩ ἀλαθές τί Blass:
ἀλαθές τί mss.: ἀλαθῆ τίς Schanz   [13] λόγον ⟨λέγοντι⟩
Diels   [14] ⟨αὐτῶν τὤνυμα, ἀλλὰ τὸ πρᾶγμα. ἐρωτάσαι
δὲ κά τις⟩ Diels: ⟨ἐρέσθαι⟩ Robinson   [15] κρίνοντι Schanz
[16] lac. post διαφέρει indic. North

5.

[1] "ταὐτὰ[1] τοὶ μαινόμενοι καὶ τοὶ σωφρονοῦντες καὶ
τοὶ σοφοὶ καὶ τοὶ ἀμαθεῖς καὶ λέγοντι καὶ πράσσοντι.
[2] καὶ πρᾶτον μὲν ὀνομάζοντι ταὐτά,[2] γᾶν καὶ ἄνθρωπον καὶ ἵππον καὶ πῦρ καὶ τἆλλα πάντα. καὶ ποιέοντι
ταὐτά,[3] κάθηνται καὶ ἔσθοντι καὶ πίνοντι καὶ κατά-
κεινται, καὶ τἆλλα καττωὐτό. [3] καὶ μὰν καὶ τὸ αὐτὸ
πρᾶγμα καὶ μέζον καὶ μῆόν ἐστι καὶ πλέον καὶ ἔλασσον καὶ βαρύτερον καὶ κουφότερον. οὕτω γὰρ ⟨κ'⟩[4]

which of the two is the one that they themselves say—if it is "false," then it is clear that these are two things; but if they answer, "true," then this same speech is also false. And if anyone has ever said something true or borne witness to it, then these same [scil. words] would therefore be false too. And if a man knows that some man is true, then also he also knows that the same man is false. [7] On the basis of this argument they say that if the event occurs then the speech is true, while if it does not, then it is false. So it is not ‹their names› that are different, ‹but the thing. One could ask› [8] the jurors again what they are judging (for they are not present at the events themselves): [9] they themselves admit that what the false is mixed in is false, what the true is mixed in, true. But this is completely different . . .[1]

[1] The text is doubtless lacunose; Robinson supplies ‹from their original thesis›.

5.

[1] "The insane and the sane, and the wise and the foolish, both say and do the same things. [2] And first, they use the same names, 'earth,' 'human,' 'horse,' 'fire,' and all the others. And they do the same things, they sit, eat, drink, and lie down, and everything else in the same way. [3] And what is more, the same thing is both larger and smaller, and more numerous and less numerous, and heavier and lighter. For in this respect all things would be the same.

---

[1] ταῦτα vel ταυτα mss., corr. North   [2,3] ταῦτα bis mss., corr. Meibom   [4] ‹κ'› Blass

εἴη ταὐτὰ[5] πάντα· [4] τὸ τάλαντόν ἐστι βαρύτερον τῆς μνᾶς καὶ κουφότερον τῶν δύο ταλάντων· τωὐτὸν ἄρα καὶ κουφότερον καὶ βαρύτερον.[6] [5] καὶ ζώει ὁ αὐτὸς ἄνθρωπος καὶ οὐ ζώει, καὶ ταὐτὰ[7] ἔστι καὶ οὐκ ἔστι· τὰ γὰρ τῇδ' ἐόντα ἐν τᾷ Λιβύᾳ οὐκ ἔστιν, οὐδέ γε τὰ ἐν Λιβύᾳ ἐν Κύπρῳ. καὶ τἆλλα κατὰ τὸν αὐτὸν λόγον. οὐκῶν καὶ ἐντὶ τὰ πράγματα καὶ οὐκ ἐντί." [6] τοὶ τῆνα[8] λέγοντες, τὼς μαινομένως καὶ[9] τὼς σοφὼς καὶ τὼς ἀμαθεῖς τωὐτὰ διαπράσσεσθαι καὶ λέγεν, καὶ τἆλλα <τὰ>[10] ἑπόμενα τῷ λόγῳ, οὐκ ὀρθῶς λέγοντι. [7] αἰ γάρ τις αὐτὼς ἐρωτάσαι[11] αἰ διαφέρει μανία σω-φροσύνης καὶ σοφία ἀμαθίης, φαντί· "ναί." [8] εὖ γὰρ καὶ ἐξ ὧν πράσσοντι ἑκάτεροι δᾶλοί ἐντι, ὡς ὁμολο-γησοῦντι. οὐκῶν αἰ[12] ταὐτὰ πράσσοντι, καὶ τοὶ σοφοὶ μαίνονται, καὶ τοὶ μαινόμενοι σοφοί, καὶ πάντα συν-ταράσσονται. [9] καὶ ἐπακτέος[13] ὁ λόγος, πότερον οἷον[14] ἐν δέοντι τοὶ σωφρονοῦντες λέγοντι ἢ τοὶ μαι-νόμενοι. ἀλλὰ γάρ φαντι ὡς ταὐτὰ[15] μὲν λέγοντι, ὅταν τις αὐτὼς ἐρωτῇ· ἀλλὰ τοὶ μὲν σοφοὶ ἐν τῷ δέοντι, τοὶ δὲ μαινόμενοι ᾇ[16] οὐ δεῖ. [10] καὶ τοῦτο λέγοντες δο-κοῦντι μικρὸν ποτιθῆναι <τὸ>[17] ᾇ[18] δεῖ καὶ μὴ δεῖ, ὥστε μηκέτι τὸ αὐτὸ ἦμεν. [11] ἐγὼ δὲ οὐ πράγματος τοσούτω ποτιτεθέντος ἀλλοιοῦσθαι δοκῶ τὰ πρά-

---

[5] ταῦτα mss., corr. Meibom   [6] lac. post βαρύτερον susp. Diels   [7] κατταντὰ mss. (κατ' αὐτὰ Y1 Y2), corr. Mul-lach   [8] τινες mss., corr. Diels   [9] καὶ <τὼς σωφρονοῦ-ντας καὶ> Blass   [10] <τὰ> Blass

[4] A talent is heavier than a mina and lighter than two talents; so that the same thing is both lighter and heavier. [5] And the same man is both alive and not alive, and the same things both are and are not: for the things that are here are not in Libya, and those that are in Libya are not in Cyprus. And the same argument applies to everything else. And so things both are and are not." [6] Those people who say this, that the insane, the wise, and the foolish do and say the same things, and everything else that follows from this argument, do not speak correctly. [7] For if one were to ask them whether insanity differs from sanity and wisdom from foolishness, they would answer, "Yes." [8] For it is quite clear, also on the basis of what both groups do, that they will agree with this. In consequence, if they do the same things, then the wise are insane too, and the insane are wise, and everything is thrown into confusion. [9] And the question should be raised whether it is the sane or the insane who speak as it were at the right moment. For when someone asks them, they answer that they say the same things, but the wise say them at the right moment, the insane when it is not right. [10] And when they say this, they seem to be making a small addition, viz. 'the right moment' and 'when it is not right,' so that it is no longer the same thing. [11] But as for me, I think that things are altered not by the addition of something

---

11 ἐρωτάσας mss., corr. Fabricius   12 καὶ mss., corr. Mullach   13 ἐπάρτεος vel ἐπ᾽ ἄρτεος mss. (ἐπ᾽ ἄργεος F2, ἐπ᾽ ἄγεος P4 P6), corr. Wilamowitz   14 ὧν Wilamowitz: secl. Koen   15 ταῦτα mss., corr. Fabricius

16 αἰ mss., corr. Blass   17 ⟨τὸ⟩ Diels

18 αἰ mss., corr. Blass

γματα, ἀλλ' ἁρμονίας διαλλαγείσας· ὥσπερ 'Γλαῦκος'
καὶ 'γλαυκός' καὶ 'Ξάνθος' καὶ 'ξανθός' καὶ 'Ξοῦθος'
καὶ 'ξουθός.' [12] ταῦτα μὲν τὴν ἁρμονίαν ἀλλάξαντα
διήνεικαν, τὰ δὲ μακρῶς καὶ βραχυτέρως ῥηθέντα.
'Τύρος' καὶ 'τυρός' 'σάκος' καὶ 'σακός,'[19] ἅτερα δὲ
γράμματα διαλλάξαντα· 'κάρτος' καὶ 'κρατός,'[20] 'ὄνος'
καὶ 'νόος.' [13] ἐπεὶ ὦν οὐκ ἀφαιρεθέντος οὐδενὸς τοσοῦτον διαφέρει, τί δή, αἴ τις ἢ ποτιτίθητί τι[21] ἢ ἀφαι-
ρεῖ; καὶ τοῦτο δείξω οἷόν ἐστιν. [14] αἴ τις ἀπὸ τῶν
δέκα ἓν ἀφέλοι,[22] οὐκέτι δέκα οὐδὲ ἓν ἂν[23] εἴη, καὶ
τἆλλα καττωὐτό.[24] [15] τὸ δὲ τὸν αὐτὸν ἄνθρωπον καὶ
ἦμεν καὶ μὴ ἦμεν, ἐρωτῶ· "τὶ ἢ τὰ πάντα ἔστιν";
οὐκῶν αἴ τις μὴ φαίη ἦμεν, ψεύδεται "τὰ πάντα" εἰ-
πών.[25] ταῦτα πάντα[26] ὦν πῇ ἐστι.

---

[19] σάκος καὶ σάκκος mss. (σάκκος καὶ σάκκος L, σάκκος
καὶ σάκος Z), corr. Weber   [20] κράτος mss., corr. Wilamowitz
[21] ἢ ποτιτιθεῖ τι mss., corr. nos: τι ποτιτίθητι Diels
[22] ἀφέλοι ‹ἢ τοῖς δέκα ἓν ποτθείη› Diels
[23] ἂν L, om. cett.   [24] καττοῦτο mss., corr. Meibom
[25] εἰπόντες mss., corr. Mullach
[26] ταὐτὰ πάντα (vel πάντως) North: ταὐτά. πάντα Diels

6.[1]

[1] λέγεται δέ τις λόγος οὔτ' ἀλαθὴς οὔτε καινός, ὅτι[2]
ἄρα σοφία καὶ ἀρετὰ οὔτε διδακτὸν εἴη οὔτε μαθητόν.
τοὶ δὲ ταῦτα λέγοντες ταῖσδε ἀποδείξεσι χρῶνται. [2]
ὡς οὐχ οἷόν τε εἴη, αἴ τι ἄλλῳ παραδοίης, τοῦτο αὐτὸν
ἔτι ἔχειν. μία μὲν δὴ αὕτα. [3] ἄλλα δέ, ὡς, αἰ δι-

of this size, but rather by a change of the accent: for example, *glaûkos* ('Glaucus') and *glaukós* ('light blue'), *xánthos* ('Xanthus') and *xanthós* ('blond'), *xoûthos* ('Xouthus') and *xouthós* ('yellow-brown'). [12] These words differ by a change in accent, the following ones by whether they are pronounced with a long or a short vowel: *Tŭros* ('Tyre') and *tūros* ('cheese'), *săkos* ('shield') and *sākos* ('enclosure'); and other ones by a change in the sequence of letters: *kartos* ('strength') and *kratos* ('of the head'), *onos* ('ass') and *noos* ('mind'). [13] So since there is such a big difference even if nothing is taken away, what will happen then, if someone were either to add or to take away something? And I shall show what sort of thing this is. [14] If someone were to take away 1 from 10, it would no longer be 10 or 1; and everything else in the same way. [15] As for the statement that the same man both is and is not, I ask: "Is he in some particular respect, or in all respects?" So that if someone says that he is not, he is making a mistake by saying "in all respects." Therefore all these things are in some way.

6.

[1] A certain argument is stated, one that is neither true nor new: viz. that wisdom and virtue can neither be taught nor learned. Those people who say this make use of the following proofs: [2] That it is not possible, if you pass something on to someone else, to still possess it yourself. This is a first proof. [3] Another one is that, if it could

---

¹ <Περὶ τᾶς σοφίας καὶ τᾶς ἀρετᾶς, αἰ διδακτόν> Stephanus   ² τίς mss., corr. Stephanus

δακτὸν ἦν, διδάσκαλοί κα ἀποδεδεγμένοι ἦν, ὡς τᾶς
μωσικᾶς. [4] τρίτα δέ, ὡς τοὶ ἐν τᾷ Ἑλλάδι γενόμενοι
σοφοὶ ἄνδρες τὰ αὑτῶν τέκνα ἂν[3] ἐδίδαξαν καὶ τὼς
φίλως.[4] [5] τετάρτα δέ, ὅτι ἤδη τινὲς παρὰ[5] σοφιστὰς
ἐλθόντες οὐδὲν ὠφέληθεν. [6] πέμπτα δέ, ὅτι πολλοὶ
οὐ συγγενόμενοι σοφισταῖς ἄξιοι λόγω γεγένηνται.
[7] ἐγὼ δὲ κάρτα εὐήθη νομίζω τόνδε τὸν λόγον· γι-
νώσκω γὰρ τὼς διδασκάλως γράμματα διδάσκοντας
ἃ καὶ αὐτὸς ἐπιστάμενος τυγχάνει, καὶ κιθαριστὰς
κιθαρίζεν. πρὸς δὲ τὰν δευτέραν ἀπόδειξιν, ὡς ἄρα
οὐκ ἐντὶ διδάσκαλοι ἀποδεδεγμένοι, τί μὰν τοὶ σοφισταὶ διδάσκοντι ἀλλ' ἢ σοφίαν καὶ ἀρετάν;[6] [8] τί δὲ
Ἀναξαγόρειοι καὶ Πυθαγόρειοι ἦεν; τὸ δὲ τρίτον, ἐδίδαξε Πολύκλειτος τὸν υἱὸν ἀνδριάντας ποιεῖν. [9] καὶ
ἂν[7] μέν τις μὴ διδάξῃ,[8] οὐ σαμῆον· αἰ δ' εἷς τις ἐδίδαξε,[9] τεκμάριον ὅτι δυνατόν ἐστι διδάξαι. [10] τέταρ-
τον δέ, αἰ μή τοι παρὰ σοφῶν[10] σοφιστῶν σοφοὶ
γίνονται· καὶ γὰρ γράμματα πολλοὶ οὐκ ἔμαθον μα-
θόντες. [11] ἔστι δέ τις καὶ φύσις, ἇ δή[11] τις μὴ μαθὼν
παρὰ σοφιστᾶν ἱκανὸς ἐγένετο, εὐφυὴς γα[12] γενόμενος, ῥαδίως συναρπάξαι τὰ πολλά, ὀλίγα μαθὼν παρ'
ὦνπερ καὶ τὰ ὀνύματα μανθάνομεν· καὶ τούτων τι ἤτοι

---

[3] τὰν αὐτῶν τέχναν Schulze   [4] καὶ τὼς φίλως L in
mg.: καὶ πῶς φίλωσι vel φίλως cett.: κα τὼς φίλως Schulze
[5] περὶ mss., corr. Stephanus   [6] post ἀρετάν; hab. mss. ἤ,
del. Wilamowitz   [7] αἰ mss., corr. Robinson
[8] ἐδίδαξε Wilamowitz   [9] δ' ἔστι vel δ' ἐστὶ (δ' ἔστιν
LZ) διδάξαι mss., corr. Wilamowitz

be taught, there would be recognized teachers of it, as there are of music. [4] A third one is that those men in Greece who showed themselves to be wise would have taught their children and friends. [5] A fourth is that it has already happened that some people who came to study with the sophists derived thereby no benefit at all. [6] A fifth is that many of those who have not studied with sophists have turned out to be noteworthy. [7] As for me, I think that this argument is extremely simpleminded. For I know that teachers teach letters that each one at that moment also knows, and that cithara players [scil. teach how] to play the cithara. Against the second proof, that there are not recognized teachers, what else do the sophists teach, if not wisdom and virtue? [8] What were the Anaxagoreans and the Pythagoreans? The third: Polyclitus taught his son how to make statues. [9] And if someone has not taught, this is not a proof: whereas if any one man has taught, this is proof that it is possible to teach. [10] The fourth, that some people do not become wise from wise sophists: it is also the case that many people have not learned to read in spite of the fact that they have studied how to. [11] But there is also a certain natural predisposition, thanks to which someone who has not learned from the sophists becomes competent, so long as he has a suitable predisposition by nature, at grasping many things easily even though he has learned only a little from the very same people from whom we also learn how to read; and among these people, one man [scil. learns] either more or

---

10 σοφῶν del. Blass   11 αἰ δέ mss., corr. Diels
12 καὶ mss., corr. Diels: κα Blass: secl. Wilamowitz

πλέον, ἤτοι ἔλασσον, ὁ μὲν παρὰ πατρός, ὁ δὲ παρὰ
ματρός. [12] αἰ δέ τῳ μὴ πιστόν ἐστι τὰ ὀνύματα μαν-
θάνεν ἁμέ,[13] ἀλλ᾿ ἐπισταμένως ἅμα γίνεσθαι, γνώτω
ἐκ τῶνδε· αἴ τις εὐθὺς γενόμενον παιδίον ἐς Πέρσας
ἀποπέμψαι καὶ τηνεῖ τράφοι, κωφὸν Ἑλλάδος φωνᾶς,
περσίζοι κα· αἴ τις τηνόθεν τῇδε κομίζοι,[14] ἑλλανίζοι
κα. οὕτω μανθάνομεν τὰ ὀνύματα, καὶ τὼς διδασκάλως οὐκ ἴσαμες.[15] [13] οὕτω[16] λέλεκταί μοι ὁ λόγος,
καὶ ἔχεις ἀρχὴν καὶ τέλος καὶ μέσαν· καὶ οὐ λέγω ὡς
διδακτόν ἐστιν, ἀλλ᾿ ὅτι οὐκ[17] ἀποχρῶντί μοι τῆναι
ταί[18] ἀποδείξεις.[19]

13 ἅμα mss. (ἅμε B P3 P4 P6 R V1), corr. Koen
14 κομίξαι Wilamowitz   15 οὐκὶ ἅμες mss. (οὐκὶ ἅμες
L), corr. Blass   16 οὐ mss., corr. Diels: οὖ North: secl. Koen
17 ἀλλ᾿ ὅτι οὐκ F2: ἀλλ᾿ ὅτι cett.: ἀλλ᾿ οὐκ Diels
18 αἱ Matth. de Varis   19 ἀποδείξιες mss., corr. Stephanus

7.

[1] λέγοντι δέ τινες τῶν δαμαγορούντων ὡς χρὴ τὰς
ἀρχὰς ἀπὸ κλάρω γίνεσθαι, οὐ βέλτιστα ταῦτα νομί-
ζοντες. [2] εἰ γάρ τις αὐτὸν ἐρωτώη τὸν ταῦτα λέγοντα, "τί δὴ σὺ τοῖς οἰκέταις οὐκ ἀπὸ κλήρω τὰ ἔργα
προστάσσεις, ὅπως ὁ μὲν ζευγηλάτας, αἴ κ᾿ ὀψοποιὸς
λάχῃ, ὀψοποιῇ, ὁ δὲ ὀψοποιὸς ζευγηλατῇ, καὶ τἆλλα
κατὰ τωὐτό;[1] [3] καὶ πῶς οὐ καὶ τὼς χαλκῆας καὶ τὼς
σκυτῆας συναγαγόντες καὶ τέκτονας καὶ χρυσοχόας
διεκλαρώσαμεν[2] καὶ ἠναγκάσαμεν, ἄν χ᾿[3] ἕκαστος
λάχῃ τέχναν ἐργάζεσθαι, ἀλλὰ μὴ ἂν ἐπίσταται; [4]

less, one from his father, another from his mother. [12]
And if someone finds it plausible not that we learn words,
but that we are born already knowing them, let him understand from the following: if a baby were sent to the
Persians as soon as he was born and were raised there, so
that he heard nothing of the Greek language, he would
speak Persian; but if he were brought from there to here,
he would speak Greek. It is in this way that we learn words,
and we do not know who our teachers are. [13] In this way
my argument has been stated, and you have the beginning,
the end, and the middle. And what I am saying is not that
they are teachable, but that those proofs are not sufficient
for me.

7.

[1] Some of the orators who make speeches to the people
say that offices should be assigned by lot; but their opinion
is not the best one. [2] For if someone were to ask the man
who says this, "Why do you not assign your house slaves
their tasks by lot, so that the ox driver, if the lot of cook
fell to him, would cook, while the cook would drive the
oxen, and everything else in the same way? [3] And how
is it that we do not bring together the blacksmiths and the
cobblers, and carpenters and goldsmiths, and make an
assignment by lot, and force each one to work at whichever
art happens to fall to him and not at the one he knows? [4]

---

¹ τοῦτο mss., corr. Koen

² διεκληρώσαμεν mss., corr. Meibom

³ ἀνάσχ' mss. (ἀ ἀν χ' L in mg.), corr. North

τωὐτὸν δὲ καὶ ἐν ἀγῶσι τὰς μωσικᾶς διακλαρῶσαι
τὼς ἀγωνιστὰς καὶ ὅ τι χ' ἕκαστος[4] λάχῃ, ἀγωνί-
ζεσθαι· αὐλητὰς κιθαριζέτω[5] τυχὸν καὶ κιθαρῳδὸς
αὐλήσει· καὶ ἐν τῷ πολέμῳ τοξότας καὶ ὁπλίτας[6] ἱπ-
πασεῖται, ὁ δὲ ἱππεὺς τοξεύσει, ὥστε πάντες ἃ οὐκ
ἐπίστανται οὐδὲ δύνανται,[7] πραξοῦντι." [5] λέγοντι δὲ
καὶ ἀγαθὸν ἦμεν καὶ δαμοτικὸν κάρτα· ἐγὼ ἥκιστα
νομίζω δαμοτικόν. ἐντὶ γὰρ ἐν ταῖς πόλεσι μισόδαμοι
ἄνθρωποι, ὧν αἵ κα τύχῃ ὁ κύαμος, ἀπολοῦντι τὸν
δᾶμον. [6] ἀλλὰ χρὴ τὸν δᾶμον αὐτὸν ὁρῶντα αἱρεῖ-
σθαι πάντας τὼς εὔνως αὐτῷ, καὶ τὼς ἐπιταδείως
στραταγέν, ἀτέρως δὲ νομοφυλακὲν καὶ τἆλλα.[8]

4 post ἕκαστος hab. mss. κα (καὶ LZ), secl. Blass

5 κιθαριξεῖ Wilamowitz: κιθαρεῖται Robinson

6 πολέμῳ τὼς τοξότας καὶ τὼς ὁπλίτας mss., corr. Wilamowitz   7 post δύνανται hab. mss. οὐδὲ, del. Schanz

8 post τἆλλα lac. pauc. litt. mss. (praeter L): ⟨ἐπιστατέν⟩
Blass: ⟨καττωὐτό⟩ Schanz

8.

[1] ⟨τῶ δ' αὐτῶ⟩[1] ἀνδρὸς καὶ τᾶς αὐτᾶς[2] τέχνας νομίζω
κατὰ βραχύ τε δύνασθαι διαλέγεσθαι,[3] καὶ ⟨τὰν⟩[4]
ἀλάθειαν τῶν πραγμάτων ἐπίστασθαι, καὶ δικάσασθαι[5] ὀρθῶς, καὶ δαμαγορεῖν οἷόν τ' ἦμεν, καὶ λόγων
τέχνας ἐπίστασθαι, καὶ περὶ φύσιος τῶν ἁπάντων ὥς
τε ἔχει καὶ ὡς ἐγένετο διδάσκεν. [2] καὶ πρῶτον μὲν ὁ
περὶ φύσιος τῶν ἁπάντων εἰδώς πῶς οὐ δυνασεῖται
περὶ πάντων ὀρθῶς[6] καὶ πράσσεν; [3] ἔτι δὲ[7] ὁ τὰς

The same thing in competitions in music too, choose the competitors by lot and, whatever happens to fall to each one, have him compete in that one: let an *aulos* player play the cithara perhaps, and a cithara player will play the *aulos*. And in war a bowmen and an infantryman will ride horseback, and the cavalryman will shoot with the bow, so that they will all do what they do not know how to do and what they are not capable of doing." [5] And they say that this is a good thing and extremely democratic; but as for me, I do not think that it is in the least bit democratic. For in the cities there are men who hate the people, and if the lot falls to them they will destroy the people. [6] But the people themselves must watch out and choose men all of whom are favorable to them, and suitable men to be generals, and other ones to be guardians of the laws, and so on.

8.

[1] I think that it belongs ⟨to the same⟩ man and to the same art to be able to discuss briefly, to know ⟨the⟩ truth of things, to judge a legal case correctly, to be able to make speeches to the people, to know the arts of speeches, and to teach about the nature of all things, both their present condition and their origins. [2] And first, how would the man who knows about the nature of all things not be able also to act correctly about all things? [3] Furthermore, the

---

¹ ⟨τῷ δ' αὐτῷ⟩ Robinson post Blass   ² κατὰ τὰς αὐτὰς mss., corr. Blass   ³ καὶ ἀλέγεσθαι mss., corr. North

⁴ ⟨τὰν⟩ Wilamowitz   ⁵ δικάσασθαι F2: διδασκάσα-σθαι cett.   ⁶ ὀρθῶς ⟨καὶ λέγεν⟩ Blass, alii alia

⁷ δὴ mss., corr. Diels

τέχνας τῶν λόγων εἰδὼς ἐπιστασεῖται καὶ περὶ πάντων ὀρθῶς λέγεν. [4] δεῖ γὰρ τὸν μέλλοντα ὀρθῶς λέγεν, περὶ ὧν ἐπίσταται, περὶ τούτων λέγεν. <περὶ>[8]
πάντων γ' ἄρ'[9] ἐπιστασεῖται. [5] πάντων μὲν γὰρ τῶν
λόγων τὰς τέχνας ἐπίσταται, τοὶ δὲ λόγοι πάντες περὶ
πάντων τῶν ἐ<όντων ἐντί>.[10] [6] δεῖ δὲ ἐπίστασθαι τὸν
μέλλοντα ὀρθῶς λέγεν περὶ ὅτων καὶ λέγοι[11] . . . ,[12]
καὶ τὰ μὲν ἀγαθὰ ὀρθῶς διδάσκεν τὴν πόλιν πράσσεν, τὰ δὲ κακὰ τὼς[13] κωλύειν. [7] εἰδὼς δέ γε ταῦτα[14]
εἰδήσει καὶ τὰ ἄτερα τούτων· πάντα γὰρ ἐπιστα-
σεῖται· ἔστι γὰρ ταῦτα[15] τῶν πάντων, τῆνα <ὁ>[16] δὲ
ποτὶ τωὐτὸν τὰ δέοντα παρέξεται, αἰ[17] χρή. [8] κἂν μὴ
ἐπίσταται[18] αὐλέν, αἰ δυνασεῖται αὐλέν, αἴ κα δέῃ
τοῦτο πράσσεν. [9] τὸν δὲ δικάζεσθαι ἐπιστάμενον δεῖ
τὸ δίκαιον ἐπίστασθαι ὀρθῶς· περὶ γὰρ τούτω ταὶ
δίκαι.[19] εἰδὼς δὲ τοῦτο, εἰδήσει καὶ τὸ ὑπεναντίον
αὐτῷ καὶ τὰ . . . <ἑ>τεροῖα.[20] [10] δεῖ δὲ αὐτὸν καὶ τὼς
νόμως ἐπίστασθαι πάντας· αἰ τοίνυν τὰ πράγματα μὴ

---

[8] <περὶ> Rohde   [9] γ' ἄρ' Robinson: γὰρ mss.: del. Diels
[10] post ἐ vel ε lac. pauc. litt. mss., corr. Orelli   [11] καὶ λέγοι
mss. (καὶ λέγει F1 F2, δεῖ λέγεν P3): κα λέγῃ Blass
[12] post λέγοι lac. 4–5 lin. mss. (ἐλλιπές τὸ χωρίον P3 in mg.),
<τὰ πράγματα> Diels   [13] κακά τως Diels: κακὰ παντῶς
Blass   [14] δέ γε αὐτὰ mss., corr. Blass: γε del. Diels
[15] ταῦτα mss., corr. Diels   [16] τῆνα P3: κεῖνα cett.: τῆνα,
<ὁ> Diels   [17] παρασσεῖται. χρὴ vel πρασσεῖται χρὴ mss.,
corr. Robinson (αἰ χρή iam Wilamowitz): πράξει, αἰ Diels

man who knows the arts of speeches will also know how
to speak correctly about all things. [4] For it is necessary
that the man who intends to speak correctly speak about
those things he knows about. Therefore he will know
⟨about⟩ all things. [5] For he knows the arts of all speeches,
and all speeches ⟨are⟩ about all of the ⟨things that are⟩.
[6] It is necessary that the man who intends to speak correctly, whatever he would speak about . . . [1] and teach the
city correctly to do beneficial things and to prevent them
from doing harmful ones. [7] Knowing all this, he will also
know what is different from this, for he will know everything: for these things are the same for all men, while in
the same way he will supply of himself what is necessary
if it is required. [8] And even if he does not know how to
play the *aulos,* he will always be able to play the *aulos,* if
it should be necessary that he do this.[2] [9] It is necessary
that a man who knows how to judge a legal case know
correctly what is just; for legal cases revolve around this.
And knowing this, he will also know what is the opposite
of it and what is . . . [3] of a different sort. [10] It is also
necessary that he know all the laws: so if he does not know

---

[1] The mss. have a lacuna of four to five lines at this point.

[2] The sentence may be corrupt; but cf. perhaps Plato, *Protagoras* 327A–C.

[3] The mss. have a lacuna of about ten letters at this point.

---

[18] κἂν μὴ ἐπίσταται mss., corr. Robinson: καὶ μὲν ἐπι-
στᾶται Diels   [19] τὰ δίκαια mss., corr. Blass
[20] καὶ vel καὶ τὰ mss. (καὶ τὼς νόμως P4 P6) tum lac. 10 fere
litt. tum τέρεια vel τερεία: ⟨ἑ⟩τεροῖα Mullach: καὶ τὰ ⟨ἄλλα
αὐτῶ ? ἑ⟩τεροῖα Robinson: καὶ τὰ ⟨τούτων⟩ ἄτερα Diels

ἐπιστασεῖται, οὐδὲ τὼς νόμως. [11] τὸν γὰρ ἐν μωσικᾷ
νόμον[21] ἐπίσταται ὅσπερ καὶ μωσικάν, ὃς δὲ μὴ μωσικάν, οὐδὲ τὸν νόμον. [12] ὅς γα ‹μὰν›[22] τὰν ἀλάθειαν
τῶν πραγμάτων ἐπίσταται, εὐπετὴς[23] ὁ λόγος, ὅτι
πάντα ἐπίσταται· [13] ὃς δὲ ‹κατὰ› βραχὺ ‹διαλέγεσθαι δύναται›,[24] δεῖ νιν ἐρωτώμενον ἀποκρίνασθαι
περὶ πάντων· οὐκῶν[25] δεῖ νιν πάντ᾽ ἐπίστασθαι.

[21] post νόμον hab. mss. τίς, del. Wilamowitz: ὡντὸς Diels
[22] ‹μὰν› Wilamowitz   [23] ἀπετὴς mss. (εὐπατής ex ἀπα-
τὴς Y2), corr. Matth. de Varis   [24] ‹κατὰ› βραχὺ ‹διαλέγεσθαι δύναται› Blass   [25] οὔκων P3 corr.: οὐκοῦν Y2:
οὔκουν cett.

9.

[1] μέγιστον δὲ καὶ κάλλιστον ἐξεύρημα εὕρηται ἐς
τὸν βίον μνάμα καὶ ἐς πάντα χρήσιμον, ἐς φιλοσο-
φίαν τε καὶ σοφίαν. [2] ἔστι δὲ τοῦτο ‹πρᾶτον›·[1] ἐὰν
προσέχῃς τὸν νοῦν, διὰ τούτω[2] παρελθοῦσα ‹ἁ›[3]
γνώμα μᾶλλον αἰσθησεῖται σύνολον ὃ ἔμαθες.[4] [3]
δεύτερον[5] δὲ[6] μελετᾶν,[7] αἴ κα ἀκούσῃς· τῷ[8] γὰρ πολλάκις ταὐτὰ ἀκοῦσαι καὶ εἶπαι ἐς μνάμαν παρεγένετο.
[4] τρίτον αἴ κα ἀκούσῃς ἐπὶ τὰ[9] οἶδας καταθέσθαι,
οἷον τόδε· δεῖ μεμνᾶσθαι Χρύσιππον, καθέμεν ἐπὶ
τὸν χρυσὸν καὶ τὸν ἵππον. [5] ἄλλο· Πυριλάμπη κατ-
θέμεν ἐπὶ ‹τὸ›[10] πῦρ καὶ τὸ λάμπειν. τάδε μὲν περὶ

[1] ‹πρᾶτον› Diels post Schanz
[2] τούτων mss., corr. Orelli
[3] ‹ἁ› Orelli

the things, he will not know the laws either. [11] For that
man knows the law in music who also [scil. knows] music,
but the man who does not [scil. know] music does not [scil.
know] its law either. [12] <Certainly,> whoever knows the
truth about things, it is easy to argue that that man knows
all things; [13] and whoever <is able to discuss> briefly
must answer, when someone questions him, about everything. And so it is necessary that he know everything.

9.

[1] A very great and fine discovery has been made for life,
viz. memory, and it is useful for everything, for philosophy
and for wisdom. [2] It is this <first of all>: if you pay attention, then your thought, passing [scil. things] in review by
this means, will better perceive the totality of what you
have learned. [3] Second: to practice, if you hear [scil.
something]; for by hearing and saying the same thing
many times, it [scil. the totality of what you have learned]
comes to be present to your memory. [4] Third: if you hear
something, connect it with what you know, as for example
the following: it is necessary to remember Chrysippus,
connect it with *khrusos* ('gold') and *hippos* ('horse'). [5] Or
another example: connect Pyrilampes with *pur* ('fire') and
lampein ('to shine'). These examples are about names. [6]

---

4 σύνολον ὃ ἔμαθες post παρεγένετο transp. Diels

5 δευτέραν mss., corr. North

6 δεῖ Robinson

7 μελέταν mss., corr. North

8 τὸ mss., corr. Schanz

9 ἔπειτα mss., corr. Matth. de Varis

10 <τὸ> Blass

τῶν ὀνυμάτων·[11] [6] τὰ δὲ πράγματα οὕτως· περὶ ἀνδρείας[12] ἐπὶ τὸν Ἄρη καὶ τὸν Ἀχιλλῆα, περὶ χαλκείας
δὲ ἐπὶ τὸν Ἥφαιστον, περὶ δειλίας ἐπὶ τὸν Ἐπειόν[13]
. . .

[11] ὠνυμάτων P3, ὀνομάτων cett.: corr. Trieber
[12] ἀνδρίας mss., corr. Stephanus
[13] post Ἐπειόν hab. P3 Σῆ: ἐλλιπὲς οὕτω καὶ τὸ ἀντίγρα-
φον, ὡς ὁρᾶτε, cett. Σῆ ὅτι τὸ ἐπίλοιπον οὐχ εὑρέθη

For things, [scil. do] as follows: about manly valor, with Ares and Achilles; about smithery, with Hephaestus; about cowardice, with Epeius . . . [1]

[1] The mss. indicate that the text breaks off at this point.

42. 'SOPHISTS' AND 'SOPHISTIC': COLLECTIVE REPRESENTATIONS AND GENERAL CHARACTERIZATIONS [SOPH.]

The present chapter gathers together a number of texts that illustrate how the loose group of fifth century intellectuals who were usually known as 'sophists' were collectively understood. It begins with passages in which the terms *sophos* ('wise man') or *sophistês* (originally 'man of learning,' 'expert') were applied to various figures—poets, sages, legislators—from the period before the fifth century, and then it goes on to illustrate some basic features attributed to most or all of the fifth-century 'sophists': the requirement that a fee be paid; travel from one city to another; personal charisma; interest in education, especially in the teaching of virtue (*aretê*) and rhetoric; various forms of oratorical disputation; writing. It also includes a number of passages in which Plato and Xenophon, in speeches they attribute to Socrates or to other characters, propose analogies intended to define, usually pejoratively, what a 'sophist' is: above all, as a prostitute, a hunter, a merchant, or a charlatan. It concludes with texts that put 'sophistic' in relation to atheism and, usually by contrast, to philosophy. Beyond the chapters on the individual 'sophists' elsewhere in this volume, in which many of the same themes are found as they apply to one figure or another, the texts in this chapter show how the term came to be specialized in order to define—most often negatively—a definite group of thinkers.

BIBLIOGRAPHY

See the titles listed in the General Introduction to Chapters 31–42.

OUTLINE OF THE CHAPTER

'SOPHISTS' AND 'SOPHISTIC': COLLECTIVE REPRESENTATIONS AND GENERAL CHARACTERIZATIONS
[cf. 79 DK]

The Earliest 'Sophists' (R1–R5)

R1 (≠ DK) Isocr. *Ant.* 313

[. . .] τοὺς μὲν καλουμένους σοφιστὰς ἐθαύμαζον καὶ τοὺς συνόντας αὐτοῖς ἐζήλουν [. . .]. μέγιστον δὲ τεκμήριον· Σόλωνα μὲν γάρ, τὸν πρῶτον τῶν πολιτῶν λαβόντα τὴν ἐπωνυμίαν ταύτην, προστάτην ἠξίωσαν τῆς πόλεως εἶναι [. . .].

R2 (≠ DK) Plut. *E ap. Delph.* 3 385D–E

[ΛΑ.] λέγουσι γὰρ ἐκείνους τοὺς σοφούς ὑπ' ἐνίων δὲ σοφιστὰς προσαγορευθέντας, αὐτοὺς μὲν εἶναι πέντε, Χίλωνα καὶ Θαλῆν καὶ Σόλωνα καὶ Βίαντα καὶ Πιττακόν [. . .].

'SOPHISTS' AND 'SOPHISTIC': COLLECTIVE REPRESENTATIONS AND GENERAL CHARACTERIZATIONS

The Earliest 'Sophists' (R1–R5)

R1 (≠ DK) Isocrates, *Antidosis*

[. . .] they [i.e. Athenians of earlier times] felt admiration for the people called 'sophists' and envy for their students [. . .]. And the greatest proof is this: they thought it right to make Solon, the first of their fellow citizens to bear this title, the head of the city [. . .].

R2 (≠ DK) Plutarch, *On the Letter E in Delphi*

[Lamprias:] For they say that those wise men (*sophoi*) whom some call 'sophists' are in fact five in number: Chilon, Thales, Solon, Bias, and Pittacus [. . .] [cf. **MOR. T35; THAL. R2**].

R3 (≠ DK) Diog. Laert. 1.12

οἱ δὲ σοφοὶ καὶ σοφισταὶ ἐκαλοῦντο· καὶ οὐ μόνον,[1]
ἀλλὰ καὶ οἱ ποιηταὶ σοφισταί, καθὰ καὶ Κρατῖνος ἐν
Ἀρχιλόχοις [cf. Frag. 2 K–A] τοὺς περὶ Ὅμηρον καὶ
Ἡσίοδον ἐπαινῶν οὕτως καλεῖ.

[1] μόνον ⟨οὗτοι⟩ Reiske

R4 (79.1a Untersteiner) Plut. *Them.* 2.4

[. . .] μᾶλλον οὖν ἄν τις προσέχοι τοῖς Μνησιφίλου
τὸν Θεμιστοκλέα τοῦ Φρεαρρίου ζηλωτὴν γενέσθαι
λέγουσιν, οὔτε ῥήτορος ὄντος οὔτε τῶν φυσικῶν κλη-
θέντων φιλοσόφων, ἀλλὰ τὴν τότε καλουμένην σοφίαν, οὖσαν δὲ δεινότητα πολιτικὴν καὶ δραστήριον
σύνεσιν, ἐπιτήδευμα πεποιημένου καὶ διασῴζοντος
ὥσπερ αἵρεσιν ἐκ διαδοχῆς ἀπὸ Σόλωνος· ἣν οἱ μετὰ
ταῦτα δικανικαῖς μείξαντες τέχναις καὶ μεταγαγόντες
ἀπὸ τῶν πράξεων τὴν ἄσκησιν ἐπὶ τοὺς λόγους, σοφισταὶ προσηγορεύθησαν.

R5 (79.1) Ael. Arist. *Or.* 3 311

ἀρχὴν δὲ οὐδ᾽ εἰδέναι μοι δοκοῦσιν οὐδ᾽ αὐτὸ τοὔνομα
τῆς φιλοσοφίας ὅπως εἶχε τοῖς Ἕλλησι καὶ ὅτι ἠδύνατο οὐδ᾽ ὅλως τῶν περὶ ταῦτ᾽ οὐδέν. οὐχ Ἡρόδοτος
Σόλωνα σοφιστὴν κέκληκεν, οὐ Πυθαγόραν πάλιν;
οὐκ Ἀνδροτίων [FGrHist 321 F69] τοὺς ἑπτὰ σοφιστὰς
προσείρηκε, λέγων δὴ τοὺς σοφούς, καὶ πάλιν αὖ Σω-

R3 (≠ DK) Diogenes Laertius

Wise men (*sophoi*) also used to be called 'sophists,' and not only they, but the poets too were 'sophists.' And so when Cratinus in his *Archilochuses* praises Homer, Hesiod, and their disciples, he calls them this.

R4 (≠ DK) Plutarch, *Themistocles*

[. . .] So one should rather pay attention to those people who say that Themistocles was a disciple of Mnesiphilus of Phrearrhi, who was neither an orator nor one of the so-called 'natural philosophers,' but who, practicing something that at that time was called 'wisdom' (*sophia*) but was really cleverness in political matters and pragmatic shrewdness, made this his profession and preserved it intact like a sect transmitted to him in succession from Solon. But those people who followed him mixed this with forensic arts and transferred its sphere of application from actions to speeches, and they were called 'sophists.'

R5 (79.1) Aelius Aristides, *Against Plato: In Defense of the Four*

It seems to me that they [i.e. the critics of oratory] do not even know anything at all either about how the very term 'philosophy' was used by the Greeks and what it signified, or in general about anything connected with it. Did not Herodotus call Solon, and again Pythagoras, a 'sophist' [*Histories* 1.29, 6.95]? Did not Androtion speak of the seven 'sophists,' meaning by that the sages (*sophoi*), and

κράτη σοφιστὴν τοῦτον τὸν πάνυ; αὖθις δ᾽ Ἰσοκράτης σοφιστὰς μὲν τοὺς περὶ τὴν ἔριν καὶ τοὺς ὡς ἂν
αὐτοὶ φαῖεν διαλεκτικούς, φιλόσοφον δ᾽ ἑαυτὸν καὶ
τοὺς ῥήτορας καὶ τοὺς περὶ τὴν πολιτικὴν ἕξιν φιλο-
σόφους; ὡσαύτως δὲ καὶ τῶν τούτῳ συγγενομένων
ὀνομάζουσί τινες. οὐ Λυσίας Πλάτωνα σοφιστὴν καλεῖ [Frag. 449 Carey] καὶ πάλιν Αἰσχίνην [VI A19 G²];
"κατηγορῶν οὗτός γε," φαίη τις ἄν. ἀλλ᾽ οὐχ οἵ γε
ἄλλοι κατηγοροῦντες ἐκείνων τῶν ἄλλων ὅμως ταυτὸν
τοῦτο προσειρήκασιν αὐτούς. ἔτι δ᾽ εἰ καὶ Πλάτωνος
ἐξῆν κατηγοροῦντα σοφιστὴν προσειπεῖν, τί τούτους
γ᾽ ἂν εἴποι τις; ἀλλ᾽ οἶμαι καὶ σοφιστὴς ἐπιεικῶς κοινὸν ἦν ὄνομα καὶ ἡ φιλοσοφία τοῦτ᾽ ἠδύνατο, φιλο-
καλία τις εἶναι καὶ διατριβὴ περὶ λόγους, καὶ οὐχ ὁ
νῦν τρόπος οὗτος, ἀλλὰ παιδεία κοινῶς [. . .]. καὶ τὸν
σοφιστὴν δοκεῖ μέν πως κακίζειν ἀεί, καὶ ὅ γε δὴ
μάλιστα ἐπαναστὰς τῷ ὀνόματι Πλάτων εἶναί μοι δοκεῖ. αἴτιον δὲ τούτου καὶ τῶν πολλῶν αὐτὸν καὶ τῶν
κατ᾽ αὐτὸν ὑπερφρονῆσαι. φαίνεται δὲ καὶ ταύτῃ εἰς
ἅπασαν εὐφημίαν τῇ προσηγορίᾳ κεχρημένος. ὃν
γοῦν ἀξιοῖ σοφώτατον εἶναι θεὸν καὶ παρ᾽ ᾧ πᾶν εἶναι
τἀληθές, τοῦτον δή που τέλεον σοφιστὴν κέκληκεν.

then again [scil. did he not call] the great Socrates a 'sophist'? Or again, [scil. did not] Isocrates [scil. call] the eristic speakers and the dialecticians (as they themselves would say) 'sophists' [cf. e.g. *Against the Sophists,* 1–8], but himself a 'philosopher,' and rhetoricians and those men involved in political activity 'philosophers' [cf. e.g. *Paneg.* 47]? Some of his associates too use the term in the same way. Does not Lysias call Plato a 'sophist,' and again Aeschines? "Yes indeed—when he accuses him," someone might say—except that the other authors call those other men [scil. the sophists] by this same name, even though they are not accusing them. Furthermore, if it was permissible to call Plato a 'sophist' when accusing him, what could one call them [i.e. the sophists]? In fact, I think that 'sophist' was a fairly general term and that 'philosophy' signified a certain love of beauty and an activity involving speeches, not in this present way, but a kind of education in general. [. . .] And Plato seems to me always somehow to be denigrating the sophist, and it is he who seems to me to attack this word most of all. The reason for this was that he despised the multitude of the people as well as his contemporaries. But it is clear that he also uses this term in an entirely positive sense. Indeed the god whom he considers to be the wisest of all and who has at his disposal all the truth [i.e. Hades] he has even called 'a perfect sophist' [*Crat.* 403e].

A Group Portrait (R6)

R6 (cf. 84 A2, ad 86 A11) Plat. *Prot.* 314e–316a

[ΣΩ.] ἐπειδὴ δὲ εἰσήλθομεν, κατελάβομεν Πρωταγόραν ἐν τῷ προστῴῳ περιπατοῦντα, ἑξῆς δ' αὐτῷ συμ-
περιεπάτουν ἐκ μὲν τοῦ ἐπὶ θάτερα Καλλίας ὁ Ἱππο-
νίκου καὶ ὁ ἀδελφὸς αὐτοῦ ὁ ὁμομήτριος, [315a]
Πάραλος ὁ Περικλέους, καὶ Χαρμίδης ὁ Γλαύκωνος,
ἐκ δὲ τοῦ ἐπὶ θάτερα ὁ ἕτερος τῶν Περικλέους Ξάν-
θιππος, καὶ Φιλιππίδης ὁ Φιλομήλου καὶ Ἀντίμοιρος
ὁ Μενδαῖος, ὅσπερ εὐδοκιμεῖ μάλιστα τῶν Πρωταγόρου μαθητῶν καὶ ἐπὶ τέχνῃ μανθάνει, ὡς σοφιστὴς
ἐσόμενος. τούτων δὲ οἳ ὄπισθεν ἠκολούθουν ἐπακού-
οντες τῶν λεγομένων τὸ μὲν πολὺ ξένοι ἐφαίνοντο—
οὓς ἄγει ἐξ ἑκάστων τῶν πόλεων ὁ Πρωταγόρας, δι'
ὧν διεξέρχεται, κηλῶν τῇ φωνῇ ὥσπερ [315b] Ὀρ-
φεύς, οἱ δὲ κατὰ τὴν φωνὴν ἕπονται κεκηλημένοι—
ἦσαν δέ τινες καὶ τῶν ἐπιχωρίων ἐν τῷ χορῷ. τοῦτον
τὸν χορὸν μάλιστα ἔγωγε ἰδὼν ἥσθην, ὡς καλῶς
ηὐλαβοῦντο μηδέποτε ἐμποδὼν ἐν τῷ πρόσθεν εἶναι
Πρωταγόρου, ἀλλ' ἐπειδὴ αὐτὸς ἀναστρέφοι καὶ οἱ
μετ' ἐκείνου, εὖ πως καὶ ἐν κόσμῳ περιεσχίζοντο
οὗτοι οἱ ἐπήκοοι ἔνθεν καὶ ἔνθεν, καὶ ἐν κύκλῳ περι-
ιόντες ἀεὶ εἰς τὸ ὄπισθεν καθίσταντο κάλλιστα.

"τὸν δὲ μετ' εἰσενόησα," ἔφη Ὅμηρος [*Od.* 11.601],
Ἱππίαν [315c] τὸν Ἠλεῖον, καθήμενον ἐν τῷ κατ' ἀντι-
κρὺ προστῴῳ ἐν θρόνῳ· περὶ αὐτὸν δ' ἐκάθηντο ἐπὶ

A Group Portrait (R6)

R6 (cf. 84 A2, ad 86 A11) Plato, *Protagoras*

[Socrates:] When we went in [scil. to Callias' house] we found Protagoras walking around in the portico, and walking around with him were on one side Callias, the son of Hipponicus, and his half brother [315a] Paralus, the son of Pericles, and Charmides, the son of Glaucon, and on the other Xanthippus, Pericles' other son, and Philippides, the son of Philomelus, and Antimoerus of Mende, who has the best reputation of Protagoras' pupils and is learning professionally so as to become a sophist. Those who were following behind these, listening to what was said, seemed to be foreigners for the most part—Protagoras leads them off from each of the cities he goes through, charming them with his voice like [315b] Orpheus, while they follow, spellbound by his voice—but there were also some locals [i.e. Athenians] in the chorus. I was extremely pleased when I saw how this chorus took such lovely care that no one ever got in Protagoras' way, but whenever he and his companions turned round, those who were listening to him divided themselves in an orderly fashion to one side and the other, and going around in a circle regrouped behind him every time in the most lovely way.

"And after him I perceived," as Homer says [*Od.* 11.601], Hippias [315c] of Elis, sitting in the opposite portico on a throne. Around him, sitting on benches, were

βάθρων Ἐρυξίμαχός τε ὁ Ἀκουμενοῦ καὶ Φαῖδρος ὁ
Μυρρινούσιος καὶ Ἄνδρων ὁ Ἀνδροτίωνος καὶ τῶν
ξένων πολῖταί τε αὐτοῦ καὶ ἄλλοι τινές. ἐφαίνοντο δὲ
περὶ φύσεώς τε καὶ τῶν μετεώρων ἀστρονομικὰ ἄττα
διερωτᾶν τὸν Ἱππίαν, ὁ δ' ἐν θρόνῳ καθήμενος ἑκά-
στοις αὐτῶν διέκρινεν καὶ διεξῄει τὰ ἐρωτώμενα.

καὶ μὲν δὴ "καὶ Τάνταλόν" γε "εἰσεῖδον" [Od.
11.582]—ἐπεδήμει γὰρ [315d] ἄρα καὶ Πρόδικος ὁ
Κεῖος—ἦν δὲ ἐν οἰκήματί τινι, ᾧ πρὸ τοῦ μὲν ὡς τα-
μιείῳ ἐχρῆτο Ἱππόνικος, νῦν δὲ ὑπὸ τοῦ πλήθους τῶν
καταλυόντων ὁ Καλλίας καὶ τοῦτο ἐκκενώσας ξένοις
κατάλυσιν πεποίηκεν. ὁ μὲν οὖν Πρόδικος ἔτι κατ-
έκειτο, ἐγκεκαλυμμένος ἐν κῳδίοις τισὶν καὶ στρώμα-
σιν καὶ μάλα πολλοῖς, ὡς ἐφαίνετο· παρεκάθηντο δὲ
αὐτῷ ἐπὶ ταῖς πλησίον κλίναις Παυσανίας τε ὁ ἐκ
Κεραμέων καὶ μετὰ Παυσανίου νέον τι ἔτι μειράκιον,
ὡς μὲν ἐγᾦμαι καλόν τε κἀγαθὸν τὴν φύσιν, τὴν δ'
οὖν ἰδέαν πάνυ καλός. ἔδοξα ἀκοῦσαι ὄνομα αὐτῷ
εἶναι Ἀγάθωνα, καὶ οὐκ ἂν θαυμάζοιμι εἰ παιδικὰ
Παυσανίου τυγχάνει ὤν. τοῦτό τ' ἦν τὸ μειράκιον, καὶ
τὼ Ἀδειμάντω ἀμφοτέρω, ὅ τε Κήπιδος καὶ ὁ Λευκο-
λοφίδου, καὶ ἄλλοι τινὲς ἐφαίνοντο· περὶ δὲ ὧν διελέ-
γοντο οὐκ ἐδυνάμην ἔγωγε μαθεῖν ἔξωθεν, καίπερ
λιπαρῶς ἔχων ἀκούειν τοῦ Προδίκου—πάσσοφος γάρ
μοι δοκεῖ ἀνὴρ εἶναι [316a] καὶ θεῖος—ἀλλὰ διὰ τὴν
βαρύτητα τῆς φωνῆς βόμβος τις ἐν τῷ οἰκήματι
γιγνόμενος ἀσαφῆ ἐποίει τὰ λεγόμενα.

Eryximachus, the son of Acumenus, and Phaedrus from Myrrinus, and Andron, the son of Androtion, and some foreigners, fellow citizens of his [i.e. Hippias] and others. They seemed to be asking Hippias a number of astronomical questions about nature and celestial phenomena, while he, sitting on his throne, answered each of them and replied to their questions in detail [cf. **HIPPIAS D34**].

And indeed "I also saw Tantalus" [cf. Homer, *Od.* 11.582], for [315d] Prodicus of Ceos too was in town. He was in a room that Hipponicus had previously used as a storeroom, but now because of the number of people staying Callias had cleared this out too and made it a guest room. Prodicus was still lying down, covered with some sheepskins and bedclothes, with a lot of them, as could be seen. On the beds next to his were sitting Pausanias from Cerameis, and with Pausanias a youth who was still quite young, fine-looking I thought and with a good (*kaloskagathos*) build. I thought I heard that his name was Agathon, and I would not be surprised if he were Pausanias' boyfriend. There was that youth, and the two Adeimantuses, the son of Cepis and the son of Leucolophides, and there seemed to be some others; but what they were talking about I was not able to understand from outside, although I was very eager to hear Prodicus—for the man seems to me to be surpassingly wise, [316a] and divine—but his deep voice produced a booming sound in the room that made what he was saying unclear [cf. **PROD. P3**].

The Sophists as Moneymakers, Travelers,
and Charismatic Figures (R7–R8)

R7 (84 A4) Plat. *Apol.* 19e–20a

[ΣΩ.] ἐπεὶ καὶ τοῦτό γέ μοι δοκεῖ καλὸν εἶναι, εἴ τις
οἷός τ᾽ εἴη παιδεύειν ἀνθρώπους ὥσπερ Γοργίας τε ὁ
Λεοντῖνος καὶ Πρόδικος ὁ Κεῖος καὶ Ἱππίας ὁ Ἠλεῖος.
τούτων γὰρ ἕκαστος [. . .] οἷός τ᾽ ἐστὶν ἰὼν εἰς ἑκάστην
τῶν πόλεων τοὺς νέους—οἷς ἔξεστι τῶν ἑαυτῶν πολιτῶν προῖκα συνεῖναι ᾧ ἂν βούλωνται—τούτους πεί-
θουσι [20a] τὰς ἐκείνων συνουσίας ἀπολιπόντας
σφίσιν συνεῖναι χρήματα διδόντας καὶ χάριν προσει-
δέναι.

R8 (≠ DK) Plat. *Prot.* 311d–e

[ΣΩ.] παρὰ δὲ δὴ Πρωταγόραν νῦν ἀφικόμενοι ἐγώ τε
καὶ σὺ ἀργύριον ἐκείνῳ μισθὸν ἕτοιμοι ἐσόμεθα τελεῖν ὑπὲρ σοῦ, ἂν μὲν ἐξικνῆται τὰ ἡμέτερα χρήματα
καὶ τούτοις πείθωμεν αὐτόν, εἰ δὲ μή, καὶ τὰ τῶν φίλων προσαναλίσκοντες. εἰ οὖν τις ἡμᾶς περὶ ταῦτα
οὕτω σφόδρα σπουδάζοντας ἔροιτο· "εἰπέ μοι, ὦ
Σώκρατές τε καὶ Ἱππόκρατες, ὡς τίνι ὄντι τῷ Πρω-
ταγόρᾳ ἐν νῷ ἔχετε χρήματα τελεῖν;" τί ἂν αὐτῷ
ἀποκριναίμεθα; τί ὄνομα ἄλλο γε λεγόμενον περὶ
Πρωταγόρου ἀκούομεν; ὥσπερ περὶ Φειδίου ἀγαλμα-
τοποιὸν καὶ περὶ Ὁμήρου ποιητήν, τί τοιοῦτον περὶ
Πρωταγόρου ἀκούομεν;

'SOPHISTS' AND 'SOPHISTIC'

The Sophists as Moneymakers, Travelers, and Charismatic Figures (R7–R8)

R7 (84 A4) Plato, *Apology*

[Socrates:] This seems to me a fine thing: to be capable of educating people, like Gorgias of Leontini, Prodicus of Ceos, and Hippias of Elis. For each of these men [. . .] is able, going into each of the cities, to persuade the young men there—who have the possibility of associating, without paying, with any of their fellow citizens they wish—to stop associating with those people, to associate instead with them, to pay money for this—and, what is more, to feel grateful for this.

R8 (≠ DK) Plato, *Protagoras*

[Socrates:] You [i.e. Hippocrates] and I are going now to Protagoras, prepared to pay money to him as a fee for your sake, spending our money if that is enough to persuade him, and if not then spending our friends' money as well. If then someone were to ask us while we are rushing off so eagerly for this purpose, "Tell me, Socrates and Hippocrates, you have in mind to pay money to Protagoras—for his being what?," how would we answer him? What other term do we hear used for Protagoras? Just as we hear 'sculptor' for Phidias and 'poet' for Homer, what term like this do we hear for Protagoras?

[Π.] σοφιστὴν δή τοι ὀνομάζουσί γε, ὦ Σώκρατες, τὸν ἄνδρα εἶναι [. . .].

[ΣΩ.] ὡς σοφιστῇ ἄρα ἐρχόμεθα τελοῦντες τὰ χρήματα;

[Π.] μάλιστα.

The Sophists as Educators (R9–R11)

R9 (≠ DK) Plat. *Rep.* 10 600c–d

[ΣΩ.] [. . .] Πρωταγόρας μὲν ἄρα ὁ Ἀβδηρίτης καὶ Πρόδικος ὁ Κεῖος καὶ ἄλλοι πάμπολλοι δύνανται τοῖς ἐφ᾽ ἑαυτῶν παριστάναι ἰδίᾳ συγγιγνόμενοι ὡς οὔτε οἰκίαν οὔτε πόλιν τὴν αὑτῶν διοικεῖν οἷοί τ᾽ ἔσονται, ἐὰν μὴ σφεῖς αὐτῶν ἐπιστατήσωσιν τῆς παιδείας, καὶ ἐπὶ ταύτῃ τῇ σοφίᾳ οὕτω σφόδρα φιλοῦνται, ὥστε μόνον οὐκ ἐπὶ ταῖς κεφαλαῖς περιφέρουσιν αὐτοὺς οἱ ἑταῖροι.

R10 (≠ DK) Plat. *Prot.* 312a–b

[ΣΩ.] ἀλλ᾽ ἄρα, ὦ Ἱππόκρατες, μὴ οὐ τοιαύτην ὑπολαμβάνεις σου τὴν παρὰ Πρωταγόρου μάθησιν [312b] ἔσεσθαι, ἀλλ᾽ οἵαπερ ἡ παρὰ τοῦ γραμματιστοῦ ἐγένετο καὶ κιθαριστοῦ καὶ παιδοτρίβου; τούτων γὰρ σὺ ἑκάστην οὐκ ἐπὶ τέχνῃ ἔμαθες, ὡς δημιουργὸς ἐσόμενος, ἀλλ᾽ ἐπὶ παιδείᾳ, ὡς τὸν ἰδιώτην καὶ τὸν ἐλεύθερον πρέπει.

[Hippocrates:] 'Sophist' certainly is the term that they apply to him, Socrates [. . .].

[Socrates:] So we are going to pay money to him for his being a sophist?

[Hippocrates:] Yes indeed.

The Sophists as Educators (R9–R11)

R9 (≠ DK) Plato, *Republic*

[Socrates:] [. . .] Protagoras of Abdera, Prodicus of Ceos, and very many other men are able to convince their contemporaries, with whom they associate in private, that they will not be able to manage their home or their city unless it is they themselves who supervise their education, and they are so beloved because of this wisdom of theirs that their companions all but carry them about on their shoulders.

R10 (≠ DK) Plato, *Protagoras*

[Socrates:] But then, Hippocrates, perhaps you think that the instruction you will receive from Protagoras is not this kind [i.e. learning how to become a sophist], but the kind you received from your grammar teacher, your cithara teacher, and your gymnastics teacher? For you did not study from these men technically so that you could become a practitioner yourself, but for the sake of your general education, as befits a layman and a free man.

[III.] πάνυ μὲν οὖν μοι δοκεῖ, ἔφη, τοιαύτη μᾶλλον εἶναι ἡ παρὰ Πρωταγόρου μάθησις.

R11 (> 80 A5) Plat. *Prot.*

a 316d–e, 317c

[ΠΡ.] ἐγὼ δὲ τὴν σοφιστικὴν τέχνην φημὶ μὲν εἶναι παλαιάν, τοὺς δὲ μεταχειριζομένους αὐτὴν τῶν παλαιῶν ἀνδρῶν, φοβουμένους τὸ ἐπαχθὲς αὐτῆς, πρόσχημα ποιεῖσθαι καὶ προκαλύπτεσθαι, τοὺς μὲν ποίησιν, οἷον Ὅμηρόν τε καὶ Ἡσίοδον καὶ Σιμωνίδην, τοὺς δὲ αὖ τελετάς τε καὶ χρησμῳδίας, τοὺς ἀμφί τε Ὀρφέα καὶ Μουσαῖον· ἐνίους δέ τινας ᾔσθημαι καὶ γυμναστικήν, οἷον Ἴκκος τε ὁ Ταραντῖνος καὶ ὁ νῦν ἔτι ὢν οὐδενὸς ἥττων σοφιστὴς Ἡρόδικος ὁ Σηλυμβριανός, τὸ δὲ ἀρχαῖον Μεγαρεύς· μουσικὴν δὲ Ἀγαθοκλῆς τε ὁ ὑμέτερος πρόσχημα ἐποιήσατο, μέγας ὢν σοφιστής, καὶ Πυθοκλείδης ὁ Κεῖος καὶ ἄλλοι πολλοί. οὗτοι πάντες, ὥσπερ λέγω, φοβηθέντες τὸν φθόνον ταῖς τέχναις ταύταις παραπετάσμασιν ἐχρήσαντο. ἐγὼ δὲ τούτοις ἅπασιν κατὰ τοῦτο εἶναι οὐ συμφέρομαι. [. . .] ἐγὼ οὖν τούτων τὴν ἐναντίαν ἅπασαν ὁδὸν ἐλήλυθα, καὶ ὁμολογῶ τε σοφιστὴς εἶναι καὶ παιδεύειν ἀνθρώπους [. . .].

b 318d–319a (= **PROT. D37**)

[ΠΡ.] οἱ μὲν γὰρ ἄλλοι λωβῶνται τοὺς νέους· τὰς γὰρ

[Hippocrates:] It seems to me, he said, that the instruction one receives from Protagoras is rather of this kind.

R11 (> 80 A5) Plato, *Protagoras*

a

[Protagoras:] I say that the sophistic art is ancient, but that those ancient men who practiced it, because they feared the annoyance it caused, employed a screen and disguised it, some using poetry, like Homer, Hesiod, and Simonides, and others initiatory rites and oracles, the followers of Orpheus and Musaeus; and certain ones, I have heard, under gymnastics too, like Iccus of Tarentum [cf. **PYTH. b T34**] and another one, still alive, as much a sophist as anyone: Herodicus of Selymbria, originally a Megarian colony. And music was the screen employed by your fellow citizen Agathocles, a great sophist, Pythocleides of Ceos, and many others. All these men, as I say, made use of these arts as façades because of their fear of ill will. But I am not in agreement with all of these. [. . .] So I myself have gone on the whole opposite path from these men, and I admit that I am a sophist and that I educate people [. . .].

b (= **PROT. D37**)

[Protagoras:] For the other people [scil. sophists] harm young men. Driving them back, despite their resistance,

τέχνας αὐτοὺς πεφευγότας ἄκοντας πάλιν αὖ ἄγοντες
ἐμβάλλουσιν εἰς τέχνας, λογισμούς τε καὶ ἀστρονο-
μίαν καὶ γεωμετρίαν καὶ μουσικὴν διδάσκοντες—καὶ
ἅμα εἰς τὸν Ἱππίαν ἀπέβλεψεν—παρὰ δ᾽ ἐμὲ ἀφικό-
μενος μαθήσεται οὐ περὶ ἄλλου του ἢ περὶ οὗ ἥκει.
τὸ δὲ μάθημά ἐστιν εὐβουλία περὶ τῶν οἰκείων, ὅπως
ἂν ἄριστα τὴν αὑτοῦ οἰκίαν διοικοῖ, καὶ περὶ τῶν τῆς
πόλεως, ὅπως τὰ τῆς πόλεως δυνατώτατος ἂν εἴη καὶ
πράττειν καὶ λέγειν.

The Sophists as Teachers of Virtue (R12–R13)

R12 (80 A5) Plat. *Prot.* 318a (= **PROT. D36**)

ὑπολαβὼν οὖν ὁ Πρωταγόρας εἶπεν· "ὦ νεανίσκε,
ἔσται τοίνυν σοι, ἐὰν ἐμοὶ συνῇς, ᾗ ἂν ἡμέρᾳ ἐμοὶ
συγγένῃ, ἀπιέναι οἴκαδε βελτίονι γεγονότι, καὶ ἐν τῇ
ὑστεραίᾳ ταὐτὰ ταῦτα· καὶ ἑκάστης ἡμέρας ἀεὶ ἐπὶ τὸ
βέλτιον ἐπιδιδόναι."

R13 (≠ DK) Plat. *Men.* 91a–b

[ΣΩ.] οὗτος γάρ, ὦ Ἄνυτε, πάλαι λέγει πρός με ὅτι
ἐπιθυμεῖ ταύτης τῆς σοφίας καὶ ἀρετῆς ᾗ οἱ ἄνθρωποι τάς τε οἰκίας καὶ τὰς πόλεις καλῶς διοικοῦσι, καὶ
τοὺς γονέας τοὺς αὑτῶν θεραπεύουσι, καὶ πολίτας καὶ
ξένους ὑποδέξασθαί τε καὶ ἀποπέμψαι ἐπίστανται
ἀξίως ἀνδρὸς ἀγαθοῦ. ταύτην οὖν τὴν ἀρετὴν[1] σκόπει
παρὰ τίνας ἂν πέμποντες αὐτὸν ὀρθῶς πέμποιμεν. ἢ

toward the arts that they have fled, they cast them upon those arts, teaching them arithmetic, astronomy, geometry, and music (and he cast a glance at Hippias) [cf. **HIPPIAS D14**]; whereas if he comes to me he will learn nothing else than what he came for. The object of my instruction is good deliberation about household matters, to know how to manage one's own household in the best way possible, and about those of the city, so as to be most capable of acting and speaking in the city's interests.

The Sophists as Teachers of Virtue (R12–R13)

R12 (80 A5) Plato, *Protagoras* (= **PROT. D36**)

Protagoras said in reply, "Young man [i.e. Hippocrates], if you study with me, this is what will happen to you: the very day that you start to study with me, you will go home having become a better man, and the same thing will happen the following day. And every day you will make progress continually toward what is better."

R13 (≠ DK) Plato, *Meno*

[Socrates:] For he [i.e. Meno] has been telling me for some time, Anytus, that he desires to acquire that wisdom and virtue by which people manage their households and cities well, take care of their parents, and know how to welcome and send off their fellow citizens and foreigners in a manner worthy of a good man. Consider then to whom we would be right to send him to learn this virtue. Is it

---

¹ post ἀρετὴν lac. stat. Cobet, μαθησόμενον vel βουλόμενοι αὐτὸν σοφὸν γενέσθαι intercidisse ratus

δῆλον δὴ κατὰ τὸν ἄρτι λόγον ὅτι παρὰ τούτους τοὺς
ὑπισχνουμένους ἀρετῆς διδασκάλους εἶναι καὶ ἀπο-
φήναντας αὐτοὺς κοινοὺς τῶν Ἑλλήνων τῷ βουλομένῳ μανθάνειν, μισθὸν τούτου ταξαμένους τε καὶ
πραττομένους;
[ΑΝ.] καὶ τίνας λέγεις τούτους, ὦ Σώκρατες;
[ΣΩ.] οἶσθα δήπου καὶ σὺ ὅτι οὗτοί εἰσιν οὓς οἱ ἄνθρωποι καλοῦσι σοφιστάς.

The Sophists as Teachers of Rhetoric (R14–R15)

R14 (≠ DK) Plat. *Prot.* 312d

[ΣΩ.] εἰ δέ τις ἐκεῖνο ἔροιτο, "ὁ δὲ σοφιστὴς τῶν τί
σοφῶν ἐστιν;" τί ἂν ἀποκρινοίμεθα αὐτῷ; ποίας ἐργα-
σίας ἐπιστάτης;
[ΙΠ.] τί ἂν εἴποιμεν αὐτὸν εἶναι, ὦ Σώκρατες, ἢ ἐπι-
στάτην τοῦ ποιῆσαι δεινὸν λέγειν;

R15 (≠ DK) Isocr. *In soph.* 9–10

[. . . = **R17**] [9] οὐ μόνον δὲ τούτοις ἀλλὰ καὶ τοῖς τοὺς
πολιτικοὺς λόγους ὑπισχνουμένοις ἄξιον ἐπιτιμῆσαι·
καὶ γὰρ ἐκεῖνοι τῆς μὲν ἀληθείας οὐδὲν φροντίζουσιν,
ἡγοῦνται δὲ τοῦτ' εἶναι τὴν τέχνην, ἢν ὡς πλείστους
τῇ μικρότητι τῶν μισθῶν καὶ τῷ μεγέθει τῶν ἐπαγγελμάτων προσαγάγωνται καὶ λαβεῖν τι παρ' αὐτῶν
δυνηθῶσιν· οὕτω δ' ἀναισθήτως αὐτοί τε διάκεινται
καὶ τοὺς ἄλλους ἔχειν ὑπειλήφασιν, ὥστε χεῖρον γρά-

not clear from the preceding argument that we should send him to those men who claim to be teachers of virtue, who declare that they are available to whoever among the Greeks wishes to learn, and who have established a fee for this and demand it?

[Anytus:] And who are these people you are talking about, Socrates?

[Socrates:] Surely you too know that these men are the ones whom people call 'sophists.'

The Sophists as Teachers of Rhetoric (R14–R15)

R14 (≠ DK) Plato, *Protagoras*

[Socrates:] If someone asked, "What is that field in which the sophist is one of the experts (*sophoi*)?" what would we answer him? What kind of thing is he in charge of making? [Hippocrates:] What else would we say that he is, Socrates, than someone who is in charge of making one clever at speaking?

R15 (≠ DK) Isocrates, *Against the Sophists*

[. . .] [9] But it is not only these men [scil. those who devote themselves to eristic] who deserve to be criticized, but also those who promise to provide political orations. For the latter too have no thought at all for the truth, but they think that this is an art, if they can attract as many people as possible by the small size of their fees and the large size of their proclamations and are able to get something from them. For they are so stupid themselves and suppose that everyone else is too, that although the speeches they

229

φοντες τοὺς λόγους ἢ τῶν ἰδιωτῶν τινες αὐτοσχεδιά-
ζουσιν, ὅμως ὑπισχνοῦνται τοιούτους ῥήτορας τοὺς
συνόντας ποιήσειν ὥστε μηδὲν τῶν ἐνόντων ἐν τοῖς
πράγμασι παραλιπεῖν. [10] καὶ ταύτης τῆς δυνάμεως
οὐδὲν οὔτε ταῖς ἐμπειρίαις οὔτε τῇ φύσει τῇ τοῦ μα-
θητοῦ μεταδιδόασιν, ἀλλά φασιν ὁμοίως τὴν τῶν λόγων ἐπιστήμην ὥσπερ τὴν τῶν γραμμάτων παραδώ-
σειν, ὡς μὲν ἔχει τούτων ἑκάτερον οὐκ ἐξετάσαντες,
οἰόμενοι δὲ διὰ τὰς ὑπερβολὰς τῶν ἐπαγγελμάτων
αὐτοί τε θαυμασθήσεσθαι καὶ τὴν παίδευσιν τὴν τῶν
λόγων πλέονος ἀξίαν δόξειν εἶναι, κακῶς εἰδότες ὅτι
μεγάλας ποιοῦσι τὰς τέχνας οὐχ οἱ τολμῶντες ἀλα-
ζονεύεσθαι περὶ αὐτῶν, ἀλλ᾽ οἵτινες ἄν, ὅσον ἔνεστιν
ἐν ἑκάστῃ, τοῦτ᾽ ἐξευρεῖν δυνηθῶσιν.

Eristic, Antilogy, Opposed Speeches (R16–R22)

R16 (≠ DK) Plat. *Theaet.* 154d–e

[ΣΩ.] οὐκοῦν εἰ μὲν δεινοὶ καὶ σοφοὶ ἐγώ τε καὶ σὺ
ἦμεν, πάντα τὰ τῶν φρενῶν ἐξητακότες, ἤδη ἂν τὸ
λοιπὸν ἐκ περιουσίας ἀλλήλων ἀποπειρώμενοι, συν-
ελθόντες σοφιστικῶς εἰς μάχην τοιαύτην, ἀλλήλων
τοὺς λόγους τοῖς λόγοις ἐκρούομεν.

R17 (≠ DK) Isocr. *In soph.* 7–8

[7] ἐπειδὰν οὖν τῶν ἰδιωτῶν τινες, ἅπαντα ταῦτα συλ-
λογισάμενοι, κατίδωσι τοὺς τὴν σοφίαν διδάσκοντας

write are worse than the ones that some laymen improvise, nonetheless they promise that they will make their students such orators that they will lack nothing in the conduct of their affairs. [10] And they ascribe this ability neither to the student's experience nor to his natural talent, but they say that they will transmit the science of speeches in exactly the same way as that of letters, without having examined the character of either of them, but on the idea that, because of the exaggerations of their proclamations, they themselves will be admired and instruction in speeches will be thought to be more valuable, not recognizing that what makes the arts great are not the people who shamelessly boast about them but the ones who are able to discover what belongs to each one.

Eristic, Antilogy, Opposed Speeches (R16–R22)

R16 (≠ DK) Plato, *Theaetetus*

[Socrates:] If you [i.e. Theaetetus] and I were clever and wise, from having examined closely everything belonging to intelligence (*phrenes*), then from now on we would spend the rest of our lives testing each other on the basis of our resources, rushing against one another like sophists in the sort of combat that is typical of them, and smiting each other's arguments with other arguments.

R17 (≠ DK) Isocrates, *Against the Sophists*

[7] When therefore certain laymen, having considered all this [scil. the misdeeds for which those who practice eris-

καὶ τὴν εὐδαιμονίαν παραδιδόντας αὐτούς τε πολλῶν
δεομένους καὶ τοὺς μαθητὰς μικρὸν πραττομένους,
καὶ τὰς ἐναντιώσεις ἐπὶ μὲν τῶν λόγων τηροῦντας,
ἐπὶ δὲ τῶν ἔργων μὴ καθορῶντας, ἔτι δὲ περὶ μὲν τῶν
μελλόντων εἰδέναι προσποιουμένους, [8] περὶ δὲ τῶν
παρόντων μηδὲν τῶν δεόντων μήτ' εἰπεῖν μήτε συμ-
βουλεῦσαι δυναμένους, ἀλλὰ μᾶλλον ὁμονοοῦντας
καὶ πλείω κατορθοῦντας τοὺς ταῖς δόξαις χρωμένους
ἢ τοὺς τὴν ἐπιστήμην ἔχειν ἐπαγγελλομένους, εἰκότως οἶμαι καταφρονοῦσι, καὶ νομίζουσιν ἀδολεσχίαν
καὶ μικρολογίαν ἀλλ' οὐ τῆς ψυχῆς ἐπιμέλειαν εἶναι
τὰς τοιαύτας διατριβάς [. . . = **R15**].

R18 (≠ DK) Arist. *SE* 11 171b25–34

οἱ μὲν οὖν τῆς νίκης αὐτῆς χάριν τοιοῦτοι ἐριστικοὶ
ἄνθρωποι καὶ φιλέριδες δοκοῦσιν εἶναι, οἱ δὲ δόξης
χάριν τῆς εἰς χρηματισμὸν σοφιστικοί· ἡ γὰρ σοφιστική ἐστιν [. . .] χρηματιστική τις ἀπὸ σοφίας φαι-
νομένης· διὸ φαινομένης ἀποδείξεως ἐφίενται, καὶ τῶν
λόγων τῶν αὐτῶν μὲν[1] οἱ φιλέριδες καὶ οἱ σοφισταί,
ἀλλ' οὐ τῶν αὐτῶν ἕνεκεν, καὶ λόγος ὁ αὐτὸς μὲν
ἔσται σοφιστικὸς καὶ ἐριστικός, ἀλλ' οὐ κατὰ ταὐτόν,
ἀλλ' ᾗ μὲν νίκης φαινομένης ⟨ἕνεκα⟩,[2] ἐριστικός, ᾗ δὲ
σοφίας, σοφιστικός. καὶ γὰρ ἡ σοφιστική ἐστι φαινομένη σοφία τις ἀλλ' οὐκ οὖσα.

---

[1] εἰσιν post μὲν hab. mss., secl. Ross   [2] ⟨ἕνεκα⟩ Ross

tic are responsible], see that those men who teach wisdom
and transmit happiness are themselves in need of many
things and demand that their students pay them only a
little, that they are on the lookout for contradictions in
words but do not see the ones in actions, and that furthermore about the future they pretend to possess knowledge
[8] but about the present they are not able either to say or
to counsel anything about what ought to be done, but that
those men who have recourse to opinions are in greater
agreement and are more successful than those who pro-
claim that they possess scientific knowledge, then it is with
good reason, I think, that they despise them and think
that this kind of occupation is mere claptrap and small-
mindedness, and not a way to care for the soul [. . .].

R18 (≠ DK) Aristotle, *Sophistic Refutations*

Therefore people who are like this [scil. who will use any
argument to win a debate] for the sake of victory are considered to be eristic and contentious, and those who do so
for the sake of reputation, in order to make money, to be
sophistic. For the sophistic art is [. . .] a certain art of making money out of what is wisdom in appearance, and that
is why they aim at what is proof in appearance. And the
contentious and the sophists both [scil. use] the same arguments, but not for the same purposes. And that is why
the sophistic argument and the eristic argument will be
identical, but not in the same regard: if it is for the sake of
what is victory in appearance, then it is eristic, but if for
what is wisdom [scil. in appearance], sophistic. For sophistic is a wisdom in appearance but not in reality [cf. **R34a**].

R19

a (≠ DK) Plat. *Men.* 80d–e

[ΜΕ.] καὶ τίνα τρόπον ζητήσεις, ὦ Σώκρατες, τοῦτο ὃ
μὴ οἶσθα τὸ παράπαν ὅτι ἐστίν; ποῖον γὰρ ὧν οὐκ
οἶσθα προθέμενος ζητήσεις; ἢ εἰ καὶ ὅτι μάλιστα
ἐντύχοις αὐτῷ, πῶς εἴσῃ ὅτι τοῦτό ἐστιν ὃ σὺ οὐκ
ᾔδησθα; [80e]
[ΣΩ.] μανθάνω οἷον βούλει λέγειν, ὦ Μένων. ὁρᾷς
τοῦτον ὡς ἐριστικὸν λόγον κατάγεις, ὡς οὐκ ἄρα
ἔστιν ζητεῖν ἀνθρώπῳ οὔτε ὃ οἶδε οὔτε ὃ μὴ οἶδε; οὔτε
γὰρ ἂν ὅ γε οἶδεν ζητοῖ—οἶδεν γάρ, καὶ οὐδὲν δεῖ τῷ
γε τοιούτῳ ζητήσεως—οὔτε ὃ μὴ οἶδεν—οὐδὲ γὰρ οἶδεν ὅτι ζητήσει.

b (≠ DK) Arist. *Metaph.* Θ8 1049b29–1050a1

διὸ καὶ δοκεῖ ἀδύνατον εἶναι οἰκοδόμον εἶναι μὴ οἰκο-
δομήσαντα μηθὲν ἢ κιθαριστὴν μηθὲν κιθαρίσαντα·
ὁ γὰρ μανθάνων κιθαρίζειν κιθαρίζων μανθάνει κιθαρίζειν, ὁμοίως δὲ καὶ οἱ ἄλλοι. ὅθεν ὁ σοφιστικὸς
ἔλεγχος ἐγίγνετο ὅτι οὐκ ἔχων τις τὴν ἐπιστήμην
ποιήσει οὗ ἡ ἐπιστήμη· ὁ γὰρ μανθάνων οὐκ ἔχει.
ἀλλὰ διὰ τὸ τοῦ γιγνομένου γεγενῆσθαί τι καὶ τοῦ

R19

a (≠ DK) Plato, *Meno*

[Meno:] And in what way will you search for this [e.g. virtue], Socrates, when you do not know at all what it is? What kind of thing, among those that you do not know, will you propose to yourself in order to be able to search for it? Or even if you are so lucky as to run into it, how will you know that it is this very thing that you did not know? [80e]

[Socrates:] I know what it is that you mean to say, Meno. You see that this is an eristic argument you are introducing, viz. that it is not possible for a person to search either for what he knows or for what he does not know? For neither could he search for what he knows—for he knows it, and such a person has no need for any search—nor for what he does not know—for he does not know what he will be searching for.

b (≠ DK) Aristotle, *Metaphysics*

That [scil. because what is generated is identical in form to its efficient cause] is why it seems impossible for someone to be a builder if he has never built anything, nor a cithara player if he has never played the cithara; for someone who learns to play the cithara learns to play the cithara by playing the cithara, and so too in all the other cases. From this arose the sophistic refutation according to which someone will do what belongs to a science without possessing the science: for he who is learning it does not possess it. But because some part of what is being generated has already been generated and some part of what is being moved as a whole has already been moved

235

ὅλως κινουμένου κεκινῆσθαί τι [. . .] [1050a1] καὶ τὸν
μανθάνοντα ἀνάγκη ἔχειν τι τῆς ἐπιστήμης ἴσως.

R20 (≠ DK) Arist. *EE* 1.8 1218b23–24

ἔτι οὐδὲ δείκνυσιν οὐθεὶς ὅτι ἀγαθὸν ἡ ὑγίεια, ἂν μὴ
σοφιστὴς ᾖ καὶ μὴ ἰατρός (οὗτοι γὰρ τοῖς ἀλλοτρίοις
λόγοις σοφίζονται) [. . .].

R21 (≠ DK) Arist. *EN* 7.2 1146a22–27

ἔτι ὁ σοφιστικὸς λόγος[1] ἀπορία· διὰ γὰρ τὸ παρά-
δοξα βούλεσθαι ἐλέγχειν ἵνα δεινοὶ ὦσιν, ὅταν ἐπιτύ-
χωσιν, ὁ γενόμενος συλλογισμὸς ἀπορία γίνεται·
δέδεται γὰρ ἡ διάνοια, ὅταν μένειν μὴ βούληται διὰ
τὸ μὴ ἀρέσκειν τὸ συμπερανθέν, προϊέναι δὲ μὴ δύ-
νηται διὰ τὸ λῦσαι μὴ ἔχειν τὸν λόγον.

[1] ψευδόμενος post λόγος hab. mss., secl. Koraïs

R22 (≠ DK) Plat. *Soph.* 232b, e

[ΞΕ.] [. . .] ἀλλ᾽ ἀναλάβωμεν ⟨ἓν⟩[1] πρῶτον τῶν περὶ
τὸν σοφιστὴν εἰρημένων. ἕν γάρ τί μοι μάλιστα κατ-
εφάνη αὐτὸν μηνῦον.
[ΘΕ.] τὸ ποῖον;
[ΞΕ.] ἀντιλογικὸν αὐτὸν ἔφαμεν εἶναί που. [. . .] ἀτὰρ
δὴ τὸ τῆς ἀντιλογικῆς τέχνης ἆρ᾽ οὐκ ἐν κεφαλαίῳ
περὶ πάντων πρὸς ἀμφισβήτησιν ἱκανή τις δύναμις
ἔοικ᾽ εἶναι;

[. . .], [1050a1] then surely it is necessary that he too who is learning possesses some part of the science.

R20 (≠ DK) Aristotle, *Eudemian Ethics*

No one demonstrates either that health is a good thing, unless he is a sophist and not a physician—for the former play tricks (*sophizesthai*) by means of irrelevant arguments [. . .].

R21 (≠ DK) Aristotle, *Nicomachean Ethics*

Again, the sophists' argument [scil. constitutes] an aporia. For because they wish to make a refutation by means of paradoxes, so that they will appear clever when they are successful, the resulting chain of argument ends up as an aporia: for the mind is blocked although it is not willing to remain stuck (because it does not approve the conclusion that has been reached) but it is not able to proceed further (because it is not able to undo the argument).

R22 (≠ DK) Plato, *Sophist*

[The stranger from Elea:] [. . .] let us return first to one of the things that we were saying about the sophist. For one thing in particular seemed to me best to reveal his nature. [Theaetetus:] Which one?
[Stranger:] We said [cf. 225b] that he is a contradictor (*antilogikos*). [. . .] But in fact would not the art of contradiction seem, in brief, to consist in a certain ability to dispute about all topics?

---

[1] <ἓν> Heindorf

The Sophists and Writing (R23–R24)

R23 (≠ DK) Plat. *Phaedr.* 257d

[ΦΑ.] καὶ σύνοισθά που καὶ αὐτὸς ὅτι οἱ μέγιστον δυνάμενοί τε καὶ σεμνότατοι ἐν ταῖς πόλεσιν αἰσχύνονται λόγους τε γράφειν καὶ καταλείπειν συγγράμματα ἑαυτῶν, δόξαν φοβούμενοι τοῦ ἔπειτα χρόνου, μὴ σοφισταὶ καλῶνται.

R24 (≠ DK) Alcid. *In soph.* 1–2

ἐπειδή τινες τῶν καλουμένων σοφιστῶν ἱστορίας μὲν καὶ παιδείας ἠμελήκασι καὶ τοῦ δύνασθαι λέγειν ὁμοίως τοῖς ἰδιώταις ἀπείρως ἔχουσι, γράφειν δὲ μεμελετηκότες λόγους καὶ διὰ βιβλίων δεικνύντες τὴν αὑτῶν σοφίαν σεμνύνονται καὶ μέγα φρονοῦσι, καὶ πολλοστὸν μέρος τῆς ῥητορικῆς κεκτημένοι δυνάμεως τῆς ὅλης τέχνης ἀμφισβητοῦσι, διὰ ταύτην τὴν αἰτίαν ἐπιχειρήσω κατηγορίαν ποιήσασθαι τῶν γραπτῶν λόγων, οὐχ ὡς ἀλλοτρίαν ἐμαυτοῦ τὴν δύναμιν αὐτῶν ἡγούμενος, ἀλλ' ὡς ἐφ' ἑτέροις μεῖζον φρονῶν καὶ τὸ γράφειν ἐν παρέργῳ μελετᾶν οἰόμενος χρῆναι, καὶ τοὺς ἐπ' αὐτὸ τοῦτο τὸν βίον καταναλίσκοντας ἀπολελεῖφθαι πολὺ καὶ ῥητορικῆς καὶ φιλοσοφίας ὑπειληφώς, καὶ πολὺ δικαιότερον ἂν ποιητὰς ἢ σοφιστὰς προσαγορεύεσθαι νομίζων.

The Sophists and Writing (R23–R24)

R23 (≠ DK) Plato, *Phaedrus*

[Phaedrus:] And you yourself [scil. Socrates] know well that the men who are the most powerful and highly regarded in the cities are ashamed to write discourses and to leave writings behind, out of fear that in later times they will be called 'sophists.'

R24 (≠ DK) Alcidamas, *On the Sophists*

Since some of the people who are called 'sophists,' although they have neglected research and education and, just like laymen, know nothing of the ability to speak, nonetheless put on airs and think themselves high and mighty for having practiced the writing of discourses and shown their own wisdom by means of books, and although they possess only a tiny part of the capacity of rhetoric, nonetheless lay a claim to the entirety of the art, for this reason I shall undertake to lodge an accusation against written discourses: not because I believe that the ability of these people is foreign to myself, but because I think myself better on other grounds: I believe that one should practice writing as a subsidiary activity, and I think that those people who devote their lives to this one activity are very lacking both in rhetoric and in philosophy, and I consider that it would be more just for them to be called 'writers' (*poiêtai,* 'poets,' literally 'makers') rather than 'sophists.'

Socratic Analogies for the Sophist (R25–R32)
Prostitute (R25)

R25 (> 79.2a) Xen. *Mem.* 1.6.13

[ΣΩ.] ὦ Ἀντιφῶν, παρ᾿ ἡμῖν νομίζεται τὴν ὥραν καὶ
τὴν σοφίαν ὁμοίως μὲν καλόν, ὁμοίως δὲ αἰσχρὸν
διατίθεσθαι εἶναι. τήν τε γὰρ ὥραν ἐὰν μέν τις ἀργυρίου πωλῇ τῷ βουλομένῳ, πόρνον αὐτὸν ἀποκαλοῦσιν, ἐὰν δέ τις, ὃν ἂν γνῷ καλόν τε κἀγαθὸν ἐραστὴν
ὄντα, τοῦτον φίλον ἑαυτῷ ποιῆται, σώφρονα νομίζο-
μεν· καὶ τὴν σοφίαν ὡσαύτως τοὺς μὲν ἀργυρίου τῷ
βουλομένῳ πωλοῦντας σοφιστὰς ὥσπερ πόρνους[1]
ἀποκαλοῦσιν, ὅστις δέ, ὃν ἂν γνῷ εὐφυῆ ὄντα, διδάσκων ὅ τι ἂν ἔχῃ ἀγαθόν, φίλον ποιεῖται, τοῦτον νομίζομεν, ἃ τῷ καλῷ κἀγαθῷ πολίτῃ προσήκει, ταῦτα
ποιεῖν.

[1] ὥσπερ πόρνους del. Ruhnken

Hunter (R26–R27)

R26 (> 79.2a) Xen. *Cyn.* 13.8–9

[8] οἱ σοφισταὶ δ᾿ ἐπὶ τῷ ἐξαπατᾶν λέγουσι καὶ γρά-
φουσιν ἐπὶ τῷ ἑαυτῶν κέρδει, καὶ οὐδένα οὐδὲν ὠφε-
λοῦσιν· οὐδὲ γὰρ σοφὸς αὐτῶν ἐγένετο οὐδεὶς οὐδ᾿
ἔστιν, ἀλλὰ καὶ ἀρκεῖ ἑκάστῳ σοφιστὴν κληθῆναι, ὅ
ἐστιν ὄνειδος παρά γε εὖ φρονοῦσι. [9] τὰ μὲν οὖν τῶν
σοφιστῶν παραγγέλματα παραινῶ φυλάττεσθαι, τὰ

Socratic Analogies for the Sophist (R25–R32)
Prostitute (R25)

R25 (> 79.2a) Xenophon, *Memorabilia*

[Socrates:] Antiphon, among us it is thought that it is possible to make use of youthful beauty and cleverness (*sophia*) in both a seemly way and an unseemly one. For if one sells one's youthful beauty for money to anyone who desires it, they call him a prostitute; but if one makes himself a friend to someone whom he knows to be a fine and honorable man, being a lover, we consider him to be temperate. And the same thing applies to cleverness (*sophia*): they call those people who sell it for money to whoever desires it 'sophists,' like prostitutes, while someone who makes himself a friend to a man whom he knows to be well endowed by nature, teaching him whatever he has that is good, we think that that man is doing what is fitting for a fine and honorable citizen.

Hunter (R26–R27)

R26 (> 79.2a) Xenophon, *On Hunting*

[8] The sophists speak in order to deceive and they write for their own profit, without doing anyone any good. For there has never been, and there is not now, any of them who is wise (*sophos*), but each one is satisfied to be called a 'sophist' (*sophistês*), which among sensible people is an insult. So my advice is to be on your guard against the declarations of the sophists, and not to disdain the reason-

241

δὲ τῶν φιλοσόφων ἐνθυμήματα μὴ ἀτιμάζειν· οἱ μὲν
γὰρ σοφισταὶ πλουσίους καὶ νέους θηρῶνται, οἱ δὲ
φιλόσοφοι πᾶσι κοινοὶ καὶ φίλοι· τύχας δὲ ἀνδρῶν
οὔτε τιμῶσιν οὔτε ἀτιμάζουσι.

R27 (79.2) Plat. *Soph.* 231d

[ΞΕ.] [. . .] τὸ πρῶτον ηὑρέθη νέων καὶ πλουσίων ἔμ-
μισθος θηρευτής.

Merchant (R28–R29)

R28 (≠ DK) Plat. *Prot.* 313c–314a

[ΣΩ.] ἆρ' οὖν, ὦ Ἱππόκρατες, ὁ σοφιστὴς τυγχάνει
ὢν ἔμπορός τις ἢ κάπηλος τῶν ἀγωγίμων, ἀφ' ὧν
ψυχὴ τρέφεται; φαίνεται γὰρ ἔμοιγε τοιοῦτός τις.
[ΙΠ.] τρέφεται δέ, ὦ Σώκρατες, ψυχὴ τίνι;
[ΣΩ.] μαθήμασιν δήπου [. . .]. καὶ ὅπως γε μή, ὦ
ἑταῖρε, ὁ σοφιστὴς ἐπαινῶν ἃ πωλεῖ ἐξαπατήσῃ
ἡμᾶς, ὥσπερ οἱ περὶ τὴν τοῦ σώματος τροφήν, ὁ
ἔμπορός τε καὶ κάπηλος. καὶ γὰρ οὗτοί που ὧν ἄγου-
σιν ἀγωγίμων οὔτε αὐτοὶ ἴσασιν ὅτι χρηστὸν ἢ πονηρὸν περὶ τὸ σῶμα, ἐπαινοῦσιν δὲ πάντα πωλοῦντες,
οὔτε οἱ ὠνούμενοι παρ' αὐτῶν, ἐὰν μή τις τύχῃ γυμ-
ναστικὸς ἢ ἰατρὸς ὤν. οὕτω δὲ καὶ οἱ τὰ μαθήματα
περιάγοντες κατὰ τὰς πόλεις καὶ πωλοῦντες καὶ κα-
πηλεύοντες τῷ ἀεὶ ἐπιθυμοῦντι ἐπαινοῦσιν μὲν πάντα
ἃ πωλοῦσιν, τάχα δ' ἄν τινες, ὦ ἄριστε, καὶ τούτων

ings of the philosophers. For the sophists hunt for rich men and young ones, while the philosophers are available to all and are the friends of all: and they neither admire men's fortunes nor disdain them.

R27 (79.2) Plato, *Sophist*

[The stranger from Elea:] [. . .] we have discovered that he [i.e. the sophist] was first of all a hired hunter of rich young men.

Merchant (R28–R29)

R28 (≠ DK) Plato, *Protagoras*

[Socrates:] Well then, Hippocrates, does the sophist turn out to be a wholesaler or retailer of the wares by which the soul is nourished? For this is the sort of person he seems to me to be.
[Hippocrates:] But what is it that the soul is nourished by, Socrates?
[Socrates:] By teachings, I suppose [. . .]. And watch out, my friend, lest the sophist deceive us by praising what he sells, just as do the wholesaler and the retailer who deal with the nourishment of the body. For even these people surely do not know which of the wares they offer are beneficial or harmful for the body, and yet they praise all of them when they sell them, and those who buy these from them do not [scil. know this] either, unless they happen to be an athletic trainer or a doctor. In the same way, those who transport teachings from city to city, and sell off and retail them to whoever desires to buy them each time, praise everything they sell, but perhaps, dear friend, some

ἀγνοοῖεν ὧν πωλοῦσιν ὅτι χρηστὸν ἢ πονηρὸν πρὸς
τὴν ψυχήν· ὡς δ᾿ αὔτως καὶ οἱ ὠνούμενοι παρ᾿ αὐτῶν,
ἐὰν μή τις τύχῃ περὶ τὴν ψυχὴν αὖ ἰατρικὸς ὤν. εἰ
μὲν οὖν σὺ τυγχάνεις ἐπιστήμων τούτων τί χρηστὸν
καὶ πονηρόν, ἀσφαλές σοι ὠνεῖσθαι μαθήματα καὶ
παρὰ Πρωταγόρου καὶ παρ᾿ ἄλλου ὁτουοῦν· εἰ δὲ μή,
ὅρα, ὦ μακάριε, [314a] μὴ περὶ τοῖς φιλτάτοις κυ-
βεύῃς τε καὶ κινδυνεύῃς.

R29 (79.2) Plat. *Soph.* 231d

[ΞΕ.] [. . . = **R27**] τὸ δέ γε δεύτερον ἔμπορός τις περὶ
τὰ τῆς ψυχῆς μαθήματα. [. . .] τρίτον δὲ ἆρα οὐ περὶ
αὐτὰ ταῦτα κάπηλος ἀνεφάνη;
[ΘΕ.] ναί, καὶ τέταρτόν γε αὐτοπώλης περὶ τὰ μαθήματα ἡμῖν ⟨ἦν⟩.[1]

[1] ⟨ἦν⟩ Heindorf

Magician and Charlatan (R30–R31)

R30 (≠ DK) Plat. *Soph.* 268c–d

[ΞΕ.] τὸ[1] δὴ τῆς ἐναντιοποιολογικῆς εἰρωνικοῦ μέρους
τῆς δοξαστικῆς μιμητικόν, τοῦ φανταστικοῦ γένους
ἀπὸ τῆς εἰδωλοποιικῆς οὐ θεῖον ἀλλ᾿ ἀνθρωπικὸν τῆς
ποιήσεως ἀφωρισμένον ἐν λόγοις τὸ θαυματοποιικὸν
μόριον, "ταύτης τῆς γενεᾶς τε καὶ αἵματος" ὃς ἂν φῇ
τὸν ὄντως σοφιστὴν εἶναι, τἀληθέστατα, ὡς ἔοικεν,
ἐρεῖ.

of these people too do not know which of the wares they
are selling is beneficial or harmful for the soul; and so too
those people who buy from them, unless they happen to
be a doctor of the soul. If then you happen to know which
of these things is beneficial and harmful, you can safely
buy teachings from Protagoras or from anyone else. But if
not, watch out, my friend, [314a] lest you play dice and
put at risk the things that are dearest to you.

R29 (79.2) Plato, *Sophist*

[The stranger from Elea:] [. . .] Secondly, [scil. we have
discovered that the sophist was] a wholesaler of teachings
for the soul. [. . .] Thirdly then, was he not revealed to be
a retailer of the same things?
[Theaetetus:] Yes, and fourthly we saw him as a seller of
his own teachings.

Magician and Charlatan (R30–R31)

R30 (≠ DK) Plato, *Sophist*

[Stranger from Elea:] Imitation of the ironic (*eironikos*)
part of the art of contradicting within opinion, belonging
to the phantasmic branch of the art of the simulacrum, not
the divine part but the human one, productive of prodigies
in the domain of discourse—whoever were to say that the
real sophist is "of this descent and blood" [Homer, *Il.*
6.211] would, it seems, be stating the perfect truth.

---

1 τὸν BT, corr. Schleiermacher

R31 (≠ DK) Plat. *Pol.*

a 291c

[ΞΕ.] [. . .] τὸν πάντων τῶν σοφιστῶν μέγιστον γόητα
καὶ ταύτης τῆς τέχνης ἐμπειρότατον, ὃν ἀπὸ τῶν
ὄντως ὄντων πολιτικῶν καὶ βασιλικῶν καίπερ παγχά-
λεπον ὄντα ἀφαιρεῖν ἀφαιρετέον [. . .].

b 303b–c

[ΞΕ.] οὐκοῦν δὴ καὶ τοὺς κοινωνοὺς τούτων τῶν πολι-
τειῶν πασῶν πλὴν τῆς ἐπιστήμονος ἀφαιρετέον ὡς
οὐκ ὄντας πολιτικοὺς ἀλλὰ στασιαστικούς, καὶ εἰδώ-
λων μεγίστων προστάτας ὄντας καὶ αὐτοὺς εἶναι τοιούτους, μεγίστους δὲ ὄντας μιμητὰς καὶ γόητας μεγίστους γίγνεσθαι τῶν σοφιστῶν σοφιστάς.

Other Images (R32)

R32 (79.2) Plat. *Soph.* 231d–e

[ΞΕ.] [. . . = **R29**] πέμπτον [. . .] τῆς γὰρ ἀγωνιστικῆς
περὶ λόγους ἦν τις ἀθλητής, τὴν ἐριστικὴν τέχνην
ἀφωρισμένος. [. . .] τό γε μὴν ἕκτον ἀμφισβητήσιμον
μέν, ὅμως δ᾽ ἔθεμεν αὐτῷ συγχωρήσαντες δοξῶν ἐμ-
ποδίων μαθήμασιν περὶ ψυχὴν καθαρτὴν αὐτὸν εἶναι.

R31 (≠ DK) Plato, *Statesman*

a

[The stranger from Elea:] [. . .] the man who is the greatest charlatan of all the sophists and the most experienced in this art, the one who must be distinguished, difficult though this is, from those who are really statesmen and of a kingly nature [. . .].

b

[The stranger from Elea:] Therefore those men who participate in all these constitutions (except for the one based on scientific knowledge) must be distinguished as being not statesmen but sectarians, presiding over the greatest images, and themselves of the same sort, men who, since they are the greatest imitators and charlatans, turn out to also be the greatest sophists among the sophists.

Other Images (R32)

R32 (79.2) Plato, *Sophist*

[The stranger from Elea:] [. . .] [. . .] fifth [scil. the sophist] was a kind of athlete in the art of contention regarding discourses, who had appropriated to himself the art of eristic. [. . .] Sixth, we had some doubts, but all the same we conceded to him and posited that he was a purifier of opinions that interfere with teachings in the soul [cf. **SOC. D29**].

Sophistic and Atheism (R33)

R33 (≠ DK) Plat. *Leg.* 10 908 d–e

[ΑΘ.] [. . .] ὁ δὲ δὴ δοξάζων μὲν καθάπερ ἅτερος, εὐφυὴς[1] δὲ ἐπικαλούμενος, δόλου δὲ καὶ ἐνέδρας πλήρης, ἐξ ὧν μάντεις τε κατασκευάζονται πολλοὶ καὶ
περὶ πᾶσαν τὴν μαγγανείαν κεκινημένοι, γίγνονται
δὲ ἐξ αὐτῶν ἔστιν ὅτε καὶ τύραννοι καὶ δημηγόροι καὶ
στρατηγοί, καὶ τελεταῖς δὲ ἰδίαις ἐπιβεβουλευκότες,
σοφιστῶν τε ἐπικαλουμένων μηχαναί. τούτων δὴ
πολλὰ μὲν εἴδη γένοιτ᾽ ἄν, τὰ δὲ νόμων ἄξια θέσεως
δύο, ὧν τὸ μὲν εἰρωνικὸν οὐχ ἑνὸς οὐδὲ δυοῖν ἄξια
θανάτοιν ἁμαρτάνον, τὸ δὲ νουθετήσεως ἅμα καὶ
δεσμῶν δεόμενον.

[1] εὐφυὴς in mg. L²O²: εὐτυχὴς ALO

Sophistic, Rhetoric, and Philosophy (R34–R36)

R34 Arist.

a (79.3) *SE.* 1 165a21

ἔστι γὰρ ἡ σοφιστικὴ φαινομένη σοφία οὖσα δ᾽ οὔ,
καὶ ὁ σοφιστὴς χρηματιστὴς ἀπὸ φαινομένης σοφίας
ἀλλ᾽ οὐκ οὔσης.

Sophistic and Atheism (R33)

R33 (≠ DK) Plato, *Laws*

[Athenian:] [. . .] He who has the same opinions as the first one [i.e. the one who does not believe in the existence of the gods], and may well be called 'well-endowed by nature,' but is full of guile and treachery, is one of those men from whom come many diviners and people who practice all kinds of trickery; and sometimes too there come from them tyrants, demagogues, and generals, and people who hatch plots in private mystery rites, and the devices of those men who are called 'sophists.' Of these last there are many species, but two in particular that require legislation: the ironic kind, whose crimes deserve more than only one death or two; and the other kind, who needs admonition together with imprisonment.

Sophistic, Rhetoric, and Philosophy (R34–R36)

R34 Aristotle

a (79.3) *Sophistic Refutations*

Sophistic (*sophistikê*) is a wisdom (*sophia*) in appearance but not in reality, and the sophist (*sophistês*) is someone who makes money from what is a wisdom in appearance but not in reality.

b (≠ DK) *Metaph.* Γ3 1004b17–26

οἱ γὰρ διαλεκτικοὶ καὶ σοφισταὶ τὸ αὐτὸ μὲν ὑποδύ-
ονται σχῆμα τῷ φιλοσόφῳ· ἡ γὰρ σοφιστικὴ φαινομένη μόνον σοφία ἐστί, καὶ οἱ διαλεκτικοὶ διαλέγονται περὶ ἁπάντων, κοινὸν δὲ πᾶσι τὸ ὄν ἐστιν,
διαλέγονται δὲ περὶ τούτων δῆλον ὅτι διὰ τὸ τῆς φιλοσοφίας εἶναι ταῦτα οἰκεῖα. περὶ μὲν γὰρ τὸ αὐτὸ
γένος στρέφεται ἡ σοφιστικὴ καὶ ἡ διαλεκτικὴ τῇ
φιλοσοφίᾳ, ἀλλὰ διαφέρει τῆς μὲν τῷ τρόπῳ τῆς δυνάμεως, τῆς δὲ τοῦ βίου τῇ προαιρέσει· ἔστι δὲ ἡ
διαλεκτικὴ πειραστικὴ περὶ ὧν ἡ φιλοσοφία γνωρι-
στική, ἡ δὲ σοφιστικὴ φαινομένη, οὖσα δ' οὔ.

R35 (≠ DK) Cic. *Brut.* 8.30–31

[30] sed ut intellectum est quantam vim haberet accurata
et facta quodam modo oratio, tum etiam magistri dicendi
multi subito exstiterunt. tum Leontinus Gorgias, Thrasymachus Chalcedonius, Protagoras Abderites, Prodicus
Cius, Hippias Elius in honore magno fuit; aliique multi
temporibus eisdem docere se profitebantur, arrogantibus
sane verbis, quem ad modum causa inferior—ita enim
loquebantur—dicendo fieri superior posset. [31] his
opposuit sese Socrates, qui subtilitate quadam disputandi
refellere eorum instituta solebat.[1] huius ex uberrimis

[1] verbis *post* solebat *hab. mss., secl. Haupt*: urbanius *Vitelli,
alii alia*

b (≠ DK) *Metaphysics*

Dialecticians and sophists clothe themselves in the same outward apparel as the philosopher does, for sophistic is wisdom only in appearance, and dialecticians discuss all subjects; and in common to all of these is what is (*to on*), and it is clear that they discuss these subjects because they belong to philosophy. For sophistic and dialectic revolve around the same kind of things as philosophy does, but it [i.e. philosophy] differs from the former in the kind of capability it possesses and from the latter in the way of life it chooses. Dialectic puts to the test the subjects about which philosophy brings knowledge, while sophistic is philosophy in appearance, but not in reality.

R35 (≠ DK) Cicero, *Brutus*

[30] But once it was understood how great a power was possessed by a discourse that had been prepared carefully and worked out in a certain way, many teachers of eloquence suddenly appeared. At that time Gorgias of Leontini, Thrasymachus of Chalcedon, Protagoras of Abdera, Prodicus of Ceos, Hippias of Elis were honored greatly; and at the same time many other men announced, in quite arrogant terms, that they taught how the weaker case—for this is how they put it—could become the stronger one by means of speech. [31] Socrates set himself in opposition to these men: by employing a certain subtlety of argumentation, he was accustomed to refute their doctrines. From

sermonibus exstiterunt doctissimi viri; primumque tum philosophia non illa de natura, quae fuerat antiquior, sed haec, in qua de bonis rebus et malis deque hominum vita et moribus disputatur, inventa dicitur.

R36 (≠ DK) Philostr. *Vit. soph.* 1

a p. 2.1–11 Kayser

τὴν ἀρχαίαν σοφιστικὴν ῥητορικὴν ἡγεῖσθαι χρὴ φιλοσοφοῦσαν· διαλέγεται μὲν γὰρ ὑπὲρ ὧν οἱ φιλοσοφοῦντες, ἃ δὲ ἐκεῖνοι τὰς ἐρωτήσεις ὑποκαθήμενοι καὶ τὰ σμικρὰ τῶν ζητουμένων προβιβάζοντες οὔπω φασὶ γιγνώσκειν, ταῦτα ὁ παλαιὸς σοφιστὴς ὡς εἰδὼς λέγει. προοίμια γοῦν ποιεῖται τῶν λόγων τὸ ῾οἶδα᾿ καὶ τὸ ῾γιγνώσκω᾿ καὶ ῾πάλαι διέσκεμμαι᾿ καὶ ῾βέβαιον ἀνθρώπῳ οὐδέν.᾿ ἡ δὲ τοιαύτη ἰδέα τῶν προοιμίων εὐγένειάν τε προηχεῖ τῶν λόγων καὶ φρόνημα καὶ κατάληψιν σαφῆ τοῦ ὄντος [. . .].

b p. 2. 22–26 Kayser

ἡ μὲν δὴ ἀρχαία σοφιστικὴ καὶ τὰ φιλοσοφούμενα ὑποτιθεμένη διῄει αὐτὰ ἀποτάδην καὶ ἐς μῆκος, διελέγετο μὲν γὰρ περὶ ἀνδρείας, διελέγετο δὲ περὶ δικαιότητος, ἡρώων τε πέρι καὶ θεῶν καὶ ὅπη ἀπεσχημάτισται ἡ ἰδέα τοῦ κόσμου [. . .].

his richly abundant colloquies arose the most learned of men. It is reported that it was at this time that philosophy was discovered—not the kind that deals with nature, which had existed previously, but this other one, which discusses what is good, what is bad, and the life and character of men.

R36 (≠ DK) Philostratus, *Lives of the Sophists*

a

Ancient sophistic should be considered to be a rhetoric of a philosophical nature. For it discusses the same things as philosophers do; but whereas the latter, posing fundamental questions and making progress in the details of what they investigate, say that they have not yet attained knowledge, the ancient sophist speaks about these matters as being someone who knows them. At any rate he begins his speeches by saying, 'I know,' 'I recognize,' 'I have observed for a long time,' and 'Nothing is certain for a human being.' This kind of beginning suggests nobility in speeches, self-assurance, and a clear grasp of the subject [. . .].

b

Ancient sophistic, even when it proposed philosophical subjects, expounded them diffusely and at length; for it discussed manly valor, it discussed justice, heroes and gods, and in what way the form of the cosmos was shaped [. . .].

c (4.17–23)

δεινότητα δὲ οἱ Ἀθηναῖοι περὶ τοὺς σοφιστὰς ὁρῶντες
ἐξεῖργον αὐτοὺς τῶν δικαστηρίων, ὡς ἀδίκῳ λόγῳ τοῦ
δικαίου κρατοῦντας καὶ ἰσχύοντας παρὰ τὸ εὐθύ, ὅθεν
Αἰσχίνης καὶ Δημοσθένης προὔφερον μὲν αὐτὸ ἀλλήλοις, οὐχ ὡς ὄνειδος δέ, ἀλλὰ ὡς διαβεβλημένον τοῖς
δικάζουσιν, ἰδίᾳ γὰρ ἠξίουν ἀπ᾿ αὐτοῦ θαυμάζεσθαι.

d (4.29–5.1)

σοφιστὰς δὲ οἱ παλαιοὶ ἐπωνόμαζον οὐ μόνον τῶν
ῥητόρων τοὺς ὑπερφωνοῦντάς τε καὶ λαμπρούς, ἀλλὰ
καὶ τῶν φιλοσόφων τοὺς ξὺν εὐροίᾳ ἑρμηνεύοντας
[. . .].

c

When the Athenians saw how clever the sophists were, they excluded them from the law courts because they were able to defeat a just speech by means of an unjust one and succeeded in prevailing against what was right. This is why Aeschines and Demosthenes call each other this term, not because it was an insult, but because it was suspect in the eyes of the jurors; for in private they thought they should be admired for this.

d

The ancients called 'sophists' not only those orators who were renowned for speaking surpassingly well, but also those philosophers who expressed themselves with fluency [. . .].

43. APPENDIX: PHILOSOPHY AND PHILOSOPHERS IN GREEK COMEDY AND TRAGEDY [DRAM.]

One striking measure of the impact of early Greek philosophy on contemporary culture is the frequency with which both the persons of philosophers and specific philosophical doctrines were represented on the stage. The present appendix gathers together a considerable number of passages drawn from Greek comic and tragic poets and thereby further documents the history of the reception of the thought of the early Greek philosophers that is presented from a doctrinal point of view in the **R** sections of the preceding chapters. Some other dramatic texts, which illustrate not the reception of early Greek philosophy but the cultural background for it, are found in chapter 3, "Reflections on Gods and Men," in volume 2 of the present edition.

The first section presents several passages in which the Sicilian comic poet Epicharmus (probably mid-sixth to mid-fifth century BC) seems to parody various concepts and modes of argumentation that can be attributed to early Greek philosophers. We also include a number of passages (printed in italics) which modern scholars generally, but not universally, consider inauthentic; we have chosen not to exclude these in part because of the uncertainty of this judgment, in part because in any case these texts importantly illustrate one form of reception of early Greek philosophy.

The second section gathers together allusions to philosophical themes and to philosophers in Attic comedy; Old Comedy is represented particularly well in its persiflage of various natural philosophers and 'sophists,' but Middle and New Comedy also supply a number of striking texts, especially regarding the Pythagorean school.

The third section collects references to philosophical themes from fifth-century Attic tragedy. Most of these involve general topics that present a greater or lesser degree of similarity with conceptions that can be attributed to one or more early Greek philosophers; but Euripides in particular also likes to reflect closely the concepts and even the language of specific philosophers such as Xenophanes, perhaps Heraclitus, Diogenes of Apollonia, Socrates, and above all certainly Anaxagoras.

In this appendix, as in the chapters dedicated to the most ancient reflections on the world (chap. 2) and on gods and men (chap. 3), the Greek texts are furnished with only a minimal critical apparatus, indicating solely our divergences, if any, from the editions of reference indicated in the first volume. Furthermore, we have only given the reference to DK when their collection cites the text in question or mentions it in a significant way, without indicating when it is not included.

BIBLIOGRAPHY

F. Egli. *Euripides im Kontext zeitgenössischer intellektueller Strömungen: Analyse der Funktion philosophischer Themen in den Tragödien und Fragmenten* (Munich, 2003).

R. Kerkhof. *Dorische Posse, Epicharm und Attische Komödie* (Munich, 2001).

L. Rodríguez-Noriega Guillén, ed. *Epicarmo de Siracusa: Testimonios y Fragmentos* (Oviedo, 1996).

OUTLINE OF THE CHAPTER

DRAMATIC APPENDIX

PHILOSOPHY AND PHILOSOPHERS IN GREEK COMEDY AND TRAGEDY

[≠ DK]

Philosophical Themes in Sicilian Comedy:
Epicharmus (T1–T9)
General Themes (T1)

T1 (23 B9) Ps.-Plut. *Cons. Ap.* 15 110A (Epich. Frag. 213 K–A)

συνεκρίθη καὶ διεκρίθη κἀπῆλθεν ὅθεν ἦλθεν
   πάλιν,
γᾶ μὲν εἰς γᾶν, πνεῦμα δ᾽ ἄνω· τί τῶνδε χαλεπόν;
   οὐδὲ ἔν.

Xenophanic Themes (T2–T3)

T2 (23 B12) Plut. *Alex. Fort.* 2.3 336B (Epich. Frag. 214 K–A)

νοῦς ὁρῆ καὶ νοῦς ἀκούει· τἆλλα κωφὰ καὶ
   τυφλά.

PHILOSOPHY AND
PHILOSOPHERS IN GREEK
COMEDY AND TRAGEDY

Philosophical Themes in Sicilian Comedy:
Epicharmus (T1–T9)[1]
General Themes (T1)

[1] For the distinction between Epicharmus and Pseudo-Epicharmus, see the introduction to this chapter.

T1 (23 B9) Ps.-Plutarch, *Consolation to Apollonius*

There was unification and division and return again
  to where it had come from,
Earth to earth, and air upward. What of these things
  is difficult? Nothing at all!

Cf. e.g. **EMP. D66–D72; ANAXAG. D30**

Xenophanic Themes (T2–T3)

T2 (23 B12) Plutarch, *On Alexander's Fortune*

Mind sees and mind hears: but everything else is deaf
  and blind.

Cf. **XEN. D17**

T3 (21 A15) Arist. *Metaph.* Γ5 1010a5–6 (Epich. Frag. 143 K–A)

διὸ εἰκότως μὲν λέγουσιν, οὐκ ἀληθῆ δὲ λέγουσιν·
οὕτω γὰρ ἁρμόττει μᾶλλον εἰπεῖν ἢ ὥσπερ Ἐπίχαρ-
μος εἰς Ξενοφάνην.

Texts of Disputed Attribution (T4–T9)
The Immortality of the Gods (T4)

T4 (23 B1) Alcimus *Contra Amynt.* in Diog. Laert. 3.10–11 (Ps.-Epich. Frag. 275 K–A)

[A.]   ἀλλ᾽ ἀεί τοι θεοὶ παρῆσαν χὐπέλιπον οὐ πώ-
         ποκα,
         τάδε δ᾽ ἀεὶ πάρεσθ᾽ ὁμοῖα διά τε τῶν αὐτῶν
         ἀεί.
[B.]   ἀλλὰ λέγεται μὰν Χάος πρᾶτον γενέσθαι
         τῶν θεῶν.
[A.]   πῶς δέ κα, μὴ ἔχον γ᾽ ἀπὸ τίνος μηδ᾽ ἐς ὅτι
         πρᾶτον μόλοι;
[B.]   οὐκ ἄρ᾽ ἔμολε πρᾶτον οὐδέν;
5 [A.]   οὐδὲ μὰ Δία δεύτερον
         τῶνδέ γ᾽ ὧν ἁμές νυν ὧδε λέγομες, ἀλλ᾽ ἀεὶ
         τάδ᾽ ἦς.

T3 (21 A15) Aristotle, *Metaphysics*

That is why they [i.e. those who say that only what is perceptible exists] say things that are plausible but are not true—for it is more fitting to speak in this way than as Epicharmus did against Xenophanes.[1]

[1] It is uncertain just what Epicharmus said; he may have claimed that Xenophanes' views were implausible but true, or that they were neither plausible nor true.

Texts of Disputed Attribution (T4–T9)
The Immortality of the Gods (T4)

T4 (23 B1) Alcimus, *Against Amyntas,* in Diogenes Laertius

[A:]   But the gods were always there and were never lacking,
        And those things are always there, similar and always in the same way.
[B:]   But Chaos is said to have been born as the first of the gods.
[A:]   How could that be? Being first, he would have nothing from which or to which he could go.
[B:]   So nothing came first?
[A:]   And not second either, by Zeus,   5
        At least of those things we are talking about now in this way, but they always were.[1]

[1] This citation continues in the manuscripts, without interruption, with **T8**.

Cf. e.g. **COSM. T11** v. 116, **T21, T22; XEN. D12**, cf. **P16**

Heraclitean Themes (T5–T8)

T5 (23 B17) Stob. 3.37.18 (Ps.-Epich. Frag. 266 K–A)

> ὁ τρόπος ἀνθρώποισι δαίμων ἀγαθός, οἷς δὲ καὶ
> κακός.

T6 (23 B4) Alcimus in Diog. Laert. 3.16 (Ps.-Epich. Frag. 278 K–A)

> Εὔμαιε, τὸ σοφόν ἐστιν οὐ καθ᾽ ἓν μόνον,
> ἀλλ᾽ ὅσσα περ ζῇ, πάντα καὶ γνώμαν ἔχει.
> καὶ γὰρ τὸ θῆλυ τᾶν ἀλεκτορίδων γένος,
> αἰ λῇς καταμαθεῖν ἀτενές, οὐ τίκτει τέκνα
> 5 ζῶντ᾽, ἀλλ᾽ ἐπῴζει καὶ ποιεῖ ψυχὰν ἔχειν.
> τὸ δὲ σοφὸν ἁ φύσις τόδ᾽ οἶδεν ὡς ἔχει
> μόνα· πεπαίδευται γὰρ αὐταύτας ὕπο.

T7 (23 B5) Alcimus in Diog. Laert. 3.16 (Ps.-Epich. Frag. 279 K–A)

> θαυμαστὸν οὐδὲν ἁμὲ ταῦθ᾽ οὕτω λέγειν
> καὶ ἁνδάνειν αὐτοῖσιν αὐτοὺς καὶ δοκεῖν
> καλῶς πεφύκειν· καὶ γὰρ ἁ κύων κυνί
> κάλλιστον εἶμεν φαίνεται καὶ βοῦς βοΐ,
> 5 ὄνος δ᾽ ὄνῳ κάλλιστον, ὗς δέ θην ὑΐ.

DRAMATIC APPENDIX

Heraclitean Themes (T5–T8)

T5 (23 B17) Stobaeus, *Anthology*

> *One's character* (tropos) *is for humans a good*
>   *divinity—but for some, also a bad one.*

Cf. **HER. D111**

T6 (23 B4) Alcimus, *Against Amyntas*, in Diogenes Laertius

> *Eumaeus, what is wise is not in one thing alone,*
> *But everything that lives also has thought.*
> *For indeed the female race of hens,*
> *If you are willing to observe intently, does not bear its*
>   *young*
> *Already living, but broods clucking on them and*   5
>   *causes them to have a soul.*
> *What is wise—this nature alone knows,*
> *For it has been educated by itself alone.*

Cf. **HER. D43–D45**

T7 (23 B5) Alcimus, *Against Amyntas,* in Diogenes Laertius

> *It is not at all surprising that we speak in this way,*
> *And are pleasing to ourselves and suppose that we*
> *Are beautiful by nature: for to a dog, the bitch*
> *Seems to be the most beautiful thing of all, and a cow*
>   *to a bull,*
> *And a she-ass to an ass is the most beautiful, and a*   5
>   *sow, obviously, to a hog.*

Cf. **XEN. D14; HER. D78–D81**

T8 (23 B2) Alcimus in Diog. Laert. 3.11 (Ps.-Epich. Frag. 276 K–A)

[A.]   αἰ πὸτ ἀριθμόν τις περισσόν, αἰ δὲ λῇς πὸτ
        ἄρτιον,
        ποτθέμειν λῇ ψᾶφον ἢ καὶ τᾶν ὑπαρχουσᾶν
        λαβεῖν,
        ἦ δοκεῖ κα τοί γ' ἔθ' ωὑτὸς εἶμεν;
[B.]   οὐκ ἐμίν γα κα.
[A.]   οὐδὲ μὰν οὐδ' αἰ ποτὶ μέτρον παχναῖον ποτ-
        θέμειν
5   λῇ τις ἕτερον μᾶκος ἢ τοῦ πρόσθ' ἐόντος
        ἀποταμεῖν,
        ἔτι χ' ὑπάρχοι κῆνο τὸ μέτρον;
[B.]   οὐ γάρ.
[A.]   ὧδε νῦν ὅρη
    καὶ τὸς ἀνθρώπους· ὁ μὲν γὰρ αὔξεθ', ὁ δέ
        γα μὰν φθίνει,
    ἐν μεταλλαγᾷ δὲ πάντες ἐντὶ πάντα τὸν χρό-
        νον.
    ὁ δὲ μεταλλάσσει κατὰ φύσιν κοὔποκ' ἐν
        τωὐτῷ μένει,
10   ἕτερον εἴη κα τόδ' ἤδη τοῦ παρεξεστακότος.
    καὶ τὺ δὴ κἀγὼ χθὲς ἄλλοι καὶ νῦν ἄλλοι
        τελέθομες,
    καὖθις ἄλλοι κοὔποχ' ωὐτοὶ καττὸν αὐτὸν αὖ
        λόγον.

DRAMATIC APPENDIX

T8 (23 B2) Alcimus, *Against Amyntas*, in Diogenes Laertius

[A:]   If to an odd number, or to an even one if you wish, someone
        Wants to add a unit [literally: a counter] or take one away from those present,
        Do you think it will still be the same?

[B:]   I certainly don't!

[A:]   Or then if to the measure of a cubit someone
        Wants to add another length or cut it off from what   5
        was there before,
        Then would that measure still remain?

[B:]   No.

[A:]   Now look in this way
        At humans too. The one grows, the other decreases,
        They are all in a state of change the whole time.
        But what changes by its nature and never remains in the same condition,
        This would be different from what has been changed,   10
        And you and I were different yesterday, and today have become different,
        And again [scil. will be] different and never the same, according to this very argument.

Pythagorean Themes (T9)

T9 (23 B56) Clem. Alex. *Strom.* 5.118.1 (Ps.-Epich. Frag. 240.1–2 K–A)

ὁ βίος ἀνθρώποις λογισμοῦ κἀριθμοῦ δεῖται
πάνυ.
ζῶμεν ἀριθμῷ καὶ λογισμῷ· ταῦτα γὰρ σῴζει
βροτούς.

*Allusions to Philosophers and Philosophical
Themes in Attic Comedy (T10–T40)
Old Comedy (T10–T32)
The Study of Celestial and Meteorological
Phenomena (T10)*

T10 Aristoph. *Nub.*

a (< 64 C1) 225–34

[ΣΩ.] ἀεροβατῶ καὶ περιφρονῶ τὸν ἥλιον.
[ΣΤ.] ἔπειτ᾽ ἀπὸ ταρροῦ τοὺς θεοὺς ὑπερφρονεῖς,
        ἀλλ᾽ οὐκ ἀπὸ τῆς γῆς, εἴπερ;
[ΣΩ.]   οὐ γὰρ ἄν ποτε
        ἐξηῦρον ὀρθῶς τὰ μετέωρα πράγματα,
        εἰ μὴ κρεμάσας τὸ νόημα καὶ τὴν φροντίδα
230   λεπτὴν καταμείξας εἰς τὸν ὅμοιον ἀέρα.
        εἰ δ᾽ ὢν χαμαὶ τἄνω κάτωθεν ἐσκόπουν,
        οὐκ ἄν ποθ᾽ ηὗρον· οὐ γὰρ ἀλλ᾽ ἡ γῆ βίᾳ

Pythagorean Themes (T9)

T9 (23 B56) Clement of Alexandria, *Stromata*

> *Human life stands in great need of calculation*
>   *(logismos) and number.*
> *We live by number and calculation. This is what*
>   *provides safety to mortals.*

Cf. **ARCHY. D4**

Allusions to Philosophers and Philosophical
Themes in Attic Comedy (T10–T40)
Old Comedy (T10–T32)
The Study of Celestial and Meteorological
Phenomena (T10)

T10 Aristophanes, *Clouds*

a (< 64 C1)

[SOCRATES:] I walk upon the air, and I scrutinize the sun.
[STREPSIADES:] So from your basket you look down on
        the gods?
        But why not from the ground, in that case?
[SOC.:]   I would never
    Have discovered the exact nature of the celestial
        phenomena
    If I had not suspended my mind and mixed
    My rarefied thought with what is similar to it, air.   230
    If I had been on the ground and examined from
        below what is on high,
    I would never have discovered anything: for the
        earth forcibly

ἕλκει πρὸς αὑτὴν τὴν ἰκμάδα τῆς φροντίδος.
πάσχει δὲ ταὐτὸ τοῦτο καὶ τὰ κάρδαμα.

b 264–66

[Σω.]   ὦ δέσποτ᾽ ἄναξ, ἀμέτρητ᾽ Ἀήρ, ὃς ἔχεις τὴν
           γῆν μετέωρον,
265   λαμπρός τ᾽ Αἰθήρ, σεμναί τε θεαὶ Νεφέλαι
           βροντησικέραυνοι,
           ἄρθητε, φάνητ᾽, ὦ δέσποιναι, τῷ φροντιστῇ
           μετέωροι.

c (cf. Nachtrag, vol. II, p. 420.14) 365–411

[Σω.]   αὗται γάρ τοι μόναι εἰσὶ θεαί, τἄλλα δὲ
           πάντ᾽ ἐστὶ φλύαρος.
[Στ.]   ὁ Ζεὺς δ᾽ ὑμῖν, φέρε, πρὸς τῆς γῆς, οὐλύμ-
           πιος οὐ θεός ἐστιν;
[Σω.]   ποῖος Ζεύς; οὐ μὴ ληρήσεις. οὐδ᾽ ἔστι Ζεύς.
[Στ.]   τί λέγεις σύ;
           ἀλλὰ τίς ὕει; τουτὶ γὰρ ἔμοιγ᾽ ἀπόφηναι
           πρῶτον ἁπάντων.
[Σω.]   αὗται δήπου· μεγάλοις δέ σ᾽ ἐγὼ σημείοις
           αὐτὸ διδάξω.
370   φέρε, ποῦ γὰρ πώποτ᾽ ἄνευ νεφελῶν ὕοντ᾽
           ἤδη τεθέασαι;
           καίτοι χρῆν αἰθρίας ὕειν αὐτόν, ταύτας δ᾽
           ἀποδημεῖν.

270

Attracts to itself the moisture of thought.
This is what happens to watercress too.

Cf. **DIOG. D44**

b

[SOCRATES:] Oh sovereign lord, boundless Air, you who
    hold the earth suspended on high,
    And shining Aether, and you, venerable goddesses,   265
    thundering-lightning Clouds,
    Arise, appear, oh mistresses, on high to this thinker!

c (cf. Nachtrag, vol. II, p. 420.14)

[SOC.:] That's because only they [i.e. the Clouds] are god-
    desses; everything else is just claptrap.
[STREPS.:] But tell me, by Earth, isn't Olympian Zeus a
    god for you people?
[SOC.:] What Zeus? Don't say stupid things. Zeus doesn't
    even exist!
[STREPS.:]   What are you saying?
    But then who makes it rain? Explain this to me
    before anything else.
[SOC.:] These do, obviously! And I will teach you how,
    with great proofs.
    Tell me: have you ever seen it rain without clouds?   370
    And yet [scil. according to you] Zeus would have to
    make it rain on a clear day, when the clouds are
    away.

[ΣΤ.] νὴ τὸν Ἀπόλλω, τοῦτό γέ τοι τῷ νυνὶ λόγῳ
    εὖ προσέφυσας·
    καίτοι πρότερον τὸν Δί᾽ ἀληθῶς ᾤμην διὰ
    κοσκίνου οὐρεῖν.
    ἀλλ᾽ ὅστις ὁ βροντῶν ἐστι φράσον, τοῦθ᾽ ὅ
    με ποιεῖ τετραμαίνειν.

[ΣΩ.] αὗται βροντῶσι κυλινδόμεναι.

375 [ΣΤ.]   τῷ τρόπῳ, ὦ πάντα σὺ τολ-
    μῶν;

[ΣΩ.] ὅταν ἐμπλησθῶσ᾽ ὕδατος πολλοῦ κἀναγκα-
    σθῶσι φέρεσθαι
    κατακριμνάμεναι πλήρεις ὄμβρου δι᾽ ἀνάγ-
    κην, εἶτα βαρεῖαι
    εἰς ἀλλήλας ἐμπίπτουσαι ῥήγνυνται καὶ πα-
    ταγοῦσιν.

[ΣΤ.] ὁ δ᾽ ἀναγκάζων ἐστὶ τίς αὐτάς—οὐχ ὁ
    Ζεύς;—ὥστε φέρεσθαι;

[ΣΩ.] ἥκιστ᾽, ἀλλ᾽ αἰθέριος δῖνος.

380 [ΣΤ.]   δῖνος; τουτί μ᾽ ἐλελήθει,
    ὁ Ζεὺς οὐκ ὤν, ἀλλ᾽ ἀντ᾽ αὐτοῦ δῖνος νυνὶ
    βασιλεύων.
    ἀτὰρ οὐδέν πω περὶ τοῦ πατάγου καὶ τῆς
    βροντῆς μ᾽ ἐδίδαξας.

[ΣΩ.] οὐκ ἤκουσάς μου τὰς νεφέλας ὕδατος μεστὰς
    ὅτι φημί
    ἐμπιπτούσας εἰς ἀλλήλας παταγεῖν διὰ τὴν
    πυκνότητα;

[ΣΤ.] φέρε, τουτὶ τῷ χρὴ πιστεύειν;

[STREPS.:] By Apollo, you have joined this point very well
   with what you said just now.
   And to think that I really used to suppose that Zeus
    was pissing through a sieve!
   But tell me, who produces the thunder that makes
    me tremble?

[SOC.:] These produce the thunder by rolling around.

[STREPS.:]   In what way, you 375
   whose audacity knows no limits?

[SOC.:] When they are filled up with a lot of water and
   drift, suspended,
   Full of water, by the effect of necessity, they smash
    into one another by their weight
   And they burst and make a crashing noise.

[STREPS.:] But the necessity that makes them drift, who
   is it? Isn't it Zeus?

[SOC.:] Not at all; it is the vortex of the aether.

[STREPS.:]   The vortex? I had not noticed 380
   That Zeus does not exist and that in his place a
    vortex is now king.
   But you still have not taught me anything about the
    crashing and thunder.

[SOC.:] Didn't you hear me? What I say is that when the
   clouds are full of water
   And smash into one another, they make a crashing
    noise because of their density.

[STREPS.:] Come on, why should anyone believe that?

385 [ΣΩ.] ἀπὸ σαυτοῦ ʼγώ σε διδάξω.

ἤδη ζωμοῦ Παναθηναίοις ἐμπλησθεὶς εἶτ᾽
ἐταράχθης

τὴν γαστέρα, καὶ κλόνος ἐξαίφνης αὐτὴν δι-
εκορκορύγησεν;

[ΣΤ.] νὴ τὸν Ἀπόλλω, καὶ δεινὰ ποεῖ γ᾽ εὐθύς μοι
καὶ τετάρακται,

χὥσπερ βροντὴ τὸ ζωμίδιον παταγεῖ καὶ
δεινὰ κέκραγεν,

390 ἀτρέμας πρῶτον "παππὰξ παππάξ," κἄπειτ᾽
ἐπάγει "παπαπαππάξ,"

χὥταν χέζω, κομιδῇ βροντᾷ "παπαπαππάξ,"
ὥσπερ ἐκεῖναι.

[ΣΩ.] σκέψαι τοίνυν ἀπὸ γαστριδίου τυννουτουὶ οἷα
πέπορδας·

τὸν δ᾽ ἀέρα τόνδ᾽ ὄντ᾽ ἀπέραντον πῶς οὐκ
εἰκὸς μέγα βροντᾶν;

[ΣΤ.] ταῦτ᾽ ἄρα καὶ τὠνόματ᾽ ἀλλήλοιν βροντὴ καὶ
πορδὴ ὁμοίω.

395 ἀλλ ὁ κεραυνὸς πόθεν αὖ φέρεται λάμπων
πυρί, τοῦτο δίδαξον,

καὶ καταφρύγει βάλλων ἡμᾶς, τοὺς δὲ ζῶ-
ντας περιφλεύει;

τοῦτον γὰρ δὴ φανερῶς ὁ Ζεὺς ἵησ᾽ ἐπὶ τοὺς
ἐπιόρκους.

[ΣΩ.] καὶ πῶς, ὦ μῶρε σὺ καὶ Κρονίων ὄζων καὶ
βεκκεσέληνε,

[SOC.:]   I'll teach you on the basis of your   385
own person.

Have you ever stuffed yourself with soup at the
Panathenaea and then had

An upset stomach, thrown into turmoil by a sudden
agitation?

[STREPS.:] By Apollo, yes! It has a terrible effect on me at
once and upsets me

And that little bit of soup crashes like thunder and
roars terribly,

At first gently, *pappax, pappax,* and then mightily,   390
papapappax;

And when I shit, it absolutely thunders, *papapappax,* just like them!

[SOC.:]   Consider then what farts you set off from your
little belly;

Isn't it only natural that this air, which is limitless,
thunders mightily?

[STREPS.:] So that's why the words *brontê* ('thunder') and
pordê ('fart') are similar!

But now explain this to me: where does the light-   395
ning bolt blazing with fire

Come from that incinerates us when it hits us and
burns the survivors?

It is obvious that it is Zeus who is hurling it against
perjurers.

[SOC.:]   What, you idiot with your antediluvian air, you
superannuated fool!

εἴπερ βάλλει τοὺς ἐπιόρκους, δῆτ᾽ οὐχὶ Σί-
μων᾽ ἐνέπρησεν

400   οὐδὲ Κλεώνυμον οὐδὲ Θέωρον; καίτοι σφόδρα
γ᾽ εἴσ᾽ ἐπίορκοι·
ἀλλὰ τὸν αὑτοῦ γε νεὼν βάλλει καὶ Σούνιον,
ἄκρον Ἀθηνέων,
καὶ τὰς δρῦς τὰς μεγάλας· τί μαθών; οὐ γὰρ
δὴ δρῦς γ᾽ ἐπιορκεῖ.

[ΣΤ.] οὐκ οἶδ᾽· ἀτὰρ εὖ σὺ λέγειν φαίνει. τί γάρ
ἐστιν δῆθ᾽ ὁ κεραυνός;

[ΣΩ.] ὅταν εἰς ταύτας ἄνεμος ξηρὸς μετεωρισθεὶς
κατακλῃσθῇ,

405   ἔνδοθεν αὐτὰς ὥσπερ κύστιν φυσᾷ, κἄπειθ᾽
ὑπ᾽ ἀνάγκης
ῥήξας αὐτὰς ἔξω φέρεται σοβαρὸς διὰ τὴν
πυκνότητα,
ὑπὸ τοῦ ῥοίβδου καὶ τῆς ῥύμης αὐτὸς ἑαυτὸν
κατακαίων.

[ΣΤ.] νὴ Δί᾽ ἐγὼ γοῦν ἀτεχνῶς ἔπαθον τουτί ποτε
Διασίοισιν,
ὀπτῶν γαστέρα τοῖς συγγένεσιν, κᾆτ᾽ οὐκ
ἔσχων ἀμελήσας·

410   ἡ δ᾽ ἄρ᾽ ἐφυσᾶτ᾽, εἶτ᾽ ἐξαίφνης διαλακήσασα
πρὸς αὐτώ
τὠφθαλμώ μου προσετίλησεν καὶ κατέκαυ-
σεν τὸ πρόσωπον.

If he is really hitting perjurers, why hasn't he burned
up Simon,

Or Cleonymus, or Theorus, given that they're the   400
worst perjurers?

On the contrary, he hits his own temple, and Su-
nium, the headland of Athens,

And the great oaks. What does he know? Certainly
an oak tree doesn't commit perjury.

[STREPS.:] I don't know; but what you say seems right.
But then what is the thunderbolt?

[SOC.:] When a dry wind arises and becomes enclosed in
these clouds,

It inflates them from inside like a bladder, and then,   405
having made them burst

By the effect of necessity, it is expelled violently
because of their density,

Igniting itself by reason of its impetuosity and force.

[STREPS.:] By Zeus, that's exactly the same thing as what
happened to me one time at the Diasia festival:

When I was cooking a paunch for my family, I forgot
to make a slit in it.

So it got inflated, and when it suddenly exploded   410
directly into my eyes

It soiled and burned my face.

Cf. e.g. **ANAXIMAND. D33**

d 329–34

[ΣΩ.]   ταύτας μέντοι σὺ θεὰς οὔσας οὐκ ᾔδεις οὐδ᾽
        ἐνόμιζες;

[ΣΤ.]   μὰ Δί᾽, ἀλλ᾽ ὁμίχλην καὶ δρόσον αὐτὰς
        ἡγούμην καὶ καπνὸν εἶναι.

[ΣΩ.]   οὐ γὰρ μὰ Δί᾽ οἶσθ᾽ ὅτι ἢ πλείστους αὗται
        βόσκουσι σοφιστάς,
        Θουριομάντεις, ἰατροτέχνας, σφραγιδονυχαρ-
            γοκομήτας·
        κυκλίων τε χορῶν ᾀσματοκάμπτας, ἄνδρας
            μετεωροφένακας,
        οὐδὲν δρῶντας βόσκουσ᾽ ἀργούς, ὅτι ταύτας
            μουσοποιοῦσιν.

Parody of an Orphic Cosmogony (T11)

T11 (1 A12) Aristoph. *Av.* 693–702

[χο.]   Χάος ἦν καὶ Νὺξ Ἔρεβός τε μέλαν πρῶτον
            καὶ Τάρταρος εὐρύς·
        γῆ δ᾽ οὐδ᾽ ἀὴρ οὐδ᾽ οὐρανὸς ἦν· Ἐρέβους δ᾽
            ἐν ἀπείροσι κόλποις
695   τίκτει πρώτιστον ὑπηνέμιον Νὺξ ἡ μελανό-
            πτερος ᾠόν,
        ἐξ οὗ περιτελλομέναις ὥραις ἔβλαστεν
            Ἔρως ὁ ποθεινός,
        στίλβων νῶτον πτερύγοιν χρυσαῖν, εἰκὼς
            ἀνεμώκεσι δίναις.

d

[SOC.:] And as for you, you didn't know that they are
goddesses, and you did not honor them?

[STREPS.:] No, by Zeus; I thought they were mist, dew,
and steam.

[SOC.:] That's because, by Zeus, you did not know that
they nourish a crowd of experts (*sophistai*):

Diviners from Thurii, medical technicians, long-
haired idlers who wear onyx rings,

And tune-bending composers of dithyrambic cho-
ruses, fraudulent astronomers,

whom, though they do nothing, they feed because
they compose music about them.

Parody of an Orphic Cosmogony (T11)

T11 (1 A12) Aristophanes, *Birds*

[CHORUS LEADER:] In the beginning, there were Chaos,
Night, black Erebus, and broad Tartarus;

Neither earth nor air nor sky existed. But in the
limitless bosom of Erebus,

Black-winged Night produced in the very begin-   695
ning a wind-egg,

From which, when the seasons had completed their
revolution, lovely Eros

Blossomed, his back gleaming with golden wings,
like swift whirlwinds.

οὗτος δὲ Χάει πτερόεντι μιγεὶς νύχιος κατὰ
   Τάρταρον εὐρύν
ἐνεόττευσεν γένος ἡμέτερον, καὶ πρῶτον ἀνή-
   γαγεν εἰς φῶς.
700   πρότερον δ᾽ οὐκ ἦν γένος ἀθανάτων, πρὶν
      Ἔρως ξυνέμειξεν ἅπαντα·
ξυμμειγνυμένων δ᾽ ἑτέρων ἑτέροις γένετ᾽
   Οὐρανὸς Ὠκεανός τε
καὶ Γῆ πάντων τε θεῶν μακάρων γένος ἄφθιτον.

698 νύχιος Halbertsma, van Herwerden: νυχίῳ fere mss.
(μυχίῳ Su. χ 84 mss. SC): μύχιος West

A Parodic Zoogony (T12)

T12 (cf. ad 64 A19) Aristoph. *Thesmo.* 9–18

[ΚΗ.]   πῶς μοι παραινεῖς; δεξιῶς μέντοι λέγεις·
10   οὐ φῂς σὺ χρῆναί μ᾽ οὔτ᾽ ἀκούειν οὔθ᾽ ὁρᾶν.
[ΕΤ.]   χωρὶς γὰρ αὐτοῖν ἑκατέρου ᾽στὶν ἡ φύσις.
[ΚΗ.]   τοῦ μήτ᾽ ἀκούειν μήθ᾽ ὁρᾶν;
[ΕΤ.]   εὖ ἴσθ᾽ ὅτι.
[ΚΗ.]   πῶς χωρίς;
[ΕΤ.]   οὕτω ταῦτα διεκρίθη τότε.
   αἰθὴρ γὰρ ὅτε τὰ πρῶτα διεχωρίζετο

12 versum del. van Herwerden

And, uniting at night with winged Chaos in broad
    Tartarus,
He hatched our race and brought us first to the light
    of day.
The race of immortals did not exist previously, be-   700
    fore Eros mixed together all things.
But when different things were mixed together with
    each other, the sky and the ocean were born,
And the earth and the immortal race of the blessed
    gods.

Cf. **COSM. T13–T18**

A Parodic Zoogony (T12)

T12 (cf. ad 64 A19) Aristophanes, *Thesmophoriazusae*

[RELATIVE OF EURIPIDES:] What are you recommending
    to me? You certainly talk cleverly!
    You say that I must neither hear nor see?   10
[EURIPIDES:] Yes, for the nature of each of these two is
    different.
[RELATIVE:] That of neither hearing nor seeing?
[EUR.:]   Yes indeed.
[RELATIVE:] But how are they different?
[EUR.:]   This is how they were distin-
    guished back then:
    For when the aether separated the elements

15   καὶ ζῴ᾽ ἐν αὐτῷ ξυνετέκνου κινούμενα,
      ᾧ μὲν βλέπειν χρὴ πρῶτ᾽ ἐμηχανήσατο
      ὀφθαλμὸν ἀντίμιμον ἡλίου τροχῷ,
      ἀκοῆς δὲ χοάνην ὦτα διετετρήνατο.

Thales (T13–T14)

T13 Aristoph. *Nub.* 177–180

[ΜΑ.]   κατὰ τῆς τραπέζης καταπάσας λεπτὴν τέ-
       φραν,
       κάμψας ὀβελίσκον, εἶτα διαβήτην λαβὼν
       ἐκ τῆς παλαίστρας θοἰμάτιον ὑφείλετο.
[ΣΤ.]   τί δῆτ᾽ ἐκεῖνον τὸν Θαλῆν θαυμάζομεν;

T14 Aristoph. *Av.* 1004–9

[ΜΕ.]   ὀρθῷ μετρήσω κανόνι προστιθείς, ἵνα
1005   ὁ κύκλος γένηταί σοι τετράγωνος κἂν μέσῳ
       ἀγορά, φέρουσαι δ᾽ ὦσιν εἰς αὐτὴν ὁδοὶ
       ὀρθαὶ πρὸς αὐτὸ τὸ μέσον, ὥσπερ δ᾽ ἀστέρος

And engendered within itself the animals endowed   15
    with motion,
It constructed first for the one that was supposed to
    see
The eye, an imitation of the wheel of the sun,
And perforated a funnel for hearing as the ears.

Thales (T13–T14)[1]

[1] Thales seems to have been a popular emblem of scientific genius in Roman comedy too: see Plautus, *Captives* 62, *Rope* 1003, *Bacchides* 122.

T13 Aristophanes, *Clouds*

[PUPIL OF SOCRATES:] Over the table he [i.e. Socrates]
    spread out fine ashes
    And bent a skewer, then taking up a spread-legged
    compass—
From the wrestling school he stole the cloak.[1]
[STREPSIADES:] Then why do we admire the great Thales?

[1] The verse is obscure.

T14 Aristophanes, *Birds*

[METON:][1] I will measure it, setting a straight ruler along-
    side, so that
    Your circle will be squared, with in the center   1005
    A marketplace, and running into it there will be
    streets,
    Straight ones, toward the very center, and just as
    from a star,

αὐτοῦ κυκλοτεροῦς ὄντος ὀρθαὶ πανταχῇ
ἀκτῖνες ἀπολάμπωσιν.

[ΠΕ.]   ἄνθρωπος Θαλῆς.

Hippo (T15–T16)

T15 (38 A2) Cratin. Πανόπται Frag. 167 K–A = Schol.
in Clem. Alex. *Protr.* 24.2 (vol. 1, p. 304.28–29 Stählin)

τοῦ δὲ Ἵππωνος [. . .] ὡς ἀσεβοῦς γενομένου μέμνηται ὁ Κρατῖνος.

T16 (38 A2)

a Aristoph. *Nub.* 94–97

[ΣΤ.]   ψυχῶν σοφῶν τοῦτ᾽ ἔστι φροντιστήριον.
95   ἐνταῦθ᾽ ἐνοικοῦσ᾽ ἄνδρες, οἳ τὸν οὐρανόν
        λέγοντες ἀναπείθουσιν ὡς ἔστιν πνιγεύς,
        κἄστιν περὶ ἡμᾶς οὗτος, ἡμεῖς δ᾽ ἄνθρακες.

b Cratin. Πανόπται Frag. 167 K–A = Schol. in Aristoph.
Nub. 96d

ταῦτα πρότερος Κρατῖνος ἐν Πανόπταις δράματι περὶ
Ἵππωνος τοῦ φιλοσόφου κωμῳδῶν αὐτὸν λέγει.

Which itself is circular, in every direction straight
Rays will beam outward.
[PISTHETAERUS:] The man is a Thales![1]

[1] A celebrated geometer and astronomer.

Hippo (T15–T16)

T15 (38 A2) Scholia on Clement of Alexandria, *Protreptic*

Cratinus mentions Hippo [. . .] and the fact that he was impious [scil. in his *Panoptai,* i.e. *Those Who See Everything*].

T16 (38 A2)

a Aristophanes, *Clouds*

[STREPSIADES:] This is the think-tank of wise souls;
This is where those men live who, speaking   95
About the heavens, persuade people that it is an
     oven,
And that it surrounds us, and that we are embers.

b Scholia on Aristophanes' *Clouds*

Cratinus said this earlier in his play *Panoptai* [i.e. *Those Who See Everything*] about the philosopher Hippo in order to make fun of him.

Parmenides? (T17)

T17 Cratin. Πανόπται Frag. 161 K–A

κρανία δισσὰ φορεῖν, ὀφθαλμοὶ δ᾿οὐκ ἀριθματοί

Protagoras (T18–T19)

T18 Eupol. Κόλακες

a (< 80 A11) Testim. ii. K–A = Athen. *Deipn.* 5.218C

ἐν οὖν τούτῳ τῷ δράματι Εὔπολις τὸν Πρωταγόραν
ὡς ἐπιδημοῦντα εἰσάγει [. . .].

b (< 80 A1, A11) Frag. 157 K–A

ἔνδον μέν ἐστι Πρωταγόρας ὁ Τήιος
ὃς ἀλαζονεύεται μὲν ἀλιτήριος
περὶ τῶν μετεώρων, τὰ δὲ χαμᾶθεν ἐσθίει.

c (< 80 A11) Frag. 158 K–A

πίνειν γὰρ αὐτὸν Πρωταγόρας ἐκέλευ᾿, ἵνα
πρὸ τοῦ κυνὸς τὸν πλεύμον᾿ ἔκπλυτον φορῇ.

DRAMATIC APPENDIX

Parmenides? (T17)

T17 Cratinus, fragment from *Panoptai* [i.e. *Those Who See Everything*]

To have two heads—and innumerable eyes

Cf. **PARM. D7.4–5**

Protagoras (T18–T19)

T18 Eupolis, *The Flatterers*

a (< 80 A11) Athenaeus, *Deipnosophists*

In this play, Eupolis brings Protagoras onto the stage as having arrived [scil. at Athens, cf. **PROT. P9**] [. . .].

b (< 80 A1, A11) Eupolis, Fragment from *Flatterers*

Inside is Protagoras of Teos,
Who boasts, the scoundrel,
About celestial phenomena, but eats what comes
    from the ground.

c (< 80 A11) Eupolis, Fragment from *Flatterers*

Then Protagoras told him [i.e. Callias] to drink
So that before the Dogstar rose
His lungs would be thoroughly moistened.

T19 Aristoph. *Nub.*

a (80 C2) 112–15

[ΣΤ.]   εἶναι παρ' αὐτοῖς φασὶν ἄμφω τὼ λόγω,
τὸν κρείττον', ὅστις ἐστί, καὶ τὸν ἥττονα.
τούτοιν τὸν ἕτερον τοῖν λόγοιν, τὸν ἥττονα,
νικᾶν λέγοντά φασι τἀδικώτερα.

b 882–85

[ΣΤ.]   ὅπως δ' ἐκείνω τὼ λόγω μαθήσεται,
τὸν κρείττον' ὅστις ἐστί καὶ τὸν ἥττονα,
ὃς τἄδικα λέγων ἀνατρέπει τὸν κρείττονα·
885   ἐὰν δὲ μή, τὸν γοῦν ἄδικον πάσῃ τέχνῃ.

c (> 80 C3) 658–93

[ΣΩ.]   ἀλλ' ἕτερα δεῖ σε πρότερα τούτου μανθάνειν,
τῶν τετραπόδων ἅττ' ἐστὶν ὀρθῶς ἄρρενα.
660   [ΣΤ.]   ἀλλ' οἶδ' ἔγωγε τἄρρεν', εἰ μὴ μαίνομαι·
κριός, τράγος, ταῦρος, κύων, ἀλεκτρυών.

T19 Aristophanes, *Clouds*

a (80 C2)

[STREPSIADES:] They say that there are both kinds of
      speeches among them,
      The stronger one, whatever that is, and the weaker
        one,
      And that of these two speeches the one that is
        weaker,
      They say, prevails by saying what is more unjust.

b

[STREPSIADES:] Make sure that he [i.e. Pheidippides]
      learns these two arguments,
      The stronger one, whatever that is, and the weaker
        one,
      The one that defends injustice and overturns the
        stronger one.
      And if not, then by all means teach him at least the   885
        unjust one![1]

[1] See also the long dispute between Just Discourse and Unjust
Discourse in *Clouds* 889–1113.

Cf. **PROT. D28**

c (> 80C3)

[SOCRATES:] But there are other things that you need to
      learn before that one:
      Among the quadrupeds, which ones are strictly
        speaking masculine?
[STREPSIADES:] But I know the masculine ones, unless I   660
      am crazy:
      Ram, billy goat, bull, dog, poultry.

[ΣΩ.] ὁρᾷς ἃ πάσχεις; τήν τε θήλειαν καλεῖς
ἀλεκτρυόνα κατὰ ταὐτὸ καὶ τὸν ἄρρενα.

[ΣΤ.] πῶς δή, φέρε;

[ΣΩ.]   πῶς; ἀλεκτρυὼν κἀλεκτρυών.

665 [ΣΤ.] νὴ τὸν Ποσειδῶ. νῦν δὲ πῶς με χρὴ καλεῖν;

[ΣΩ.] ἀλεκτρύαιναν, τὸν δ' ἕτερον ἀλέκτορα.

[ΣΤ.] ἀλεκτρύαιναν; εὖ γε, νὴ τὸν Ἀέρα·
ὥστ' ἀντὶ τούτου τοῦ διδάγματος μόνου
διαλφιτώσω σου κύκλῳ τὴν κάρδοπον.

670 [ΣΩ.] ἰδοὺ μάλ' αὖθις, τουθ' ἕτερον· τὴν κάρδοπον
ἄρρενα καλεῖς θήλειαν οὖσαν.

[ΣΤ.]   τῷ τρόπῳ;
ἄρρενα καλῶ 'γὼ κάρδοπον;

[ΣΩ.]   μάλιστά γε,
ὥσπερ γε καὶ Κλεώνυμον.

[ΣΤ.]   πῶς δή; φράσον.

[ΣΩ.] ταὐτὸν δύναταί σοι κάρδοπος Κλεωνύμῳ.

675 [ΣΤ.] ἀλλ', ὦγάθ', οὐδ' ἦν κάρδοπος Κλεωνύμῳ,
ἀλλ' ἐν θυείᾳ στρογγύλῃ γ' ἀνεμάττετο.
ἀτὰρ τὸ λοιπὸν πῶς με χρὴ καλεῖν;

[ΣΩ.]   ὅπως;
τὴν καρδόπην, ὥσπερ καλεῖς τὴν Σωστρά-
την.

[ΣΤ.] τὴν καρδόπην, θήλειαν;

[ΣΩ.]   ὀρθῶς γὰρ λέγεις.

680 [ΣΤ.] ἐκεῖνο δ' ἦν ἄν 'καρδόπη Κλεωνύμη'.

[SOC.:]   Do you see what is happening to you? You call the
          female 'poultry' just like the male.

[STREPS.:] What's that? Let's see!

[SOC.:]   What's that? Poultry and poultry.

[STREPS.:] Quite so, by Poseidon. But just what am I sup-   665
          posed to call them?

[SOC.:]   'Poultress,' and the other one 'poultry.'

[STREPS.:] 'Poultress'? Very good, by Air!
          So that, for this lesson alone,
          I'll fill up your bowl (*kardopos*) with barley all
          around.

[SOC.:]   You see? Here's another one. You call the bowl   670
          masculine,
          Though the word is feminine.

[STREPS.:]   How so?
          Do I call the bowl masculine?

[SOC.:]   Absolutely, just like when you say, "Cleonymus."

[STREPS.:]   What's that? Tell me.

[SOC.:]   For you, 'bowl' and 'Cleonymus' have the same
          value.

[STREPS.:] But, my dear fellow, Cleonymus didn't even   675
          have a bowl;
          It was in a round mortar that he did *his* kneading!
          But how am I supposed to say it from now on?

[SOC.:]   How? 'Bowless' (*kardopê*), just as you say 'Sos-
          tratê.'

[STREPS.:] *Kardopê* in the feminine?

[SOC.:]   Indeed: that is how to speak correctly.

[STREPS.:] So this is what I should say: *kardopê, Cle-*   680
          onymê.

291

[ΣΩ.] ἔτι δέ γε περὶ τῶν ὀνομάτων μαθεῖν σε δεῖ,
   ἅττ᾽ ἄρρεν᾽ ἐστίν, ἅττα δ᾽ αὐτῶν θήλεα.

[ΣΤ.] ἀλλ᾽ οἶδ᾽ ἔγωγ᾽ ἃ θήλε᾽ ἐστίν.

[ΣΩ.]   εἰπὲ δή.

[ΣΤ.] Λύσιλλα, Φίλιννα, Κλειταγόρα, Δημητρία.

685 [ΣΩ.] ἄρρενα δὲ ποῖα τῶν ὀνομάτων;

[ΣΤ.]   μυρία.
   Φιλόξενος, Μελησίας, Ἀμυνίας.

[ΣΩ.] ἀλλ᾽ ὦ πόνηρε, ταῦτά γ᾽ ἔστ᾽ οὐκ ἄρρενα.

[ΣΤ.] οὐκ ἄρρεν᾽ ὑμῖν ἐστιν;

[ΣΩ.]   οὐδαμῶς γ᾽, ἐπεί
   πῶς ἂν καλέσειας ἐντυχὼν Ἀμυνίᾳ;

690 [ΣΤ.] ὅπως ἄν; ὡδί· "δεῦρο δεῦρ᾽, Ἀμυνία."

[ΣΩ.] ὁρᾷς; γυναῖκα τὴν Ἀμυνίαν καλεῖς.

[ΣΤ.] οὔκουν δικαίως, ἥτις οὐ στρατεύεται;
   ἀτὰρ τί ταῦθ᾽ ἃ πάντες ἴσμεν μανθάνω;

Gorgias (T20–T21)

T20 (82 A5a) Aristoph. *Av.* 1694–705

[ΧΟ.] ἔστι δ᾽ ἐν Φάναισι πρὸς τῇ
1695   Κλεψύδρᾳ πανοῦργον Ἐγ-
   γλωττογαστόρων γένος,

[SOC.:] But you still have to learn, regarding proper names,

Which ones are masculine and which ones feminine.

[STREPS.:] But I know which ones are feminine.

[SOC.:] Then tell me.

[STREPS.:] Lysilla, Philinna, Cleitagora, Demetria.

[SOC.:] And the masculine ones, which names are they? 685

[STREPS.:] Innumerable ones:

Philoxenus, Melesias, Amynias.

[SOC.:] But those are not masculine, you fool!

[STREPS.:] Those don't count as masculine for you people?

[SOC.:] Not in the least. For

How would you call Amynias if you ran into him?

[STREPS.:] How I would call him? Like this: "Over here, 690

over here, Amynia!"

[SOC.:] You see? You're calling that 'Amynia' by a woman's name.

[STREPS.:] But isn't that appropriate, since she doesn't serve in the army?

But why do I have to learn these things? We all know them.

Cf. **PROT. D23–D25**

Gorgias (T20–T21)

T20 (82 A5a) Aristophanes, *Birds*

[CHORUS:] There exists in Phanae by the

Clepsydra a race of wicked people 1695

That live by their tongues,

293

οἳ θερίζουσίν τε καὶ σπεί-
ρουσι καὶ τρυγῶσι ταῖς γλώτ-
ταισι συκάζουσί τε·
1700   βάρβαροι δ᾽ εἰσὶν γένος,
Γοργίαι τε καὶ Φίλιπποι,
κἀπὸ τῶν Ἐγγλωττογαστό-
ρων ἐκείνων τῶν Φιλίππων
πανταχοῦ τῆς Ἀττικῆς ἡ
1705   γλῶττα χωρὶς τέμνεται.

T21 (82 A5a) Aristoph. *Vesp.* 420–21

[ΞΑ.] Ἡράκλεις, καὶ κέντρ᾽ ἔχουσιν. οὐχ ὁρᾷς, ὦ
δέσποτα;

[ΒΔ.] οἷς γ᾽ ἀπώλεσαν Φίλιππον ἐν δίκῃ τὸν Γορ-
γίου.

Prodicus (T22–T24)

T22 (> 84 A5) Aristoph. *Nub.* 360–61

[ΧΟ.] [. . .] οὐ γὰρ ἂν ἄλλῳ γ᾽ ὑπακούσαιμεν τῶν
νῦν μετεωροσοφιστῶν
πλὴν ἢ Προδίκῳ, τῷ μὲν σοφίας καὶ γνώμης
οὕνεκα [. . . = **T28**].

Who with their tongues
Reap and sow
And gather in grapes and figs:
They are a race of people who do not speak good   1700
    Greek (*barbaroi*),
Gorgiases and Philippuses,
And it is by reason of those Phillipuses
That live by their tongues
That everywhere in Attica
The tongue is cut off separately [scil. in sacrifices].   1705

T21 (82 A5a) Aristophanes, *Wasps*

[XANTHIAS:] By Heracles, they have stings too, don't you
    see, master?
[BDELYCLEON:] Yes, and with these they destroyed Gor-
    gias' son Philippus in a trial.

Prodicus (T22–T24)

T22 (> 84 A5) Aristophanes, *Clouds*

[CHORUS LEADER:] [. . .] For we would not listen to any
    other one of our present-day meteorosophists
    Except for Prodicus, on account of his wisdom and
    intelligence [. . .].

T23 (cf. 84 A5) Aristoph. *Av.* 690–92

[χο.] [. . .] ἵν᾽ ἀκούσαντες πάντα παρ᾽ ἡμῶν ὀρθῶς περὶ τῶν μετεώρων,
φύσιν οἰωνῶν γένεσίν τε θεῶν ποταμῶν τ᾽
Ἐρέβους τε Χάους τε
εἰδότες ὀρθῶς, Προδίκῳ παρ᾽ ἐμοῦ κλάειν
εἴπητε τὸ λοιπόν. [. . . = **T11**]

T24 (84 A5) Aristoph. Ταγηνισταί Frag. 506 K–A

τοῦτον τὸν ἄνδρ᾽ ἢ βιβλίον διέφθορεν
ἢ Πρόδικος ἢ τῶν ἀδολεσχῶν εἷς γέ τις.

1 τοῦτον τὸν ἄνδρ᾽ ἢ Hermann: τὸν ἄνδρα τόνδ᾽ ἢ Schol.
in *Nub.* 361a, Suda Π.2366.

Thrasymachus (T25)

T25 (85 A4) Aristoph. Δαιταλῆς Frag. 205.3–9 K–A

[Α.] ἦ μὴν ἴσως σὺ καταπλιγήσῃ τῷ χρόνῳ.
[Β.] τὸ καταπλιγήσῃ τοῦτο παρὰ τῶν ῥητόρων.
5 [Α.] ἀποβήσεταί σοι ταῦτά ποι τὰ ῥήματα.
[Β.] παρ᾽ Ἀλκιβιάδου τοῦτο τἀποβήσεται.
[Α.] τί ὑποτεκμαίρῃ καὶ κακῶς ἄνδρας λέγεις
καλοκἀγαθίαν ἀσκοῦντας;
[Β.]   οἴμ᾽, ὦ Θρασύμαχε,
τίς τοῦτο τῶν ξυνηγόρων τερατεύεται;

DRAMATIC APPENDIX

T23 (cf. 84 A5) Aristophanes, *Birds*

[CHORUS OF BIRDS:] [. . .] So that, once you have heard
correctly everything we say about celestial phenomena,
And know correctly the nature of birds, the birth of
the gods, rivers, Erebus, and Chaos,
you [i.e. humans] can tell Prodicus from me hence-
forth to go to hell! [. . .]

T24 (84 A5) Fragment from *Fry Cooks*

This man here—either a book ruined him,
Or else Prodicus, or some one of those idle talkers.

Thrasymachus (T25)

T25 (85 A4) Aristophanes, Fragment from *Banqueters*

[A:] You will certainly be tripped up sooner or later.
[B:] This 'tripped up' you have gotten from the orators.
[A:] Where will these words finish up for you?   5
[B:] This 'finish up' you have gotten from Alcibiades.
[A:] What are these insinuations and slanders against
gentlemen
Who cultivate refinement?
[B:]   Well, Thrasymachus,
Who among the lawyers uses this extreme subtlety?

Socrates (T26–T32)

T26 (I A 3 G²) Aristoph. *Nub. prior.* Frag. 392 K–A

Εὐριπίδῃ δ᾽ ὁ τὰς τραγῳδίας ποιῶν
τὰς περιλαλούσας οὗτός ἐστι, τὰς σοφάς.

T27 (I A 5 G²) Aristoph. *Av.* 1280–83

1280 [ΚΗ.] πρὶν μὲν γὰρ οἰκίσαι σε τήνδε τὴν πόλιν,
ἐλακωνομάνουν ἅπαντες ἄνθρωποι τότε,
ἐκόμων, ἐπείνων, ἐρρύπων, ἐσωκράτων,
σκυτάλι᾽ ἐφόρουν [. . .].

T28 (> 64 C1) Aristoph. *Nub.*

a 361–63

[ΧΟ.]   [. . . = **T22**] σοὶ δέ,
ὅτι βρενθύει τ᾽ ἐν ταῖσιν ὁδοῖς καὶ τὠφθαλμὼ
παραβάλλεις
κἀνυπόδητος κακὰ πόλλ᾽ ἀνέχει κἀφ᾽ ἡμῖν
σεμνοπροσωπεῖς.

DRAMATIC APPENDIX

Socrates (T26–T32)[1]

[1] For some other brief jibes at Socrates, cf. Aristophanes, *Birds* 1553–55, *Frogs* 1491–99.

T26 (I A 3 G²) Aristophanes, Fragment from the first version of *Clouds*

> This is the man [scil. Socrates] who makes the tragedies
> For Euripides, the ones that chatter excessively, the clever ones.

T27 (I A 5 G²) Aristophanes, *Birds*

[HERALD:] Before you [i.e. Pisthetaerus] built this city   1280
[i.e. Cloudcuckooland],
> The people were all crazy about the Spartan way of life:
> They grew their hair long, they went hungry, they were filthy, they Socratized,
> They carried little cudgels [. . .].

T28 (> 64 C1) Aristophanes, *Clouds*

a

[CHORUS LEADER:]   [. . .] and you [i.e. Socrates] too,
> Because you go strutting along through the streets and casting your eyes to the sides
> And go barefoot and endure lots of sufferings and look down solemnly on us.

b 826–37

[ΣΤ.]	ὁρᾷς οὖν ὡς ἀγαθὸν τὸ μανθάνειν;
	οὐκ ἔστιν, ὦ Φειδιππίδη, Ζεύς.
[ΦΕ.]	ἀλλὰ τίς;
[ΣΤ.]	Δῖνος βασιλεύει τὸν Δί' ἐξεληλακώς.
[ΦΕ.]	αἰβοῖ· τί ληρεῖς;
[ΣΤ.]	ἴσθι τοῦθ' οὕτως ἔχον.

830

[ΦΕ.]	τίς φησι ταῦτα;
[ΣΤ.]	Σωκράτης ὁ Μήλιος
	καὶ Χαιρεφῶν, ὃς οἶδε τὰ ψυλλῶν ἴχνη.
[ΦΕ.]	σὺ δ' εἰς τοσοῦτον τῶν μανιῶν ἐλήλυθας
	ὥστ' ἀνδράσιν πείθει χολῶσιν;
[ΣΤ.]	εὐστόμει
	καὶ μηδὲν εἴπῃς φλαῦρον ἄνδρας δεξιοὺς

835

	καὶ νοῦν ἔχοντας, ὧν ὑπὸ τῆς φειδωλίας
	ἀπεκείρατ' οὐδεὶς πώποτ' οὐδ' ἠλείψατο
	οὐδ' εἰς βαλανεῖον ἦλθε λουσόμενος [. . .].

c 627

[ΣΩ.]	μὰ τὴν Ἀναπνοήν, μὰ τὸ Χάος, μὰ τὸν Ἀέρα
	[. . .].

T29 (I A 10 G²) Diog. Laert. 2.28 = Ameips. Κόννος (?) Frag. *9 K–A

Ἀμειψίας δ' ἐν τρίβωνι παράγων αὐτὸν φησὶν οὕτως·

b

[STREPSIADES:] Now do you see that learning is a good
       thing?
       Zeus does not exist, Phidippides.
[PHEIDIPPIDES:]   Then who does exist?
[STREPS.:] Vortex (*Dînos*) is king, he has kicked out Zeus.
[PHEID.:] Bah! What is this nonsense?
[STREPS.:]   You should know that that's
       how it is.
[PHEID.:] Who says this?   830
[STREPS.:]   Socrates the Melian,
       And Chaerephon, who's an expert on the footsteps
          of fleas.
[PHEID.:] Have you become so crazy
       That you trust these bilious guys?
[STREPS.:]   Watch what you say,
       And don't denigrate these clever
       And intelligent men, who are so frugal   835
       That none of them has ever cut his hair or oiled
          himself
       Or gone to the baths to wash himself [. . .].

Cf. e.g. **ANAXAG. D27; EMP. D73.289, D116–D117; ATOM.
D13, D80b**

c

[SOCRATES:] By Respiration, by Chaos, by Air [. . .].

T29 (I A 10 G^2) Diogenes Laertius

Ameipsias brings him [i.e. Socrates] onto the stage in
threadbare clothes [in *Connus*?] and says:

a

Σώκρατες ἀνδρῶν βέλτιστ᾽ ὀλίγων, πολλῶν δὲ
ματαιόταθ᾽, ἥκεις
καὶ σὺ πρὸς ἡμᾶς; καρτερικός γ᾽ εἶ. πόθεν ἄν σοι
χλαῖνα γένοιτο;

b

τουτὶ τὸ κακὸν τῶν σκυτοτόμων κατ᾽ ἐπήρειαν
γεγένηται.

c

οὗτος μέντοι πεινῶν οὕτως οὐπώποτ᾽ ἔτλη
κολακεῦσαι.

T30 (I A 2 G²) Callias Πεδῆται Frag. 15 K–A

[A.]   τί δὴ σὺ σεμνὴ καὶ φρονεῖς οὕτω μέγα;
[B.]   ἔξεστι γάρ μοι· Σωκράτης γὰρ αἴτιος.

T31 (I A 12 G²) Eupol. Frag. 386 K–A

μισῶ δὲ καὶ ⟨τὸν⟩ Σωκράτην
τὸν πτωχὸν ἀδολέσχην,
ὃς τἆλλα μὲν πεφρόντικεν,
ὁπόθεν δὲ καταφαγεῖν ἔχοι
τούτου κατημέληκεν.

1 μισῶ δὲ καὶ ⟨τὸν⟩ Σωκράτην Dindorf: μισῶ δὲ καὶ
Σωκράτην Asclep. In Metaph., p. 135.23–24 Hayduck, Procl.
In Parm., p. 656.18–19: τί δῆτα ἐκεῖνον Olymp. In Parm. 70B
(p. 137.5–7 Westerink)

a

Socrates, the best of the few, the most foolish of the
many, have you come,
You too, to us? You're pretty courageous. Where will
you get yourself a cloak from?

b

This wretchedness [probably: Socrates' notorious
habit of going barefoot] is an insult to the
shoemakers.

c

And yet this man, poor as he is, has never submitted
to flattering people.

T30 (I A 2 G²) Callias, Fragment from *Men in Shackles*

[A:] Why are you so solemn and so pompous?
[B:] Because I can be—for Socrates is the reason.

T31 (I A 12 G²) Eupolis, Fragment from an unidentified
play (the *Flatterers?*)

And I hate Socrates too,
That beggarly chatterbox,
Who has figured out everything else,
But where he could get something to eat from—
To this he has paid no attention.

T32 (I A 1 G²) Telecl.

a Frag. 41 K–A

Μνησίλοχός ἐστ᾽ ἐκεῖνος ὅς φρύγει τι δρᾶμα
  καινόν
Εὐριπίδῃ, καὶ Σωκράτης τὰ φρύγαν᾽ ὑποτίθησιν.

b Frag. 42 K–A

Εὐριπίδης σωκρατογόμφος

σωκρατογόμφους mss., corr. Casaubon

Middle Comedy (T33–T39)
Heraclitus (T33)

T33 (T136 Mouraviev) Antiphan. Κᾶρες Frag. 111.1–3
K–A

  οὐχ ὁρᾷς ὀρχούμενον
ταῖς χερσὶ τὸν βάκηλον; οὐδ᾽ αἰσχύνεται
ὁ τὸν Ἡράκλειτον πᾶσιν ἐξηγούμενος [. . .].

T32 (I A 1 G²) Telecleides, Fragments from unidentified plays

a

> Mnesilochus[1] is that man, who is roasting some
>   newfangled drama
> For Euripides, and Socrates is putting firebrands
>   under it.

[1] Euripides' father-in-law.

b

> Euripides, bolted together by Socrates

Middle Comedy (T33–T39)
Heraclitus (T33)

T33 (T136 Mouraviev) Antiphanes, fragment from *Carians*

>   Don't you see him dancing,
> That eunuch, on his hands? Is he not ashamed,
> He who explains Heraclitus[1] to everyone [. . .]?

[1] Some scholars take this to be an allusion to Heraclides of Pontus; cf. **HER. R1a, b.**

Democritus (T34)

T34 (68 C1) Damox. Σύντροφοι Frag. 2.12–34 K–A

[A.] διόπερ μάγειρον ὅταν ἴδῃς ἀγράμματον
      μὴ Δημόκριτόν τε πάντα διανεγνωκότα,
      μᾶλλον δὲ κατέχοντα καταγέλα ὡς κενοῦ,

15   καὶ τὸν Ἐπικούρου Κανόνα, μινθώσας ἄφες
      ὡς ἐκ διατριβῆς. τοῦτο δεῖ γὰρ εἰδέναι,
      τίν' ἔχει διαφορὰν πρῶτον, ὦ βέλτιστε σύ,
      γλαυκίσκος ἐν χειμῶνι καὶ θέρει, πάλιν
      ποῖος περὶ δύσιν Πλειάδος συνειδέναι

20   ἰχθὺς ὑπὸ τροπάς τ' ἐστὶ χρησιμώτατος.
      αἱ μεταβολαὶ γὰρ αἵ τε κινήσεις κακόν
      ἠλίβατον ἀνθρώποισιν ἀλλοιώματα
      ἐν ταῖς τροφαῖς ποιοῦσι, μανθάνεις; τὸ δέ
      ληφθὲν καθ' ὥραν ἀποδίδωσι τὴν χάριν.

25   τίς παρακολουθεῖ ταῦτα; τοιγαροῦν στρόφοι
      καὶ πνευμάτια γινόμενα τὸν κεκλημένον
      ἀσχημονεῖν ποιοῦσι. παρὰ δ' ἐμοὶ τρέφει
      τὸ προσφερόμενον βρῶμα καὶ λεπτύνεται,
      ὀρθῶς τε διαπνεῖ. τοιγαροῦν εἰς τοὺς πόρους

30   ὁ χυμὸς ὁμαλῶς πανταχοῦ συνίσταται—

14 versum cacometrum del. Hermann

Democritus (T34)

T34 (68 C1) Damoxenus, Fragment from *The Foster Brothers*

[A:]   And that is why, when you see an unlettered cook

Who has not read through all of Democritus—

Or rather, even though he possesses him, laughs at
    him as being void—

And Epicurus' *Canon,* then cover him with shit and   15
    send him away

As if from school: for you must know this,

First what the difference is, dear sir,

Between a grayfish in winter and in summer, and
    then

You must understand what kind of fish is best

Around the setting of the Pleiades and near the   20
    solstices.

For transformations and changes, which are a pre-
    cipitous evil

For human beings, bring about alterations

In foodstuffs, you understand? But what is

Consumed in the right season produces pleasure.

Who pays close attention to these matters? And so   25
    indigestion

And flatulence occur and make the invited guest

Disgrace himself; but in my case

The food that is consumed nourishes, makes a man
    slender,

And passes through correctly. And so the humor

Is composed homogeneously everywhere in the   30
    pores.

[B.]   χυμός;

[A.]   λέγει Δημόκριτος—οὐδ᾽ ἐμφράγματα
        γινόμενα ποιεῖ τὸν φαγόντ᾽ ἀρθριτικόν.

[B.]   καὶ τῆς ἰατρικῆς τι μετέχειν μοι δοκεῖς.

[A.]   καὶ πᾶς ὁ φύσεως ἐντός. [. . .]

Pythagoreans (T35–T39)

T35 (58E.1) Alexis

a Πυθαγορίζουσα Frag. 201 K–A

(a) [A.] ἡ δ᾽ ἑστίασις ἰσχάδες καὶ στέμφυλα
        καὶ τυρὸς ἔσται· ταῦτα γὰρ θύειν νόμος
        τοῖς Πυθαγορείοις.

[B.]   νὴ Δί᾽, ἱερεῖον μὲν οὖν
        ὁποῖον ἂν κάλλιστον, ὦ βέλτιστ᾽, ἔχῃ.

(b)   ἔδει θ᾽ ὑπομεῖναι μικροσιτίαν, ῥύπον,
        ῥῖγος, σιωπήν, στυγνότητ᾽, ἀλουσίαν.

b Ταραντῖνοι Frag. 223 K–A

(a) [A.] οἱ πυθαγορίζοντες γάρ, ὡς ἀκούομεν,
        οὔτ᾽ ὄψον ἐσθίουσιν οὔτ᾽ ἄλλ᾽ οὐδὲ ἕν
        ἔμψυχον, οἶνόν τ᾽ οὐχὶ πίνουσιν μόνοι.

[B.]   Ἐπιχαρίδης μέντοι κύνας κατεσθίει,
        τῶν Πυθαγορείων εἷς.

[B:] The humor?
[A:]   That's what Democritus says: the obstructions
don't occur
That give the man who eats a case of gout.
[B:] To me you seem to have some knowledge of medi-
cine too.
[A:] And [scil. so does] every expert on nature. [. . .]

Pythagoreans (T35–T39)

T35 (58E.1) Alexis

a Fragments from *The Female Pythagorean*

(a) [A:] The banquet will consist of dried figs, pressed
olives,
And cheese: for it is the Pythagoreans' custom
To sacrifice these things.
[B:]   By Zeus, dear sir,
That is the finest sacrifice there is!

(b) A meager diet, filth, cold, silence, gloominess,
And grime—all this had to be endured.

b Fragments from *Men from Tarentum*

(a) [A:] For the Pythagoreans, according to what we are
told,
Eat neither fish nor anything else
That has a soul, and they are the only people who
do not drink wine.
[B:] But Epicharides eats dogs,
And he is one of the Pythagoreans!

[A.]   ἀποκτείνας γέ που·
οὐκέτι γάρ ἐστ' ἔμψυχον.

(b) [A.]   πυθαγορισμοὶ καὶ λόγοι
λεπτοὶ διεσμιλευμέναι τε φροντίδες
τρέφουσ' ἐκείνους, τὰ δὲ καθ' ἡμέραν τάδε·
ἄρτος καθαρὸς εἷς ἑκατέρῳ, ποτήριον
ὕδατος· τοσαῦτα ταῦτα.

[B.]   δεσμωτηρίου
λέγεις δίαιταν. πάντες οὕτως οἱ σοφοί
διάγουσι καὶ τοιαῦτα κακοπαθοῦσιν;

[A.]   οὔ·
τρυφῶσιν οὗτοι πρὸς ἑτέρους. ἆρ' οἶσθ' ὅτι
Μελανιππίδης ἑταῖρός ἐστι καὶ Φάων
καὶ Φυρόμαχος καὶ Φᾶνος, οἳ δι' ἡμέρας
δειπνοῦσι πέμπτης ἀλφίτων κοτύλην μίαν;

T36 (58E.1) Antiphan.

a Μνήματα Frag. 158 K–A

τῶν Πυθαγορικῶν δ' ἔτυχον ἄθλιοί τινες
ἐν τῇ χαράδρᾳ τρώγοντες ἅλιμα καὶ κακά
τοιαῦτα συλλέγοντες ἐν τῷ κωρύκῳ.

b Κώρυκος Frag. 133 K–A

πρῶτον μὲν ὥσπερ πυθαγορίζων ἐσθίει
ἔμψυχον οὐδέν, τῆς δὲ πλείστης τοὐβολοῦ
μάζης μελαγχρῆ μερίδα λαμβάνων λέπει.

[A:]   But he kills it first—
For that way there is no longer any soul in it.

(b) [A:]   Pythagorisms, subtle discourses,
And finely chiseled meditations
Are what nourish those men, but their daily diet is
    this:
One plain loaf of bread for each one and a cup
Of water. And that is all.
[B:]   That's prison fare
You're talking about. Do all those wise men
Spend their lives in this way and endure such evils?
[A:]   No:
Compared to the others, these men revel in luxury.
    Don't you know that
Melanippides is a disciple, as well as Phaon,
And Phyromachus and Phanus, and that every four
    days
They dine on a half-pint of barley meal?

T36 (58E.1) Antiphanes

a *The Tombs*

Some of those wretched Pythagoreans happened
To be gnawing purslanes in a torrent and
Gathering together awful things like this in their
    leather sack.

b *The Leather Sack*

First, being a Pythagorean, he eats
Nothing that has a soul, but from the cheapest barley
    cake he can find
He takes the blackened part and eats that.

T37 Aristophon Πυθαγοριστής

a (58E.2) Frag. 9 K–A

πρὸς τῶν θεῶν, οἰόμεθα τοὺς πάλαι ποτέ,
τοὺς Πυθαγοριστὰς γινομένους ὄντως ῥυπᾶν
ἑκόντας ἢ φορεῖν τρίβωνας ἡδέως;
οὐκ ἔστι τούτων οὐδέν, ὡς ἐμοὶ δοκεῖ·
5   ἀλλ' ἐξ ἀνάγκης, οὐκ ἔχοντες οὐδὲ ἕν,
τῆς εὐτελείας πρόφασιν εὑρόντες καλήν
ὅρους ἔπηξαν τοῖς πένησι χρησίμους.
ἐπεὶ παράθες αὐτοῖσιν ἰχθῦς ἢ κρέας,
κἂν μὴ κατεσθίωσι καὶ τοὺς δακτύλους,
10   ἐθέλω κρέμασθαι δεκάκις.

b (58E.3) Frag. 12 K–A

(a) [Α.] ἔφη καταβὰς εἰς τὴν δίαιταν τῶν κάτω
ἰδεῖν ἑκάστους, διαφέρειν δὲ πάμπολυ
τοὺς Πυθαγοριστὰς τῶν νεκρῶν· μόνοισι γὰρ
τούτοισι τὸν Πλούτωνα συσσιτεῖν ἔφη
5   δι' εὐσέβειαν.
[Β.]   εὐχερῆ θεὸν λέγεις
εἰ τοῖς ῥύπου μεστοῖσιν ἥδεται συνών.

(b)   ἐσθίουσί τε
λάχανά τε καὶ πίνουσιν ἐπὶ τούτοις ὕδωρ·

T37 Aristophon, Fragments from *The Pythagorean*

a (58E.2)

> By the gods, do we suppose that those men of old,
> Those who were really Pythagoreans, were voluntarily
> Filthy or took pleasure in wearing threadbare
>   clothes?
> Not at all, in my opinion!
> They did this by necessity, since they possessed   5
>   absolutely nothing:
> Having found a fine pretext for their shabbiness,
> They established standards appropriate for beggars.
> For if you set before them fish or meat
> And they don't eat it up, and their fingers too,
> Then I am willing to be hanged ten times!   10

b (58E.3)

(a) [A:] He said that he descended to observe the way of
>   life
>   Of those below, each one, and that the Pythagore-
>   ans
>   Were completely different from the [scil. other?]
>   dead: for, he said,
>   Pluto dines together with them alone
>   Because of their piety.   5
> [B:]   You are speaking of a tolerant god,
>   If he takes pleasure in the company of people full
>   of filth.

(b)   And they eat
>   Vegetables and drink water to top them off;

φθεῖρας δὲ καὶ τρίβωνα τήν τ' ἀλουσίαν
οὐδεὶς ἂν ὑπομείνειε τῶν νεωτέρων.

T38 (58E.3) Cratinus Junior

a Diog. Laert. 8.37 (Πυθαγορίζουσα Frag. 6 K–A)

ἔσκωψε δ' αὐτὸν Κρατῖνος μὲν ἐν Πυθαγοριζούσῃ·
[. . .].

b Ταραντῖνοι Frag. 7 K–A

ἔθος ἐστὶν αὐτοῖς, ἄν τιν' ἰδιώτην ποθέν
λάβωσιν εἰσελθόντα, διαπειρωμένοις
τῆς τῶν λόγων ῥώμης ταράττειν καὶ κυκᾶν
τοῖς ἀντιθέτοις, τοῖς πέρασι, τοῖς παρισώμασιν,
τοῖς ἀποπλάνοις, τοῖς μεγέθεσιν νουβυστικῶς.

T39 (58E.3) Mnesim. Ἀλκμαίων Frag. 1 K–A

ὡς Πυθαγοριστὶ θύομεν τῷ Λοξίᾳ,
ἔμψυχον οὐδὲν ἐσθίοντες παντελῶς.

New Comedy (T40)
Diogenes of Apollonia? (T40)

T40 (64 C4) Philemo Frag. 95 K–A

ὃν οὐδὲ εἷς λέληθεν οὐδὲ ἓν ποιῶν,
οὐδ' αὖ ποιήσων οὐδὲ πεποιηκὼς πάλαι,

And their lice, their threadbare clothes, and their
    grime—
None of the younger people could stand that!

T38 (58E.3) Cratinus the Younger

a Diogenes Laertius

Cratinus made fun of him [i.e. Pythagoras] in *The Female
Pythagorean* [. . .].

b Fragment from *Men from Tarentum*

They have a custom: if they catch a private person
Who arrives from somewhere else, they cause him
    trouble and confusion
By testing the strength of his reasonings,
By using antitheses, limits, equations,
Fallacies, magnitudes—all full of ingenuity.

T39 (58E.3) Mnesimachus, Fragment from *Alcmaeon*

In accordance with the Pythagorean way, we sacrifice
    to Loxias,
We who eat nothing whatsoever that is living.

New Comedy (T40)
Diogenes of Apollonia? (T40)

T40 (64 C4) Philemon, Fragment from an unidentified
play

He who does not fail to notice whatever any man does,
In the present or in the future or formerly in the
    past,

οὔτε κακὸν οὔτε γ᾽ ἐσθλόν, οὗτός εἰμ᾽ ἐγώ,
Ἀήρ, ὃν ἄν τις ὀνομάσειε καὶ Δία.
5   ἐγὼ δ᾽, ὃ θεοῦ ᾽στιν ἔργον, εἰμὶ πανταχοῦ,
ἐνταῦθ᾽ ἐν Ἀθήναις, ἐν Πάτραις, ἐν Σικελίᾳ,
ἐν ταῖς πόλεσι πάσαισιν, ἐν ταῖς οἰκίαις
πάσαις, ἐν ὑμῖν πᾶσιν· οὐκ ἔστιν τόπος,
οὗ μή ᾽στιν Ἀήρ· ὁ δὲ παρὼν ἀπανταχοῦ
10   πάντ᾽ ἐξ ἀνάγκης οἶδε πανταχοῦ παρών.

Philosophical References in
Attic Tragedy (T41–T84)
General Themes (T41–T71)
Epistemological Considerations (T41–T42)

T41 Soph. *Alead.* Frag. 86.3 R

τό τοι νομισθὲν τῆς ἀληθείας κρατεῖ.

T42 Eur. *Helen*

a 117–19, 121–22

[ΗΛ.]   εἶδες σὺ τὴν δύστηνον, ἢ κλύων λέγεις;
[ΤΕ.]   ὥσπερ σέ γ᾽, οὐδὲν ἧσσον, ὀφθαλμοῖς ὁρῶ.

Whether evil or good—that is what I am,
Air, whom one could also call Zeus.
I am everywhere—what is a god's job—   5
Here in Athens, in Patras, in Sicily,
In all the cities, in all the dwellings,
And in all of you. There is no place
In which Air does not exist; and, being present everywhere,
By necessity he knows all things, being everywhere   10
present.

Cf. **DIOG. D10**

Philosophical References in
Attic Tragedy (T41–T84)
General Themes (T41–T71)
Epistemological Considerations (T41–T42)

T41 Sophocles, Fragment from *The Sons of Aleus*

What is believed prevails over the truth.

T42 Euripides, *Helen*

a

[HELEN:] Did you see the wretched woman,[1] or are you
speaking from hearsay?
[TEUCER:] I saw her with my eyes, just as I see you, not
less.

[1] Teucer thinks that it was the real Helen whom the Greeks
captured in Troy at the end of the war; the real Helen, who is
speaking with him, knows that it was only a phantom.

[ΗΛ.]   σκοπεῖτε μὴ δόκησιν εἴχετ᾽ ἐκ θεῶν. [. . .]

[ΗΛ.]   οὕτω δοκεῖτε τὴν δόκησιν ἀσφαλῆ;

[ΤΕ.]   αὐτὸς γὰρ ὅσσοις εἰδόμην, καὶ νοῦς ὁρᾷ.

119 σκοπεῖτε ms.: σκόπει δὲ A. Y. Campbell
121–22 del. W. Ribbeck

b 1138–42

[ΧΟ.]   ὅτι θεὸς ἢ μὴ θεὸς ἢ τὸ μέσον
        τίς φησ᾽ ἐρευνήσας βροτῶν;
1140   μακρότατον πέρας ηὗρεν ὃς τὰ θεῶν ἐσορᾷ
        δεῦρο καὶ αὖθις ἐκεῖσε καὶ πάλιν ἀντιλόγοις
        πηδῶντ᾽ ἀνελπίστοις τύχαις.

The Study of Nature (T43)

T43 Eur.

a (59 A30) Frag. 910 K

[ΧΟ.]   ὄλβιος ὅστις τῆς ἱστορίας
        ἔσχε μάθησιν,
        μήτε πολιτῶν ἐπὶ πημοσύνῃ
        μήτ᾽ εἰς ἀδίκους πράξεις ὁρμῶν,
        ἀλλ᾽ ἀθανάτου καθορῶν φύσεως
        κόσμον ἀγήρων, πῇ τε συνέστη
        καὶ ὅπῃ καὶ ὅπως.
        τοῖς δὲ τοιούτοις οὐδέποτ᾽ αἰσχρῶν
        ἔργων μελέτημα προσίζει.

[HELEN:] Watch out, you might have received some ap-
      pearance sent by the gods. [. . .]
[HELEN:] And so you think that this appearance is reliable?
[TEUCER:] Yes, for I myself saw her with my own eyes.
      And the mind (*nous*) sees.

b

[CHORUS:] What is god, or not god, or in the middle—
      Who of mortals can search this out and say it?
      That man has discovered the farthest limit, he who   1140
        sees that what comes from the gods
      Is here, then there, then in turn leaps
      With contradictory, unexpected turns of fortune.

The Study of Nature (T43)

T43 Euripides

a (59 A30) Fragment from an unidentified play (*Anti-ope?*)

[CHORUS:] Happy the man who, having attained
      The knowledge deriving from inquiry,
      Aspires neither to trouble for his fellow citizens
      Nor to unjust deeds,
      But observes immortal nature's
      Unaging order, where it was formed,
      In what way, and how.
      Never to men like this does the practice
        Of shameful actions come near.

b (59 A20) Frag. 913 K

τίς [. . .] . . . οθεος [κ]αὶ [. . .]ραδαίμῳ[ν];
ὃς τάδε λεύσσων οὐ προδιδάσκει,
ψυχὴν αὑτοῦ θεὸν ἡγεῖσθαι,
μετεωρολόγων δ᾽ ἑκὰς ἔρριψεν
σκολιὰς ἀπάτας; ὧν τολμηρά
γλῶσσ᾽ εἰκοβολεῖ περὶ τῶν ἀφανῶν
οὐδὲν γνώμης μετέχουσα;

The Naturalization of the Gods (T44–T50)

T44 (cf. 22 A16, 59 A48, 64 C2) Eur. *Tro.* 884–88

[ΗΚ.] ὦ γῆς ὄχημα κἀπὶ γῆς ἔχων ἕδραν,
885   ὅστις ποτ᾽ εἶ σύ, δυστόπαστος εἰδέναι,
    Ζεύς, εἴτ᾽ ἀνάγκη φύσεος εἴτε νοῦς βροτῶν,
    προσηυξάμην σε· πάντα γὰρ δι᾽ ἀψόφου
    βαίνων κελεύθου κατὰ δίκην τὰ θνήτ᾽ ἄγεις.

T45 Eur.

a Frag. 877 K

ἀλλ᾽ αἰθὴρ τίκτει σε, κόρα,
Ζεὺς ὃς ἀνθρώποις ὀνομάζεται.

b (59 A20) Fragment from an unidentified play

Who †. . .†,
Who when he sees these things does not begin by
    teaching
His soul to conceive of god,
And casts far away the crooked deceptions of those
    who study the heavens,
Whose audacious tongue guesses at random about
    invisible matters
                without having any share in judgment?

The Naturalization of the Gods (T44–T50)

T44 (cf. 22 A16, 59 A48, 64 C2) Euripides, *The Trojan
Women*

[HECUBA:] Oh you, who sustain the earth and are en-
    throned on the earth,
    Whoever you are, most unfathomable to know,   885
    Zeus, whether you are the necessity of nature or the
        intelligence of mortals,
    I pray to you: for it is you who, walking along a silent
        path,
    Lead all mortal affairs according to justice.

T45 Euripides, Fragments from unidentified plays

a

But you, maiden [scil. Helen?], were born from the
    aether,
Which is called Zeus by humans.

b Frag. 941 K

ὁρᾷς τὸν ὑψοῦ τόνδ᾽ ἄπειρον αἰθέρα
καὶ γῆν πέριξ ἔχονθ᾽ ὑγραῖς ἐν ἀγκάλαις;
τοῦτον νόμιζε Ζῆνα, τόνδ᾽ ἡγοῦ θεόν.

T46 Soph. Frag. 752 R

Ἥλι᾽, οἰκτίροις ἐμέ,
ὃν οἱ σοφοὶ λέγουσι γεννητὴν θεῶν
πατέρα τε πάντων.

T47 Eur. Frag. 919 K

κορυφὴ δὲ θεῶν ὁ περὶ χθόν᾽ ἔχων
φαεννὸς αἰθήρ

T48 (59 A20b) Eur. Frag. 944 K

[. . .]
καὶ Γαῖα μῆτερ· Ἑστίαν δέ σ᾽ οἱ σοφοὶ
βροτῶν καλοῦσιν ἡμένην ἐν αἰθέρι.

T49 Critias (?) *Peirithous* Frag.

a (88 B18) Frag. 43 F 3 Snell

ἀκάμας τε χρόνος περί τ᾽ ἀενάῳ
ῥεύματι πλήρης φοιτᾷ τίκτων
αὐτὸς ἑαυτόν, δίδυμοί τ᾽ ἄρκτοι

b

> Do you see this unlimited aether up on high,
> Which holds the earth all around in its moist
>   embrace?
> Consider this to be Zeus, think that this is a god.

T46 Sophocles, Fragment from an unidentified play

>   Sun, take pity on me,
> You whom wise man call the begetter of the gods
> And the father of all things.

T47 Euripides, Fragment from an unidentified play

> Summit of the gods, that which surrounds the earth:
> Bright aether

T48 (59 A20b) Euripides, Fragment from an unidentified play

> [. . .]
> And mother Earth; the wise among mortals
> Call you Hestia, you who are seated in the aether.

T49 Critias (?), Fragments from *Pirithous*[1]

---

[1] The ancient authors who cite these lines attribute them to
Euripides.

a (88 B18)

> Time, indefatigable and filled with an ever-flowing
> Stream, moves along, himself bringing to birth
> Himself; and the twin Bears,

ταῖς ὠκυπλάνοις πτερύγων ῥιπαῖς
τὸν Ἀτλάντειον τηροῦσι πόλον.

b (88 B19) Frag. 43 F 4 Snell

σὲ τὸν αὐτοφυῆ, τὸν ἐν αἰθερίῳ
ῥύμβῳ πάντων φύσιν ἐμπλέξανθ᾽,
ὃν πέρι μὲν φῶς, πέρι δ᾽ ὀρφναία
νὺξ αἰολόχρως ἄκριτός τ᾽ ἄστρων
ὄχλος ἐνδελεχῶς ἀμφιχορεύει.

T50 Eur. *Bacch.* 274–83

[TE.]   δύο γάρ, ὦ νεανία,
275   τὰ πρῶτ᾽ ἐν ἀνθρώποισι· Δημήτηρ θεά—
         Γῆ δ᾽ ἐστίν, ὄνομα δ᾽ ὁπότερον βούλει κάλει·
         αὕτη μὲν ἐν ξηροῖσιν ἐκτρέφει βροτούς·
         ὃς δ᾽ ἦλθ᾽ ἔπειτ᾽, ἀντίπαλον ὁ Σεμέλης γόνος
         βότρυος ὑγρὸν πῶμ᾽ ηὗρε κεἰσηνέγκατο
280   θνητοῖς, ὃ παύει τοὺς ταλαιπώρους βροτοὺς
         λύπης, ὅταν πλησθῶσιν ἀμπέλου ῥοῆς,

With the swift beating of their wings,
Observe the celestial pole of Atlas [i.e. which Atlas
    holds up].

b (88 B19)

You [i.e. the world?],[1] the self-generated, you who
    have woven
The nature of all things in the vortex of the aether,
You around whom the light, around whom the
    gloomy
Spangled night and the innumerable
Swarm of stars perpetually dance!

[1] Clement, who cites these lines, says that the invocation is
addressed to Mind, the demiurge of the world.

T50 Euripides, *Bacchae*

[TEIRESIAS:]   For, young man [scil. Pentheus],
    two things
    Are of first importance among humans: the goddess   275
        Demeter—
    She is Earth, but you can call her by whichever of
        these two names you wish—
    She nourishes mortals with dry food;
    And the one who came after, the son of Semele [i.e.
        Dionysus], discovered
    A counterpart, the moist drink of the grapevine, and
        introduced it
    To mortals—it relieves wretched humans   280
    Of their pain, whenever they are full of the liquid
        of the grapevine,

ὕπνον τε λήθην τῶν καθ᾽ ἡμέραν κακῶν
δίδωσιν, οὐδ᾽ ἔστ᾽ ἄλλο φάρμακον πόνων.

The Gods and Chance (T51–T52)

T51 Eur. *Phrixus* B Frag. 820b K

ὦ θνητὰ παραφρονήματ᾽ ἀνθρώπων, μάτην
οἳ φασιν εἶναι τὴν τύχην, ἀλλ᾽ οὐ θεούς·
ὡς οὐδὲν ἴστε, κεἰ λέγειν δοκεῖτέ τι·
εἰ μὲν γὰρ ἡ τύχη 'στιν, οὐδὲν δεῖ θεῶν,
εἰ δ᾽ οἱ θεοὶ σθένουσιν, οὐδὲν ἡ τύχη.

T52 Eur. Frag. 901 K

[χο.] πολλάκι μοι πραπίδων διῆλθε φροντίς,
εἴτε τύχα τις εἴτε δαίμων τὰ βρότεια κραίνει
παρά τ᾽ ἐλπίδα καὶ παρὰ δίκαν
τοὺς μὲν ἀπ᾽ οἴκων †δ᾽ ἐναπίπτοντας
ἀτὰρ θεοῦ†, τοὺς δ᾽ εὐτυχοῦντας ἄγει

And it gives sleep, forgetfulness of the evils of the
    day,
And there is no other remedy for pains.

Cf. **PROD. D15–D16**

The Gods and Chance (T51–T52)

T51 Euripides, Fragment from *Phrixus* B

Oh, the mortal delusions of humans, who say
In vain that chance exists, but not the gods!
For you [scil. men] know nothing, even if you think
    you are saying something.
For if chance exists, there is no need of gods;
But if the gods are strong, then chance is nothing.

T52 Euripides, Fragment from an unidentified play

[CHORUS:] Often this worry has passed through my mind
        (*prapides*):
        Whether it is some chance or a divinity that brings
            mortal affairs to accomplishment
        Against expectation and against justice,
        The ones from their homes †. . .
        . . .† and leads others to prosperity

Cf. also **SOC. P27**

Law (nomos) *and Nature* (phusis) *(T53–T55)*

T53 Eur. *Bacch.* 893–96

[ΧΟ.] κούφα γὰρ δαπάνα νομίζειν ἰσχὺν τόδ᾽ ἔχειν,
ὅτι ποτ᾽ ἄρα τὸ δαιμόνιον,
τό τ᾽ ἐν χρόνῳ μακρῷ νόμιμον
ἀεὶ φύσει τε πεφυκός.

895

T54 Eur. *Auge* Frag. 265a.1 K

ἡ φύσις ἐβούλεθ᾽, ᾗ νόμων οὐδὲν μέλει.

T55 Eur. *Dictys* Frag. 346 K

εἷς γάρ τις ἔστι κοινὸς ἀνθρώποις νόμος—
καὶ θεοῖσι τοῦτο δόξαν, ὡς σαφῶς λέγω—
θηρσίν τε πᾶσι τέκν᾽ ἃ τίκτουσιν φιλεῖν.
τὰ δ᾽ ἄλλα χωρὶς χρώμεθ᾽ ἀλλήλων νόμοις.

τέκν᾽ ἃ Paris. 1985 (B) teste Gaisford: τέκνα cett.

The Progress of Civilization (T56–T63)

T56 Aesch. *Palamedes* Frag. **181a R

[ΠΑ.] ἔπειτα πάσης Ἑλλάδος καὶ ξυμμάχων
βίον διῴκησ᾽ ὄντα πρὶν πεφυρμένον
θηρσίν θ᾽ ὅμοιον· πρῶτα μὲν τὸν πάνσοφον
ἀριθμὸν ηὕρηκ᾽ ἔξοχον σοφισμάτων.

DRAMATIC APPENDIX

Law (nomos) *and Nature* (phusis) *(T53–T55)*

T53 Euripides, *Bacchae*

[CHORUS:]   For slight is the expense to think
     That this it is that possesses strength:
     Everything that is divine, whatever it is,
     What over long time has always possessed   895
     The sanction of law and exists by nature.

T54 Euripides, Fragment from *Auge*

   It was the wish of nature, which does not care at all
     about laws.

T55 Euripides, Fragment from *Dictys*

   For there is a single law in common for humans—
   And this is approved by the gods, as I assert clearly—
   And for all animals: to love the offspring they bring to
     birth.
   For the rest, we make use of various laws that differ
     from one another.

The Progress of Civilization (T56–T63)

T56 Aeschylus, Fragment from *Palamedes*

[PALAMEDES:] Then I organized the life, which earlier
     had been confused
   And similar to that of the animals.
   Of all of Greece and its allies. First I discovered
     supremely ingenious (*pansophos*)
   Number, the most eminent of all artifices (*sophis-
     mata*).

T57 Aesch. (?), *Prom.* 442–44, 447–68, 476–506

[ΠΡ.]   τἀν βροτοῖς δὲ πήματα
443 ἀκούσαθ', ὡς σφας νηπίους ὄντας τὸ πρίν
  ἔννους ἔθηκα καὶ φρενῶν ἐπηβόλους. [. . .]
447 οἳ πρῶτα μὲν βλέποντες ἔβλεπον μάτην,
  κλύοντες οὐκ ἤκουον, ἀλλ' ὀνειράτων
  ἀλίγκιοι μορφῇσι τὸν μακρὸν βίον
450 ἔφυρον εἰκῇ πάντα, κοὔτε πλινθυφεῖς
  δόμους προσείλους ᾖσαν, οὐ ξυλουργίαν,
  κατώρυχες δ' ἔναιον ὥστ' ἀήσυροι
  μύρμηκες ἄντρων ἐν μυχοῖς ἀνηλίοις.
  ἦν δ' οὐδὲν αὐτοῖς οὔτε χείματος τέκμαρ
455 οὔτ' ἀνθεμώδους ἦρος οὔτε καρπίμου
  θέρους βέβαιον, ἀλλ' ἄτερ γνώμης τὸ πᾶν
  ἔπρασσον, ἔστε δή σφιν ἀντολὰς ἐγώ
  ἄστρων ἔδειξα τάς τε δυσκρίτους δύσεις.
  καὶ μὴν ἀριθμόν, ἔξοχον σοφισμάτων,
460 ἐξηῦρον αὐτοῖς, γραμμάτων τε συνθέσεις,
  μνήμην ἁπάντων, μουσομήτορ' ἐργάνην.
  κἄζευξα πρῶτος ἐν ζυγοῖσι κνώδαλα,
  ζεύγλῃσι δουλεύοντα σώμασίν θ' ὅπως
  θνητοῖς μεγίστων διάδοχοι μοχθημάτων
465 γένοινθ'· ὑφ' ἅρμά τ' ἤγαγον φιληνίους

---

1 Scholars disagree on whether or not *Prometheus Bound* is to
be attributed to Aeschylus, among whose works it is transmitted.

T57 Aeschylus (?), *Prometheus Bound*[1]

[PROMETHEUS:]   Hear the sufferings

That prevailed among men, how they had earlier   443
been foolish,

But I made them mindful and possessed of thinking. [. . .]

For at first, though they saw, they saw in vain,   447

Though they heard, they did not listen, but,

Like the shapes of dreams, throughout a long life

They mixed everything up at random, and they   450
knew

Neither bricked sun-warmed houses nor wood-
working;

They dwelt underground like nimble

Ants in the sunless recesses of caves.

They had no certain sign for winter

Nor for flowering spring nor for crop-laden   455

Summer, but they did everything

Without a plan, until I taught them the risings

Of the stars and their settings, hard to distinguish.

And further, number, the most eminent of all artifices (*sophismata*),

I discovered for them, and the combinations of let-   460
ters—

Memory of all things, mother of the Muses, crafts-
woman.

And I was the first to yoke for them beasts in harness

As slaves to yoke loops and pack saddles, so that

They would be the substitutes for mortals

In grievous toils, and I harnessed to the chariot   465

ἵππους, ἄγαλμα τῆς ὑπερπλούτου χλιδῆς.
θαλασσόπλαγκτα δ᾽ οὔτις ἄλλος ἀντ᾽ ἐμοῦ
λινόπτερ᾽ ηὗρε ναυτίλων ὀχήματα. [. . .]

476   τὰ λοιπά μου κλύουσα θαυμάσῃ πλέον,
οἵας τέχνας τε καὶ πόρους ἐμησάμην.
τὸ μὲν μέγιστον, εἴ τις ἐς νόσον πέσοι,
οὐκ ἦν ἀλέξημ᾽ οὐδέν, οὔτε βρώσιμον,

480   οὐ χριστόν, οὐδὲ πιστόν, ἀλλὰ φαρμάκων
χρείᾳ κατεσκέλλοντο, πρίν γ᾽ ἐγώ σφισιν
ἔδειξα κράσεις ἠπίων ἀκεσμάτων
αἷς τὰς ἁπάσας ἐξαμύνονται νόσους.
τρόπους τε πολλοὺς μαντικῆς ἐστοίχισα,

485   κἄκρινα πρῶτος ἐξ ὀνειράτων ἃ χρή
ὕπαρ γενέσθαι, κληδόνας τε δυσκρίτους
ἐγνώρισ᾽ αὐτοῖς ἐνοδίους τε συμβόλους,
γαμψωνύχων τε πτῆσιν οἰωνῶν σκεθρῶς
διώρισ᾽, οἵτινές τε δεξιοὶ φύσιν

490   εὐωνύμους τε, καὶ δίαιταν ἥντινα
ἔχουσ᾽ ἕκαστοι, καὶ πρὸς ἀλλήλους τίνες
ἔχθραι τε καὶ στέργηθρα καὶ ξυνεδρίαι,
σπλάγχνων τε λειότητα, καὶ χροιὰν τίνα
ἔχουσ᾽ ἂν εἴη δαίμοσιν πρὸς ἡδονήν

495   χολή, λοβοῦ τε ποικίλην εὐμορφίαν·
κνίσῃ τε κῶλα ξυγκαλυπτὰ καὶ μακράν

Rein-loving horses, the pride of over-wealthy lux-
   ury.
And no one other than myself discovered the sea-
   struck
Sail-winged conveyances of ships. [. . .]
When you hear the rest you [i.e. the Chorus] will be   476
   even more astonished,
What crafts and resources I devised.
The greatest of all: if someone fell ill,
There was no protection at all, neither food
Nor ointment, nothing that would be reliable, but   480
   for lack of drugs
They were withering away—until I showed them
The compounding of soothing remedies,
By which they warded off all illnesses.
And I cataloged all the forms of divination,
And I was the first to separate from dreams what   485
   must
Come to pass as waking visions; and ominous utter-
   ances,
Hard to distinguish, I identified for them, and
   omens on the road.
And the flight of crooked-taloned birds I defined
With precision, which ones are propitious by nature
And good-omened, and what way of life   490
Each one possesses, and what are the antagonisms
Of each for each, their love charms, and their as-
   sociations;
And the smoothness of their entrails, and what color
Their bile should be to please the deities,
And the varieties of the well-shaped liver lobe.   495
And by burning thighs wrapped in fat and the long

333

ὀσφῦν πυρώσας δυστέκμαρτον εἰς τέχνην
ὥδωσα θνητούς, καὶ φλογωπὰ σήματα
ἐξωμμάτωσα πρόσθεν ὄντ᾽ ἐπάργεμα.
500 τοιαῦτα μὲν δὴ ταῦτ᾽· ἔνερθε δὲ χθονός
κεκρυμμέν᾽ ἀνθρώποισιν ὠφελήματα,
χαλκόν, σίδηρον, ἄργυρον χρυσόν τε, τίς
φήσειεν ἂν πάροιθεν ἐξευρεῖν ἐμοῦ;
οὐδείς, σάφ᾽ οἶδα, μὴ μάτην φλῦσαι θέλων.
505 βραχεῖ δὲ μύθῳ πάντα συλλήβδην μάθε·
πᾶσαι τέχναι βροτοῖσιν ἐκ Προμηθέως.

T58 Soph. *Ant.* 332–75

[xo.] πολλὰ τὰ δεινὰ κοὐδὲν ἀν-
θρώπου δεινότερον πέλει·
τοῦτο καὶ πολιοῦ πέραν
335 πόντου χειμερίῳ νότῳ
χωρεῖ, περιβρυχίοισιν
περῶν ὑπ᾽ οἴδμασιν, θεῶν
τε τὰν ὑπερτάταν, Γᾶν
ἄφθιτον, ἀκαμάταν ἀποτρύεται,
340 ἰλλομένων ἀρότρων ἔτος εἰς ἔτος,
ἱππείῳ γένει πολεύων.

κουφονόων τε φῦλον ὀρ-
νίθων ἀμφιβαλὼν ἄγει
καὶ θηρῶν ἀγρίων ἔθνη

334

Loins, I set mortals on the path of this enigmatic
    craft;
And I opened their eyes to the blazing constella-
    tions,
Which earlier had been veiled to their sight.
So much for these things. But hidden   500
Beneath the earth, what provides benefits for hu-
    mans,
Bronze, iron, silver, and gold—who
Could claim to have discovered these before I did?
No one, I know it well, who does not want to prattle
    in vain.
Learn the whole thing briefly in a few words: 505
All crafts came to mortals from Prometheus.

T58 Sophocles, *Antigone*

[CHORUS:] Many are the things that are eerie,
    And nothing is eerier than man.
    This thing travels beyond the gray
    Sea with its wintery blast,   335
    Making his crossing
    On its engulfing swells.
    And the greatest of the gods, Earth,
    The indestructible, the unwearied—her he wears
      down
    As the plows move back and forth, year after year,   340
    Turning up the soil with the aid of the equine race.

    And the tribe of light-minded birds
    He snares and leads off,
    And the nations of wild beasts

345
πόντου τ' εἰναλίαν φύσιν
σπείραισι δικτυοκλώστοις,
περιφραδὴς ἀνήρ· κρατεῖ
δὲ μηχαναῖς ἀγραύλου

350
θηρὸς ὀρεσσιβάτα, λασιαύχενά θ'
ἵππον ὀχμάζεται ἀμφὶ λόφον ζυγῷ
οὔρειόν τ' ἀκμῆτα ταῦρον.

355
καὶ φθέγμα καὶ ἀνεμόεν φρόνημα καὶ ἀστυ-
νόμους
ὀργὰς ἐδιδάξατο καὶ δυσαύλων
πάγων ὑπαίθρεια καί
δύσομβρα φεύγειν βέλη

360
παντοπόρος· ἄπορος ἐπ' οὐδὲν ἔρχεται
τὸ μέλλον· Ἅιδα μόνον
φεῦξιν οὐκ ἐπάξεται·
νόσων δ' ἀμηχάνων φυγάς
ξυμπέφρασται.

365
σοφόν τι τὸ μηχανόεν τέχνας ὑπὲρ ἐλπίδ'
ἔχων
τοτὲ μὲν κακόν, ἄλλοτ' ἐπ' ἐσθλὸν ἕρπει.
νόμους παρείρων χθονός
θεῶν τ' ἔνορκον δίκαν

370
ὑψίπολις· ἄπολις ὅτῳ τὸ μὴ καλόν
ξύνεστι τόλμας χάριν·
μήτ' ἐμοὶ παρέστιος
γένοιτο μήτ' ἴσον φρονῶν
375
ὃς τάδ' ἔρδοι.

336

And the salty progeny of the sea,   345
With the twisted coils of his nets—
Surpassingly ingenious man! He rules
With his devices the mountain-roaming
Wild animal, the shaggy-maned   350
Horse he harnesses, yoking it around the neck,
And the tireless mountain bull.

And utterance, wind-swift thought, and the disposi- 355
   tions
That govern the city, he has learned,
And how to flee the open-sky,
Stormy shafts of inhospitable frosts—
Man full of resources! Without resources toward 360
   nothing
That might happen does he set forth.
For Hades alone will he find for himself no escape;
But he has contrived means of escape from incur-
   able diseases.

Possessing what he has ingeniously devised beyond 365
   any expectation,
His crafts, he moves at one time toward evil, at
   another toward good:
When he inserts [scil. into his actions?] the laws of
   the land
And the gods' oath-bound justice,
He soars high with his city; but cityless he, whom- 370
   ever depravity
Joins because of his rashness.
He who does such things—may he not
Share my hearth nor think thoughts equal [scil. to 375
   mine].

T59 Soph. *Nauplius* Frag. *432 R

[NA.]   οὗτος δ᾿ ἐφηῦρε τεῖχος Ἀργείων στρατῷ,
        σταθμῶν, ἀριθμῶν καὶ μέτρων εὑρήματα
        τάξεις τε ταύτας οὐράνιά τε σήματα.
        κἀκεῖν᾿ ἔτευξε πρῶτος, ἐξ ἑνὸς δέκα
5   κἀκ τῶν δέκ᾿ αὖθις ηὗρε πεντηκοντάδας
        †ὃς χίλι(α) εὐθὺς ὃς† στρατοῦ φρυκτωρίαν
        ἔδειξε κἀνέφηνεν οὐ δεδειγμένα.
        ἐφηῦρε δ᾿ ἄστρων μέτρα καὶ περιστροφάς,
        ὕπνου †φυλάξει(ς) (στι)θόα† σημαντήρια
10   νεῶν τε ποιμαντῆρσιν ἐνθαλασσίοις
        ἄρκτου στροφάς τε καὶ κυνὸς ψυχρὰν δύσιν.

T60 Soph. *Palamedes* Frag. 479 R

        οὐ λιμὸν οὗτος τῶνδ᾿ ἔπαυσε, σὺν θεῷ
        εἰπεῖν, χρόνου τε διατριβὰς σοφωτάτας
        ἐφηῦρε φλοίσβου μετὰ κόπον καθημένοις,
        πεσσοὺς κύβους τε, τερπνὸν ἀργίας ἄκος;

T59 Sophocles, Fragment from *Nauplius*

[NAUPLIUS:] It was he [i.e. Palamedes] who invented the
    wall for the Argives' army,
    And the inventions of weights, numbers, and mea-
      sures,
    These military formations and the celestial signs.
    And these things too he was the first to make: ten
      from one
    And from ten in turn he discovered fifty   5
    †He who a thousand straightaway† the army's signal
      beacon
    He showed, and he revealed what before had not
      been revealed.
    He discovered the measures and revolutions of the
      celestial bodies,
    Of sleep †guardings† signs
    And for the seafaring shepherds of ships   10
    The turnings of the Bear and the chilly setting of
      the Dog Star.

T60 Sophocles, Fragment from *Palamedes*

    Did he not stop their famine—to say it
    With god's permission—and did he not discover for
      them,
    Resting after their exertions with the waves, the
      cleverest pastimes:
    Drafts and dice, an enjoyable remedy for inaction?

T61 Soph. Frag. 843 R

τὰ μὲν διδακτὰ μανθάνω, τὰ δ' εὑρετά
ζητῶ, τὰ δ' εὐκτὰ παρὰ θεῶν ᾐτησάμην.

T62 Eur. *Palamedes* Frag. 578 K

[ΠΑ.] τὰ τῆς γε λήθης φάρμακ' ὀρθώσας μόνος,
ἄφωνα καὶ φωνοῦντα, συλλαβὰς τιθείς,
ἐξηῦρον ἀνθρώποισι γράμματ' εἰδέναι,
ὥστ' οὐ παρόντα ποντίας ὑπὲρ πλακός
τἀκεῖ κατ' οἴκους πάντ' ἐπίστασθαι καλῶς,
παισίν τ' ἀποθνῄσκοντα χρημάτων μέτρον
γράψαντα λείπειν, τὸν λαβόντα δ' εἰδέναι.
ἃ δ' εἰς ἔριν πίπτουσιν ἀνθρώποις κακά,
δέλτος διαιρεῖ, κοὐκ ἐᾷ ψευδῆ λέγειν.

T63 (88 B25) Critias (?) *Sisyphus* Frag. 43 F 19 Snell

ἦν χρόνος ὅτ' ἦν ἄτακτος ἀνθρώπων βίος
καὶ θηριώδης ἰσχύος θ' ὑπηρέτης,
ὅτ' οὐδὲν ἆθλον οὔτε τοῖς ἐσθλοῖσιν ἦν
οὔτ' αὖ κόλασμα τοῖς κακοῖς ἐγίγνετο.
5   κἄπειτά μοι δοκοῦσιν ἄνθρωποι νόμους
θέσθαι κολαστάς, ἵνα δίκη τύραννος ᾖ

---

1 Some of the ancient authors who cite these lines attribute them to Critias, some to Euripides; modern scholars disagree on whom they are to be assigned to.

T61 Sophocles, Fragment from an unidentified play

What can be taught, I learn; what can be discovered,
I seek; but for what is the object of prayer, I asked
    this of the gods.

T62 Euripides, Fragment from *Palamedes*

[PALAMEDES:] I alone, establishing remedies for forget-
    ting,
    Speechless and speaking [i.e. consonants and vow-
      els?], creating syllables,
    I invented for men the knowledge of writing,
    So that a man who was absent beyond the sea's plain
    Could know exactly everything back there in his
      house,
    And a man who was dying could write the measure
      of his wealth
    And leave it to his sons, and the man who inherited
      it would know.
    And men's evils, when they fall to quarreling—
    A written tablet decides them and does not allow
      people to tell lies.

T63 Critias (?), Fragment from the satyr-play *Sisyphus*[1]

There was a time when the life of humans was
    disordered
And animal-like, and subservient to force,
When neither was there any prize for good men
Nor inversely any punishment for evil ones.
And then, it seems to me, humans established laws   5
To punish, so that justice would be the absolute ruler
    (*turannos*)

<. . . .> τήν θ᾽ ὕβριν δούλην ἔχῃ·
ἐζημιοῦτο δ᾽ εἴ τις ἐξαμαρτάνοι.
ἔπειτ᾽ ἐπειδὴ τἀμφανῆ μὲν οἱ νόμοι
10   ἀπεῖργον αὐτοὺς ἔργα μὴ πράσσειν βίᾳ,
λάθρᾳ δ᾽ ἔπρασσον, τηνικαῦτά μοι δοκεῖ
<. . . .> πυκνός τις καὶ σοφὸς γνώμην ἀνήρ
θεῶν δέος θνητοῖσιν ἐξευρεῖν, ὅπως
εἴη τι δεῖμα τοῖς κακοῖσι, κἂν λάθρᾳ
15   πράσσωσιν ἢ λέγωσιν ἢ φρονῶσί τι.
ἐντεῦθεν οὖν τὸ θεῖον εἰσηγήσατο,
ὡς ἔστι δαίμων ἀφθίτῳ θάλλων βίῳ
νόῳ τ᾽ ἀκούων καὶ βλέπων, φρονῶν τε καὶ
προσέχων τε ταῦτα καὶ φύσιν θείαν φορῶν,
20   ὃς πᾶν τὸ λεχθὲν ἐν βροτοῖς ἀκούσεται,
τὸ δρώμενον δὲ πᾶν ἰδεῖν δυνήσεται.
ἐὰν δὲ σὺν σιγῇ τι βουλεύῃς κακόν,
τοῦτ᾽ οὐχὶ λήσει τοὺς θεούς· τὸ γὰρ φρονοῦν
<. . . .> ἔνεστι. τούσδε τοὺς λόγους λέγων
25   διδαγμάτων ἥδιστον εἰσηγήσατο
ψευδεῖ καλύψας τὴν ἀλήθειαν λόγῳ.
ναίειν δ᾽ ἔφασκε τοὺς θεοὺς ἐνταῦθ᾽ ἵνα
μάλιστ᾽ ἂν ἐξέπληξεν ἀνθρώπους ἄγων,
ὅθεν περ ἔγνω τοὺς φόβους ὄντας βροτοῖς
30   καὶ τὰς ὀνήσεις τῷ ταλαιπώρῳ βίῳ,
ἐκ τῆς ὕπερθε περιφορᾶς, ἵν᾽ ἀστραπάς

⟨   ⟩ and it would hold arrogance enslaved;
And if anyone committed a transgression he would be
     punished.
Then, as the laws prevented them
From committing acts of violence in public   10
But they did commit them in secret, at that time, it
     seems to me,
⟨   ⟩ some man who was shrewd and wise in his
     planning
Discovered for mortals fear of the gods, so that
There would be an object of terror for evil men, even
     if it was in secret
That they committed, said, or thought something.   15
And that was how the divine was introduced,
[scil. The idea] that there is a divinity flourishing with
     immortal life
Who listens and watches with his mind (noos), and
     thinks and
Pays attention to these things and is possessed of a
     divine nature,
Who will hear everything that is said among mortals,   20
And will be able to see everything that is done.
And if you plan some evil deed in silence,
This will not escape the gods' notice: for thought
⟨   ⟩ is present. By saying these things,
He introduced the most delightful of teachings,   25
Concealing the truth in a false speech.
He said that the gods live in the place where
He could most terrify humans by setting them there,
From where, he knew, fears come for mortals
And benefits for their miserable life,   30
From the circumference up above, where, he saw,

343

κατεῖδον οὔσας, δεινὰ δὲ κτυπήματα
βροντῆς τό τ᾽ ἀστερωπὸν οὐρανοῦ δέμας,
Χρόνου καλὸν ποίκιλμα, τέκτονος σοφοῦ,
35   ὅθεν τε λαμπρὸς ἀστέρος στείχει μύδρος
ὅ θ᾽ ὑγρὸς εἰς γῆν ὄμβρος ἐκπορεύεται.
τοίους πέριξ ἔστησεν ἀνθρώποις φόβους,
δι᾽ οὓς καλῶς τε τῷ λόγῳ κατῴκισεν
τὸν δαίμον᾽ οὗτος ἐν πρέποντι χωρίῳ,
40   τὴν ἀνομίαν τε τοῖς νόμοις κατέσβεσεν.
< . . . >
οὕτω δὲ πρῶτον οἴομαι πεῖσαί τινα
θνητοὺς νομίζειν δαιμόνων εἶναι γένος.

The Power of Speech (T64–T67)

T64 Soph. *Phil.* 96–99

[ΟΙ.] ἐσθλοῦ πατρὸς παῖ, καὐτὸς ὢν νέος ποτέ
γλῶσσαν μὲν ἀργόν, χεῖρα δ᾽ εἶχον ἐργάτιν·
νῦν δ᾽ εἰς ἔλεγχον ἐξιὼν ὁρῶ βροτοῖς
τὴν γλῶσσαν, οὐχὶ τἄργα, πάνθ᾽ ἡγουμένην.

There are lightning flashes, and terrifying crashes
Of thunder, and the starry expanse of the heavens,
The lovely embroidery of Time, that wise builder,
From where the gleaming mass of the heavenly body   35
    [i.e. the sun] proceeds
And the moist rain rushes toward the earth.
These were the kinds of terrors with which he
    surrounded humans,
By means of which this man established divinity,
By a well-made speech, in a suitable place,
And extinguished lawlessness by means of the laws   40
‹. . .›
And it was in this way, I think, that someone first
    persuaded
Mortals to believe that there exists a race of
    divinities.

The Power of Speech (T64–T67)

T64 Sophocles, *Philoctetes*

[ODYSSEUS:] You [i.e. Neoptolemus], child of a noble fa-
    ther, when I was young,
      I too would keep my tongue inactive and my hand
        busy;
      But now when I go out to put things to the test, I
        see that for mortals
      It is the tongue, not deeds, that rules all things.

T65 Eur. *Hec.* 814–19

[ΗΚ.] τί δῆτα θνητοὶ τἄλλα μὲν μαθήματα

815 μοχθοῦμεν ὡς χρὴ πάντα καὶ ματεύομεν,
πειθὼ δὲ τὴν τύραννον ἀνθρώποις μόνην
οὐδέν τι μᾶλλον ἐς τέλος σπουδάζομεν
μισθοὺς διδόντες μανθάνειν, ἵν᾽ ἦν ποτε
πείθειν ἅ τις βούλοιτο τυγχάνειν θ᾽ ἅμα;

T66 (ad 90 1.1) Eur. *Antiope* Frag. 189 K

[ΑΜ.?] ἐκ παντὸς ἄν τις πράγματος δισσῶν λόγων
ἀγῶνα θεῖτ᾽ ἄν, εἰ λέγειν εἴη σοφός.

T67 (88 B22) Critias (?) *Peirithous* Frag. 43 F 11 Snell

τρόπος δὲ χρηστὸς ἀσφαλέστερος νόμου·
τὸν μὲν γὰρ οὐδεὶς ἂν διατρέψαι ποτέ
ῥήτωρ δύναιτο, τὸν δ᾽ ἄνω τε καὶ κάτω
λόγοις ταράσσων πολλάκις λυμαίνεται.

T65 Euripides, *Hecuba*

[HECUBA:] Why do we mortals exert ourselves to study
    All the other fields of knowledge as we should,   815
    But persuasion, the sole absolute ruler (*turannos*)
        for human beings—
    We take no further trouble, by paying a fee,
    To learn this thoroughly, so that it would be possible
        someday
    To persuade whatever one wished and at the same
        to achieve it!

Cf. e.g. **GORG. D24 [8–14]**

T66 (ad 90 1.1) Euripides, Fragment from *Antiope*

[AMPHION?:] On every subject a man could establish a
    contest
    Between two arguments, if he were skilled at speak-
    ing.

Cf. e.g. **PROT. D26; DISS.**

T67 (88 B22) Critias (?), Fragment from *Pirithous*

An honest character is surer than the law:
For the former, no orator could ever pervert it;
While the latter, he often ruins it
By agitating it up and down with his speeches.

The Relativity of Values (T68)

T68 Eur. *Phoen.* 499–502

[ET.]   εἰ πᾶσι ταὐτὸν καλὸν ἔφυ σοφόν θ᾽ ἅμα,
500   οὐκ ἦν ἂν ἀμφίλεκτος ἀνθρώποις ἔρις·
          νῦν δ᾽ οὔθ᾽ ὅμοιον οὐδὲν οὔτ᾽ ἴσον βροτοῖς
          πλὴν ὀνόμασιν· τὸ δ᾽ ἔργον οὐκ ἔστιν τόδε.

Can Virtue Be Taught? (T69–T71)

T69 Eur. *Hipp.* 79–81

[III.]   [. . .]
          ὅσοις διδακτὸν μηδὲν ἀλλ᾽ ἐν τῇ φύσει
80   τὸ σωφρονεῖν εἴληχεν ἐς τὰ πάντ᾽ ἀεί,
          τούτοις δρέπεσθαι, τοῖς κακοῖσι δ᾽ οὐ θέμις.

T70 Eur. *Hec.* 592–602

[HK.]   οὔκουν δεινόν, εἰ γῆ μὲν κακὴ
            τυχοῦσα καιροῦ θεόθεν εὖ στάχυν φέρει,
            χρηστὴ δ᾽ ἁμαρτοῦσ᾽ ὧν χρεὼν αὐτὴν τυχεῖν
595   κακὸν δίδωσι καρπόν, ἄνθρωποι δ᾽ ἀεί
            ὁ μὲν πονηρὸς οὐδὲν ἄλλο πλὴν κακός,
            ὁ δ᾽ ἐσθλὸς ἐσθλὸς οὐδὲ συμφορᾶς ὕπο

348

The Relativity of Values (T68)

T68 Euripides, *Phoenician Women*

[ETEOCLES:] If for all men the same thing were by nature
    fine and wise,
    There would be no disputatious contention among   500
    humans:
    But as it is, nothing is similar or equal for mortals
    Except for the name—but this is not the thing itself
    (*ergon*).

Cf. **DISS. [2]**

Can Virtue Be Taught? (T69–T71)

T69 Euripides, *Hippolytus*

[HIPPOLYTUS:] [. . .]
    For all those who have received temperance in all
    regards
    Not from instruction, but in their nature, forever,   80
    For these it is lawful to pluck [scil. flowers from the
    meadow of Reverence], but for the wicked it is
    not.

T70 Euripides, *Hecuba*

[HECUBA:] Is it not dreadful that poor soil
    Bears a good crop if a god provides favorable cir-
    cumstances,
    While good land, if it lacks what it needs to receive,
    Produces a bad harvest—and yet that among hu-   595
    mans
    The wicked one is always nothing else than evil,

349

    φύσιν διέφθειρ᾽ ἀλλὰ χρηστός ἐστ᾽ ἀεί;
    ἆρ᾽ οἱ τεκόντες διαφέρουσιν ἢ τροφαί;

600   ἔχει γε μέντοι καὶ τὸ θρεφθῆναι καλῶς
    δίδαξιν ἐσθλοῦ· τοῦτο δ᾽ ἤν τις εὖ μάθῃ,
    οἶδεν τό γ᾽ αἰσχρὸν κανόνι τοῦ καλοῦ μα-
    θών.

599–602 del. Sakorraphos

T71 (> ad 80 B3) Eur. *Suppl.* 911–17

[ΑΔ.] τὸ γὰρ τραφῆναι μὴ κακῶς αἰδῶ φέρει·
    αἰσχύνεται δὲ τἀγάθ᾽ ἀσκήσας ἀνήρ
    κακὸς γενέσθαι πᾶς τις. ἡ δ᾽ εὐανδρία
    διδακτόν, εἴπερ καὶ βρέφος διδάσκεται

915   λέγειν ἀκούειν θ᾽ ὧν μάθησιν οὐκ ἔχει.
    ἃ δ᾽ ἂν μάθῃ τις, ταῦτα σῴζεσθαι φιλεῖ
    πρὸς γῆρας. οὕτω παῖδας εὖ παιδεύετε.

Reflections of Specific Doctrines
in Euripides (T72–T84)
Reflections of Xenophanes (T72–T73)

T72 (21 C1) Eur. *Her. Fur.* 1341–46

[ΗΡ.] ἐγὼ δὲ τοὺς θεοὺς οὔτε λέκτρ᾽ ἃ μὴ θέμις
    στέργειν νομίζω δεσμά τ᾽ ἐξάπτειν χεροῖν

The noble one noble, and that misfortune
Does not ruin his nature, but he remains always
    virtuous?
Is it the parents that differ, or the upbringing?
Surely, a good upbringing teaches what is noble too;   600
And whoever has learned this well knows
What is shameful, since he has learned it by the
    criterion of the good.

T71 (> ad 80 B3) Euripides, *Suppliant Women*

[ADRASTUS:] To be educated correctly brings a sense of
    shame;
And every man who has been trained in good things
    is ashamed
To behave badly. Manly courage
Is something that can be taught, since even an in-
    fant is taught
To speak and to hear things about which he is igno-   915
    rant.
And what someone learns, he tends to preserve this
Until old age. So teach your children well.

Reflections of Specific Doctrines
in Euripides (T72–T84)
Reflections of Xenophanes (T72–T73)

T72 (21 C1) Euripides, *Heracles*

[HERACLES:] I myself believe that the gods do not desire
    unlawful sexual unions
Or bind one another's hands with fetters—

οὔτ᾽ ἠξίωσα πώποτ᾽ οὔτε πείσομαι
οὐδ᾽ ἄλλον ἄλλου δεσπότην πεφυκέναι.
1345   δεῖται γὰρ ὁ θεός, εἴπερ ἔστ᾽ ὀρθῶς θεός,
οὐδενός· ἀοιδῶν οἵδε δύστηνοι λόγοι.

T73 (21 C2) Eur. *Autolycus* Frag. 282 K

κακῶν γὰρ ὄντων μυρίων καθ᾽ Ἑλλάδα
οὐδὲν κάκιόν ἐστιν ἀθλητῶν γένους.
οἳ πρῶτον οἰκεῖν οὔτε μανθάνουσιν εὖ
οὔτ᾽ ἂν δύναιντο· πῶς γὰρ ὅστις ἔστ᾽ ἀνήρ
5   γνάθου τε δοῦλος νηδύος θ᾽ ἡσσημένος
κτήσαιτ᾽ ἂν ὄλβον εἰς ὑπερβολὴν πατρός;
οὐδ᾽ αὖ πένεσθαι κἀξυπηρετεῖν τύχαις
οἷοί τ᾽· ἔθη γὰρ οὐκ ἐθισθέντες καλά
σκληρῶς μεταλλάσσουσιν εἰς τἀμήχανον.
10   λαμπροὶ δ᾽ ἐν ἥβῃ καὶ πόλεως ἀγάλματα
φοιτῶσ᾽· ὅταν δὲ προσπέσῃ γῆρας πικρόν,
τρίβωνες ἐκβαλόντες οἴχονται κρόκας.
ἐμεμψάμην δὲ καὶ τὸν Ἑλλήνων νόμον,
οἳ τῶνδ᾽ ἕκατι σύλλογον ποιούμενοι

I have never believed this, and never will I be per-
  suaded,
Nor that one god is naturally ruler over another.
For a god, if he rightly is a god, has no need   1345
Of anything. These are the miserable tales of singers.

Cf. **XEN. D8–D9**

T73 (21 C2) Euripides, Fragment from the satyr-play
Autolycus

For of the countless evils that afflict Greece,
None is worse than the race of athletes.
First, they neither learn how to run a household well,
Nor would they be capable of doing so: for how could
  a man
Who is slave to his jaws and is subservient to his   5
  stomach
Acquire wealth surpassing that of his father?
Nor, again, are they capable of being poor or sub-
  mitting to misfortune;
For since they have not been trained to have good
  habits,
They find it hard to fall into a condition of being
  without resources.
In their youth, they strut around illustriously, the   10
  idols of the city;
But when bitter old age falls upon them, they are
  goners,
Threadbare tatters whose nap has worn off.
I have also criticized the custom among the Greeks,
Who assemble together to show respect to these men

353

15   τιμῶσ᾽ ἀχρείους ἡδονὰς δαιτὸς χάριν.
          τίς γὰρ παλαίσας εὖ, τίς ὠκύπους ἀνήρ
          ἢ δίσκον ἄρας ἢ γνάθον παίσας καλῶς
          πόλει πατρῴᾳ στέφανον ἤρκεσεν λαβών;
          πότερα μαχοῦνται πολεμίοισιν ἐν χεροῖν
20   δίσκους ἔχοντες ἢ δι᾽ ἀσπίδων χερί
          θείνοντες ἐκβαλοῦσι πολεμίους πάτρας;
          οὐδεὶς σιδήρου ταῦτα μωραίνει πέλας
          †στάς. ἄνδρας χρὴ σοφούς τε κἀγαθούς
          φύλλοις στέφεσθαι, χὤστις ἡγεῖται πόλει
25   κάλλιστα σώφρων καὶ δίκαιος ὢν ἀνήρ,
          ὅστις τε μύθοις ἔργ᾽ ἀπαλλάσσει κακά
          μάχας τ᾽ ἀφαιρῶν καὶ στάσεις· τοιαῦτα γάρ
          πόλει τε πάσῃ πᾶσί θ᾽ Ἕλλησιν καλά.

Reflections of Heraclitus or of the Orphics (T74)

T74 Eur.

a *Polyidus* Frag. 638 K

    τίς δ᾽ οἶδεν εἰ τὸ ζῆν μέν ἐστι κατθανεῖν,
    τὸ κατθανεῖν δὲ ζῆν κάτω νομίζεται;

And honor useless pleasures for the benefit of a   15
   banquet.
For even if a man has wrestled well, or is swift of
   foot,
Or has thrown the discus or punched someone's jaw
   well—
How has he ever defended the city of his fathers by
   winning a garland?
Will they fight against enemies by holding in their
   hands
A discus, or is it by striking with shields in their hand   20
That they will drive away the enemies from their
   fatherland?
When the weapon approaches, no one is such a fool.
Men who are wise and virtuous should be crowned
With garlands, and the man who guides the city
Best of all, as someone who is temperate and just,   25
And the man who wards off evil deeds by his words,
By banishing contention and civic strife. For this is
   what
Is good for the whole city and for all the Greeks.

Cf. **XEN. D61**

Reflections of Heraclitus or of the Orphics (T74)

T74 Euripides, Fragments

a from *Polyidus*

Who knows whether to be alive is to be dead,
While to be dead is considered to be alive down
   below?

355

b *Phrixus* A aut B Frag. 833.1–2 K

[ΦΡ.]   τίς δ᾽ οἶδεν εἰ ζῆν τοῦθ᾽ ὃ κέκληται θανεῖν,
      τὸ ζῆν δὲ θνῄσκειν ἐστί; [. . .]

Reflections of Anaxagoras (T75–T80)

T75

a (59 A20) Schol. in Pind. *Ol.* 1.91 (1.38.10–39.1 Drachmann)

περὶ δὲ τοῦ ἡλίου οἱ φυσικοί φασιν ὡς λίθος καλεῖται
ὁ ἥλιος· καὶ Ἀναξαγόρου δὲ γενόμενον τὸν Εὐριπίδην
μαθητὴν πέτρον εἰρηκέναι τὸν ἥλιον διὰ τῶν προεκ-
κειμένων·

[ΗΛ.]   ὁ γὰρ μακάριος, κοὐκ ὀνειδίζω τύχας,
      Διὸς πεφυκὼς, ὡς λέγουσι, Τάνταλος
      κορυφῆς ὑπερτέλλοντα δειμαίνων πέτρον
      ἀέρι ποτᾶται καὶ τίνει ταύτην δίκην.

καὶ πάλιν δι᾽ ἄλλων βῶλον λέγοντα οὕτως·

[ΗΛ.]   μόλοιμι τὰν οὐρανοῦ
      μέσον χθονός τε τεταμέναν
      αἰωρήμασι
      πέτραν ἁλύσεσι χρυσέαισι,
      φερομέναν δίναισι,
      βῶλον ἐξ Ὀλύμπου [. . .].

b from *Phrixus* A or B

[PHRIXUS:] Who knows whether what is called death
is life,
And life is death? [. . .]

Cf. **HER. D70**; cf. **MOR. T32–T34**

Reflections of Anaxagoras (T75–T80)

T75

a (59 A20) Scholia on Pindar's *Olympians*

Concerning the sun, the natural philosophers say that
what is called 'the sun' is a stone, and Euripides, who was
Anaxagoras' student, said that the sun is a rock in the opening verses [scil. *Orestes* 4–7]:

[ELECTRA:] For the prosperous (and I do not blame
chance)
Tantalus, born of Zeus, as they say,
Suspended in the air, dreads the rock
Hanging over his head and pays his penalty.

And again in other verses [scil. *Orestes* 982–84] he calls it
a clod, speaking as follows:

[ELECTRA:] If only I could go
To the stone that extends,
Suspended
In the middle between heaven and earth,
Carried by golden chains, in vortices,
A clod from Olympus [. . .].

Cf. **ANAXAG. D4[6]**

b (< 59 A1) Diog. Laert. 2.10 (*Phaethon* Frag. 783 K)

[. . .] ὅθεν καὶ Εὐριπίδην μαθητὴν ὄντα αὐτοῦ, ʽχρυσέαν βῶλον᾽ εἰπεῖν τὸν ἥλιον ἐν τῷ Φαέθοντι.

T76 (59 A91) Eur. *Hel.* 1–3

[ΗΛ.]   Νείλου μὲν αἵδε καλλιπάρθενοι ῥοαί,
       ὃς ἀντὶ δίας ψακάδος Αἰγύπτου πέδον
       λευκῆς τακείσης χιόνος ὑγραίνει γύας.

T77 (59 A62) Eur. Μελανίππη ἡ Σοφή Frag. 484 K

κοὐκ ἐμὸς ὁ μῦθος, ἀλλ᾽ ἐμῆς μητρὸς πάρα,
ὡς οὐρανός τε γαῖά τ᾽ ἦν μορφὴ μία·
ἐπεὶ δ᾽ ἐχωρίσθησαν ἀλλήλων δίχα,
τίκτουσι πάντα κἀνέδωκαν εἰς φάος·
δένδρη, πετεινά, θῆρας, οὕς θ᾽ ἅλμη τρέφει
γένος τε θνητῶν.

T78 (59 A112) Eur. *Chrysippus* Frag. 839 K

[ΧΟ.]   Γαῖα μεγίστη καὶ Διὸς Αἰθήρ,
       ὁ μὲν ἀνθρώπων καὶ θεῶν γενέτωρ,

b (59 A1) Diogenes Laertius

. . . [scil. they say] that this is why Euripides, who was his [i.e. Anaxagoras'] student, called the sun "golden clod" in his *Phaethon*.

T76 (59 A91) Euripides, *Helen*

[HELEN:] These are the streams of the Nile with its beautiful nymphs,
Which, instead of divine rain, waters the lands
Of the plain of Egypt when the white snow has
melted.

Cf. **ANAXAG. D66**

T77 (59 A62) Euripides, Fragment from *The Wise Mela-
nippe*

And the tale is not mine, but it comes from my
mother [i.e. Hippo, a mythical astrologer]:
That heaven and earth once had a single form;
But when they were separated from each other,
They gave birth to all things and sent them up into
the light—
Trees, birds, wild beasts, and the ones that the salt
sea nourishes
And the race of mortals.

Cf. **ANAXAG. D9**

T78 (59 A112) Euripides, Fragment from *Chrysippus*

[CHORUS:] Mightiest Earth, and Aether, son of Zeus—
The latter is the begetter of humans and of gods,

ἡ δ᾽ ὑγροβόλους σταγόνας νοτίας
παραδεξαμένη τίκτει θνητούς,

5   τίκτει βοτάνην φῦλά τε θηρῶν·
ὅθεν οὐκ ἀδίκως
    μήτηρ πάντων νενόμισται.
χωρεῖ δ᾽ ὀπίσω
τὰ μὲν ἐκ γαίας φύντ᾽ εἰς γαῖαν,

10   τὰ δ᾽ ἀπ᾽ αἰθερίου βλαστόντα γονῆς
εἰς οὐράνιον πάλιν ἦλθε πόλον·
θνήσκει δ᾽ οὐδὲν τῶν γιγνομένων,
διακρινόμενον δ᾽ ἄλλο πρὸς ἄλλου
μορφὴν ἑτέραν ἀπέδειξεν.

T79 Eur.

a *Oenomaus* Frag. 574 K

    τεκμαιρόμεσθα τοῖς παροῦσι τἀφανῆ

b *Phoenix* Frag. 811 K

            τἀφανῆ
    τεκμηρίοισιν εἰκότως ἁλίσκεται

The former receives the wet drops of water
And gives birth to mortals,
Gives birth to plants and the tribes of animals: 5
This is why it is not unjust
That she is considered the mother of all things.
What grows out of the earth
Goes back again to the earth,
What sprouts forth from an aethereal seed   10
Returns once again to the pole of the heavens.
Nothing of what is born dies,
But one thing, separating from another,
Presents a different shape.

Cf. **ANAXAG. D15**

T79 Euripides, Fragments

a from *Oenomaus*

We make conjectures (*tekmairesthai*) from things that
are present about things that are invisible

b from *Phoenix*

Things that are invisible
Are detected according to plausibility from signs
(*tekmêria*)

Cf. **ALCM. D4; ANAXAG. D6**

T80 (59 A33) Eur. Frag. 964 K

[ΘΗ.]   ἐγὼ δὲ παρὰ σοφοῦ τινος μαθών
εἰς φροντίδας νοῦν συμφοράς τ᾽ ἐβαλλόμην
φυγάς τ᾽ ἐμαυτῷ προστιθεὶς πάτρας ἐμῆς
θανάτους τ᾽ ἀώρους καὶ κακῶν ἄλλας ὁδούς,
ἵν᾽ εἴ τι πάσχοιμ᾽ ὧν ἐδόξαζον φρενί,
μή μοι νεῶρες προσπεσὸν μᾶλλον δάκοι

A *Reflection of Diogenes of Apollonia (T81)*

T81 (59 A48) Eur. Frag. 1018 K

ὁ νοῦς γὰρ ἡμῶν ἐστιν ἐν ἑκάστῳ θεός.

Reflections of Protagoras

See **PROT. P23**

T80 (59 A33) Euripides, Fragment from an unidentified play

[THESEUS:] Having learned from a certain wise man,
    I would habitually set my mind upon anxieties and
        misfortunes,
    Imagining for myself exiles from my country,
    Untimely deaths, and other ways of evils,
    So that if I suffered any of the things I was imagin-
        ing in my mind,
    It would not gnaw me more by falling upon me
        unexpected.

Cf. **ANAXAG. D15**

A Reflection of Diogenes of Apollonia (T81)

T81 (59 A48) Euripides, Fragment from an unidentified play

For our intelligence (*nous*) is a god in each of us.

Cf. **DIOG. D13**

Reflections of Protagoras

See **PROT. P23**

Reflections of Socrates? (T82–T84)

T82 Eur. *Med.* 1078–80

[ΜΗ.] καὶ μανθάνω μὲν οἷα δρᾶν μέλλω κακά,
θυμὸς δὲ κρείσσων τῶν ἐμῶν βουλευμάτων,

1080 ὅσπερ μεγίστων αἴτιος κακῶν βροτοῖς.

versus 1078–80 cum 1056–77 del. Bergk ut interpolatos

T83 Eur. *Hippol.* 380–83

380 [ΦΑ.] τὰ χρήστ᾽ ἐπιστάμεσθα καὶ γιγνώσκομεν,
οὐκ ἐκπονοῦμεν δ᾽, οἱ μὲν ἀργίας ὕπο,
οἱ δ᾽ ἡδονὴν προθέντες ἀντὶ τοῦ καλοῦ
ἄλλην τιν᾽.

T84 Eur. *Chrysippus* Frag. 841 K

αἰαῖ· τόδ᾽ ἤδη θεῖον ἀνθρώποις κακόν,
ὅταν τις εἰδῇ τἀγαθόν, χρῆται δὲ μή.

DRAMATIC APPENDIX

Reflections of Socrates? (T82–T84)

T82 Euripides, *Medea*

[MEDEA:] And I know full well what evils I am going to
  commit,
  But my ardor (*thumos*) is stronger than my plans—
  Ardor, the cause of the greatest evils for mortals.   1080

T83 Euripides, *Hippolytus*

[PHAEDRA:] We know and understand what is virtuous   380
  But we do not put it into practice, some out of lazi-
  ness,
  Others because they set something else above vir-
  tue,
  Some pleasure.

T84 Euripides, Fragment from *Chrysippus*

  Alas! This is truly an evil for humans sent by the
  gods,
  When one knows what is good, but does not make
  use of it.

See also **SOC. P27.1**